The Israeli Memory Struggle

History and Identity in the Age of Globalization

Jakob Feldt

The Israeli Memory Struggle

History and Identity in the Age of Globalization

University Press of Southern Denmark
2007

© The author and University Press of Southern Denmark 2007
Set by DTP-funktionen, University of Southern Denmark
Printed by Narayana Press
Cover design by Anne Charlotte Mouret, UniSats
EAN 9788776742188

University of Southern Denmark Studies in History and Social Sciences vol. 340

University Press of Southern Denmark
Campusvej 55
DK-5230 Odense M
Phone: +45 6615 7999
Fax: +45 6615 8126
Press@forlag.sdu.dk
www.universitypress.dk

Distribution in the United States and Canada:
International Specialized Book Services
5804 NE Hassalo Street
Portland, OR 97213-3644 USA
www.isbs.com

Distribution in the United Kingdom:
Gazelle
White Cross Mills
Hightown
Lancaster
LA1 4 XS
U.K.
www.gazellebooks.co.uk

Table of Contents

Foreword ... 7
History, Imagination, Discourse ... 11
  History and Theory ... 11
    What is History? ... 17
    History as Rhetoric ... 18
    Discourse and Society ... 27
  Discourses of Israeli State and Citizenship ... 31
    Israel in the 1990s ... 36
Post-Nationalist Discourse on Israeli History: ... 45
  The Ghost of 1948; Benny Morris and the Palestinian Refugee Problem ... 45
    Discourse and Tropes in Benny Morris ... 47
  There is no History, Only Historians: Ilan Pappé. ... 62
    A War Decided in Advance: Ilan Pappé and 1948 ... 64
  The Collusion ... 70
  Final Comments ... 74
History and Irony ... 79
  Introduction ... 79
  The Israeli Literary Tradition and Zionist History ... 81
    Hebrew Writing and History ... 84
  Satire and Irony in the 1990s ... 88
    Orly Castel-Bloom's *Dolly City* ... 88
  The Liberal Ironist – Etgar Keret ... 95
  Human Parts: Castel-Bloom's Return to Realism ... 104
  History and Irony in *Human Parts* ... 106
  Final Remarks ... 113
Replacing History and Identity: Back to the Diaspora ... 119
  Introduction ... 119
    Diaspora as Non-History ... 124
    The Jewishness- Israeliness Dilemma ... 129
    Re-Invigorating the Diaspora ... 131

    Post-Colonial Diasporism as Identity Politics 140
        Zionism Psychoanalyzed 149
    An Israeli-Palestinian Homeland past Territory 158
    Final Comments 170
History on TV: The *Tekumah* series 175
    Introduction 175
    Commemorative History 181
    The Tekumah-series 183
        Contextualizing *Tekumah* 196
    Final Comments 201
**Post-Nationalist Discourse, Globalization and
a New Jewish Ethnoscape – Postscripts** 205
    The New Historians and post-Nationalist Discourse 210
    Irony and Liberalism in the 1990s 212
    Diaspora 217
Bibliography 221

Foreword

This study of Israeli historical discourses is located within the field of cultural studies. It analyses historical discourses from the perspective of their contributions to the identities and ideologies of the Israeli social domain. Accordingly, this study does not engage in discussions over the factuality or reality of the historical discourses presented, or aim to empower a particular body of knowledge within modern Jewish history. This study focuses on the way Jewish-Israeli historical discourses in historical works, literature, philosophy and TV create identities, space and give indications to social change in a period of cultural crisis.

Cultural studies cannot be considered a discipline with its own specific theories or specific methodology. Rather, its significance is a matter of perspective and a cross-disciplinary, multi-theoretical approach to the areas of the social domain that has to do with culture in a wider sense. An ongoing interest of the field of cultural studies is the formation of human identities, subjects, and the conditions of life experiences within a social domain. Issues of race, gender, sexuality, cultural stereotypes and otherness are among the central concerns of this field. Often, cultural studies are represented as being academic work in the interest of certain historically suppressed communities such as the people formerly living under colonialism or minorities of different kinds. This is also the perspective of the new Jewish cultural studies launched by Daniel and Jonathan Boyarin.[1] They state that new Jewish cultural studies can assist in the enhancement of the riches of Jewish culture. This might be so but from the perspective of this present study, such empowerment cannot be the purpose of critical academic studies. In the perspective of this study, the perspective of cultural studies on minorities and the social formation of human categories is a critical perspective concerned with the effects of power and violence. Accordingly, this study wholeheartedly supports the integration of Jewish studies with cultural studies, but it is

---

1. Boyarin 1997: VII-XXI.

not intended to empower any collective or ideology of togetherness. This is not a claim to objectivity, but a combination of the perspective of cultural studies with a Richard Rortyan ironism that makes it impossible to offer the re-descriptions of this study as an answer or a solution to any position.[2] Cultural studies do not consider academic work a protected environment from the general social domain and accordingly works of history, sociology and philosophy are treated as central aspects of the constitution of social categories and "reality" instead of as descriptions of reality. This view is also shared by this present study of Israeli historical discourses. Having located this study within a field of studies, I will proceed with a few comments on style.

This study consists of six essays. The essays can in principle be read independently of each other, but together they form a series of inquiries into different historical discourses of a Jewish-Israeli social domain. I have chosen the form of the essay because it has connotations of a freer and more "un-disciplined" inquiry than a conventional monograph. Accordingly, the essays do not follow a uniform interpretive strategy as a mathematical formula for the solution to a problem, and they do not refer to each other as a case building. Each essay is initiated by a quite elaborate introduction, which presents the perspective of the essay and provides the re-descriptions that serve as the background for my statements about the treated topic. The philosophical positions that anyhow permeate these essays are presented in the first essay entitled *History, Imagination, Discourse*. I have made use of some texts in other languages than English, mostly Hebrew texts. As a rule, I have translated quotes from other languages than English into English to the benefit of most readers and the homogeneity of the text itself. If a translation already exists into English, I follow this and indicate both the source of the translation and the original. This has been done in the recognition that professional translators most often do a better job translating/re-writing than I do. If there is no indication of an English translation in the notes, the translation is my own. In the bibliography, all titles are translated into English but I have noted the language of the version I have used.

These essays are all permeated by a dialectic between the general and the specific, the theoretical and the empirical. In this regard, I will para-

---

2. Rorty 1999: 91.

phrase Virginia Dominguez and state that these essays are and are not about Israel. They are about historical discourses and identity through an inquiry into Israeli historical discourses primarily of the 1990s.[3]

***

I would like to thank the following friends and colleagues for their interest in my work: Judith Winther, Jakob Skovgaard-Petersen, Annette Haaber Ihle, Rasmus Alenius Boserup, Michael Irving Jensen and Carmit Romano. I would in particular like to thank Laura Feldt, Claus V. Pedersen, Joel Haviv and Gal Bar-Emet for giving me their time and support when necessary. My deepest gratitude goes to Liv Egholm for being a wonderful friend, critic, colleague and partner. Finally, thanks to the people at the Carsten Niebuhr Department, Institute for Cross-Cultural and Regional Studies at University of Copenhagen and Centre for Contemporary Middle East Studies at University of Southern Denmark.

---

3. Dominguez 1989: 19.

History, Imagination, Discourse

"Thesis Ten: The idea of method is, etymology suggests, the idea of a road which takes you from the starting-point of inquiry to its goal. The best translation of the Greek meth' odo is "on track". Representationalists, because they believe that there are objects which are what they are apart from the way they are described, can take seriously this picture the picture of a track leading from subject to object. Anti-representationalists cannot. They see inquiry not as crossing a gap but as a gradual reweaving of individual or communal beliefs and desires under the pressure of causal impacts made by the behavior of people and things. Such reweaving dissolves problems as often as it solves them. The idea that the problems of philosophy stay the same but the methods of dealing with them change begs the metaphilosophical question at issue between representationalists and non-representationalists. It is much easier to formulate specific "philosophical problems" if, with Kant, you think that there are concepts which stay fixed regardless of historical change rather than, with Hegel, that concepts change as history moves along. Hegelian historicism and the idea that the philosopher's job is to draw out the meanings of our statements cannot easily be reconciled."[4]

History and Theory

The present essays are all about Israeli discourses of history in the 1990s. Four categories of texts have been selected for discussion. They are the new Israeli historians, authors Orly Castel-Bloom and Etgar Keret, Diasporic philosophy and finally Israel's 50th anniversary in 1998 in the shape of the TV series *Tekumah*. Furthermore, the present essays are all philosophical in character. The basic motivation that guides the work is a deep seated interest in the philosophy of history and the conviction that Hayden White was absolutely right when he in his *Meta-History. The*

---

4. Rorty 1999: 16.

Historical Imagination in Nineteenth Century Europe (1973) stated that: "There can be no "proper history" which is not at the same time "philosophy of history"".⁵ Hence, the interests of these essays are as much theoretical or philosophical as they are of the specific texts and contexts dealt with. The philosopher who to my mind most clearly has expressed such as perspective in a general way is Richard Rorty. The work of Richard Rorty and in particular his *Contingency, Irony and Solidarity* (1989) has had a profound influence on the essays though only one essay directly debates Rorty in connection with Israeli discourses of history.⁶ There are of course many other philosophical influences throughout the essays and these will figure in context. Here I will attempt to explain the most basic understandings that guide the work in general. The present essay is to be considered not a method or an external explanatory frame for the treatment of "sources" but as a fully integrated and inseparable dimension of the work in general. The "sources" have nothing to say apart from what their use in our discourses ascribes to them; they are not messages. This is why emphasis is placed on discourse and why my own philosophical discourse cannot be separated from the meanings I attribute to statements of others.

In the above citation, Rorty in a very basic way explains the difference between philosophical positions that figure prominently in the present essays. The position taken by Rorty and myself is the one of the non-representationalist. Representationalists understand method as something more than just sets of conventions for procedure among specific expert cultures such a nuclear physicists, linguists or historians. They think that methods and their innovation can direct us to a truer or more accurate description of an object as it really is apart from the way this object is described by language. Non-representationalists understand research as a "re-weaving", in Rorty's word, or a re-description of individual and communal beliefs. Accordingly, we do not progressively come closer to how things really are but we gradually re-describe them under the influence of many other things. In Israel in the 1990s a number of interesting re-descriptions surfaced and came to be central to the historical and cultural debates of that decade. These re-descriptions were highly influenced by "people and things" such as the political situa-

---

5. White 1973: XI.
6. The essay *History and Irony*.

tion and socio-economic development. The present essays focus on the re-descriptions themselves but attempt also to also describe the impact of context both specifically in the essays and as a heuristic framing of a certain "social plot" that hopefully will provide the essays with a context and a base. In line with the view of research borrowed from Rorty, the perspective on the character of Israel's social development through the 1990s is equally re-descriptive. The second half of this essay is devoted to re-description of a sociology of Israel in the 1990s based on the works of critical Israeli sociologists. The intention is that this part of the essay provides the reader with both a presentation of the way these sociologists understand Israeli society and the way their descriptions also are the Israel of the 1990s of these essays. Thus, I do not mean to indicate that I find sociology a less philosophical or re-descriptive discipline than the other categories of texts treated in the essays. Sociology is the description of the base, structures and categories of a society and that is why it is interesting to see how the sociology of the critical sociologists have discursive similarities to the more "speculative" texts of history, literature and philosophy.

Within this non-representationalist perspective real academic problems cannot be constructed. The construction of an academic problem implicates a stability of concepts and objects of inquiry and the idea that method is the path we walk between stable concepts and corresponding objects. In the above citation, Rorty refers to this perspective as Kantian. Rather, concepts and objects, mutually dependant they are, change in the course of time and social settings. The relativity of these times and social settings are equally the researcher's lot. I prefer to speculate on the academic problem of these essays in terms of a subjective encounter with texts that caught my attention and out of this meeting evolved gradually both concepts and objects for the present studies.[7] Thus, I

---

7. Here I draw on an understanding of reading suggested by Keith Jenkins through Jenkins' reading of Jacques Derrida and Geoffrey Bennington (Jenkins 2003: 26). This reading strategy consists of two steps. The first is a faithful reading to what the texts want and the second step is a rewriting. The second step interrupts the text and focuses on words, concepts, sentences that the text itself has not closed. Basically, when we have something to say about a text beyond mere summary we address places that are open in the text and refigure this place for it to be intelligible. This rewriting will not be the same as the text. These places are rewritten and rethought to make sense for the reader and thus the

make no claim to any degree of closure in the treatment of this topic or to have documented how things really were in the 1990s Israel. My hope is that I have accomplished an informed and coherent inquiry into the uses of history in Israeli texts from the 1990s which will finally lead to a discussion of whether or not these uses of history can be characterized as post-nationalist discourse. Throughout the essays I discuss the relationship between history, nation and collective identity and accordingly if changes in the historical imagination of Israelis occur in a relationship with globalization, post-modernity and its cultural logic. The post-nationalist discourses of the 1990s might then be conceptualized as attempts at articulating a new Jewish "ethnoscape" for a post-national era, following the arguments about imagination and identities in the era of increased globalization of Arjun Appadurai.[8] Therefore, these essays appear as an investigation of historical discourse in Israel in the 1990s with the aim of discussing discursive tendencies that point to a Jewish history and identity after Zionism.

The topic of Israeli discourse on history in the 1990s has attracted considerable attention since the so-called new Israeli historians rose to fame at the early end of the decade. A new historian, Benny Morris, started the debate already in 1988 with articles in the Israeli press and foreign journals. The debate about the new historians and their revisions of Israeli history soon spilled over into other academic areas such as sociology, literature, geography and philosophy. Several different tendencies highly critical towards Israeli political, social and cultural practices emerged under a category invented for the moment, namely post-Zionism.[9] As

---

text deconstructs itself by being subjected to reading. In this perspective, texts are not messages they are rather like unfinished vocabularies. Accordingly, I do not in these essays represent the authors of the texts that I read but I use the texts as inspiration for the development of my own vocabulary/discourse. Obviously, this is quite in opposition to traditional virtues of historians like being faithful to what the "sources" want to express and to write as clearly, unambiguously and commonsensical as possible. I should stress that I consider the past a text that can be read in the above manner.

8. Appadurai 2003: 32. Appadurai's perspective will be discussed in the essay *Replacing History and Identity*.
9. Among these tendencies I count the critical sociologists, some of whom will figure in the second half of this essay, the journals *Theory and Criticism* and *Hagar*, younger authors such as Orly Castel-Bloom and Etgar Keret and the increased focus on *Mizrahi* (Eastern) Jews within Israeli cultural studies. I do not intend to name these tendencies post-Zionist as this term has outworn

far as I have been able to detect, the term post-Zionist appeared in a 1993 compilation of Israeli sociology edited by Uri Ram.[10] Ram applies the term as a name for a sociological segment of Israeli society and this category's worldview and ideology. In popular usage, though, the term simply became an umbrella for leftwing criticism of Israel after the death of communism and socialism in the early 1990s.[11]

The debate over the new Israeli historians and post-Zionism has resulted in numerous articles and special issues of journals and a couple of books. I consider the vast majority of articles on the issue as direct participants in the debates with the aim of supporting either "the post-Zionists" or "the old historians". As such, the majority of articles are highly contextual arguments in a quite local Israeli memory struggle.[12] Some works, anyhow, deserve mention and these are the special issue of *History & Memory* (7, 1 1995), Laurence J. Silberstein's *The Post-Zionism Debates* (1999), the special issue on Israeli historical revisionism of *The Journal of Israeli History* (20, 2/3 2001) and Efraim Nimni's *The Challenge of Post-Zionism* (2003).[13] In Hebrew, consideration should be given to the entire production of *Theory and Criticism* (1991-) and the collection *From Vision to Revision* (1997) edited by Yechiam Weitz.[14] Newspaper articles and interviews from the entire decade with prominent post-Zionists or their opponents such Ilan Pappé, Benny Morris, Uri Ram,

---

itself in the debates and now only serves a purpose as a sociological category in the texts of sociologist Uri Ram (Ram 1993, 1999, 2003).

10. Ram 1993.
11. As clearly articulated by Ilan Pappé in his series of articles in *Journal of Palestine Studies*. These articles will discussed in the essay *History on TV*. Pappé 1997a, 1997b, 1997c.
12. Surely, no treatment of the topic is value-free. I attempt, though, to read the texts in a principled, theoretical, and open manner that will not simply dismiss other points of view. Any reader will easily detect my own affinities.
13. As mentioned there are numerous works that deal with the topic one way or the other. Of the ones attempting to establish what really happened in history Shlaim and Rogan's *The War for Palestine* (2000) and Pappé's *The Israel/Palestine Question* (2002) are worth mentioning and as highly polemical opponents to the new historians Efraim Karsh's *Fabricating Israeli History* (1999) and Yoram Hazony's *The Struggle for the Jewish State* (2000) ought to be mentioned.
14. I do not only mention works that I use in the present essays but works that I consider interesting or valuable for the understanding of the topic. Of course, I do not do justice to the many single and good articles on aspects of this topic in both English and Hebrew.

Aharon Megged, Amnon Rubinstein and Anita Shapira have also had a significant influence on the cultural debates regarding Israeli history and identity. I will make mention of some of these public statements if it seems appropriate without representing the entire scope of public debate over these issues.

In the special issue of *History & Memory* (7, 1 1995), two articles in particular have paved the way for some of the arguments of these essays. Baruch Kimmerling's article *Academic History Caught in the Crossfire* (1995) has been valuable for a clarification of key issues in Zionist history and Anita Shapira's article *Politics and Collective Memory; the Debate over the "New Historians" in Israel* (1995) has been valuable as a sensible criticism of the new history. Silberstein's *The Post-Zionism Debates* (1999) was the first comprehensive work to deal with aspects of this topic. The book has a survey character and does not go into any depth with detailed aspects of the topic.[15] The quality of Silberstein's book lies in its use of a discourse theoretical perspective and its strategy of mapping post-Zionist discourse which has been a great help in getting an idea of the magnitude of the shift in Israeli culture over the decade. I consider these present essays to be related to Silberstein's book without making much concrete use of it.

The definition of a field such as historical discourse is intimately related to which idea of history is appropriated. I have selected the texts that I read in the present essays neither to represent the range of Israeli historical debates nor to correspond to a reality as perceived by any group of Israelis. Accordingly, any claim to the significance of these chosen texts is purely my own and the field of inquiry is thus defined by my aforementioned idea of how academic problems appear. Other texts, histories, structures or institutions of 1990s Israel could have been chosen to give a picture of the changes of historical discourse of the 1990s with equal strength but basically the ones treated in these essays are the ones that I have an issue with. Anyhow, topics such as the new historians and the *Tekumah* series have received scholarly attention and my treatment of these topics surely engages in, and hopefully expands,

---

15. The book was seriously criticised by Emanuele Ottolenghi in his review of it for lacking interpretive coherence and being superficial. I find the criticism to an extent justifiable though I'm still quite fond of Silberstein's book. Ottolenghi 2003.

this particular production of knowledge. My inquiry into post-modern Diasporic philosophy and the historical discourse of authors Castel-Bloom and Keret has not the same entangled body of texts as I have not seen other treatments of these topics within a historical perspective.

What is History?
The question of what history really is and how it should be worked with has engaged historians since the invention of modern history in the 19th century. Still, historians have rarely engaged in philosophical reflections over their vocation but focused on debating the methods of reaching the clearest and most unmediated connection to past things and events. The Rankian quest of finding out how it really was has dominated and still dominates the discipline of history despite many methodological innovations and crystallizations of different historical schools since the 19th century. Historians are usually representationalists and realists and understand such views as the very raison d'etre of their discipline. Thus, we cannot approach the matter of historical discourse from the perspective of an historian. Instead, we will approach historical discourse from a philosophical and discourse theoretical perspective that enables an appreciation of historical discourse without consideration to the truthfulness of its representations or its correspondence to reality.

The perspective on history as a discourse crystallized in earnest in the 1950s and 1960s with the brands of continental European thinking commonly known as structuralism and post-structuralism. Roland Barthes, Michel Foucault and Jacques Derrida as well as others have played key roles in criticizing conventional history and attempting to rethink history in ways to avoid or supersede the pitfalls they saw in conventional history.[16] The results of these criticisms and re-workings are diverse and can hardly be reduced to any simple explanations and neither can the differences between their proponents. I have found the perspectives on history of Michel Foucault and Jacques Derrida particularly beneficial for the entire inquiry presented here. The relevant aspects of their philosophies will be explained in context. The basic problem is that of historicity in its broadest and most radical sense. History appears in every construction of meaning, in every language, as a relation between past, present

---

16. Se Attridge, Bennington and Young 1987: 1-11. Foucault and Derrida will be discussed in further detail in context in the present essays.

and future and as the utopian dimension of every discourse. The very meaningfulness of a word or a thing is due to a difference between this word or thing and other words or things. This difference is not only spatial but also temporal. The world or time is not the source of history but language is.[17] Conventional history is based on the opposite view that it is indeed the past in itself that is reflected in historical writings. This language that makes histories makes identities and categories which are maps of the social domains we inhabit. Language, its construction of identities and categories are themselves historical in as much as they change and fluctuate and have no origins only relations to other words and things. The coming into being of a history as that of a nation, a collective, an era, an institution or a proper name is an attempt to close the un-closable and this history comes to exist as a social institution. It becomes an ideology of identity and will be fought over because whoever controls it controls very important aspects of the social domain; the plot of its sense of togetherness and the contexts of experience. Histories in the shape of academic works about the past, philosophies about history and identity, news stories, interact with a social domain, shape it and is shaped by it, in a process where our efforts to achieve a stable description of it can never avoid to participate in the play. This participation is not about truth but it has truth-effects that have a huge influence on our perception of the world. Rather, this participation is an ethical, or aesthetical, statement ultimately installed by our imagination of things. We put our imagination of things into action in our social domains by way of communication, by way of discourse. The present studies make an inquiry into the ways Israeli historical discourses act as imaginations of self and collective in an Israeli social domain in a historical moment in Israeli history when hegemonic Zionism seemed challenged by both cultural and real-political developments. The most dominant relation of these discourses is still Zionism but they are all occupied with the possibilities of Israeli history and identity in a period of a waning Zionist regime of truth.

History as Rhetoric
In this section, we will go into some detail with Hayden White's rhetorical studies of writings of history. White has been instrumental to the

---

17. Ibid. 8.

specific study of historical discourse as a genre, a type of literature and as rhetorical constructions. The philosophy of history of Hayden White can be considered a concretization of post-structuralist perspectives on history manifested as direct studies of historical works and many of their details in an elaborate, systematic and coherent way. Virtually all of White's articles and books on history are among the key works of critical historiography and his influence has for a long time gone beyond mere philosophy of history. He is now widely read on theoretical courses of conventional history, literature and anthropology at many universities. The aspects of White's work that are important for the present essays are his fundamental divisions of historical discourses into archetypical plots, his ideas of the historical imagination and his particular version of the study of tropes (tropology). The concepts developed by White are used in context throughout these essays though most directly in the essay *Readings of the New Israeli Historians*. Therefore, it seems appropriate with a more elaborate discussion of this particular theoretical aspect of the study.

In his key work, *Meta-History; the Historical Imagination of Nineteenth Century Europe* (1973), Hayden White sets out to analyze the founding fathers of the realistic, representationalist, modern writing of history and their speculative counterparts in the philosophy of history from a literary and rhetorical perspective. The detailed analysis of Michelet, Ranke, Tocqueville and Burckhardt as the realists and Hegel, Marx, Nietzsche and Croce as the philosophers leads, roughly put, to the following conclusions:

> "(1) there can be no "proper" history which is not at the same time "philosophy of history"; (2) the possible modes of historiography are the same as the possible modes of speculative philosophy of history, (3) these modes, in turn, are in reality *formalizations* of poetic insights that analytically precede them and that sanction the particular theories used to give historical accounts the aspect of an "explanation"; (4) there are no apodictically certain theoretical grounds on which one can legitimately claim an authority for any one of the modes over the others as being more "realistic", (5) as a consequence of this, we are indentured to a *choice* among contending interpretive strategies in any effort to reflect on history-in-general; (6) as a corollary of this, the best grounds for choosing one perspective on history rather than another are ultimately aesthetic or moral rather than epistemological; and,

> finally, (7) the demand for the scientization of history represents only the statement of a preference for a specific modality of historical conceptualization, the grounds of which are either moral or aesthetic, but the epistemological justification of which still remains to be established."[18]

Accordingly, the basic conclusions of White, rephrased, refer to a view on history as a type of literary or narrative imagination. Historians who write realistically about the past and philosophers who speculate about its laws, structures and nature have the same literary/narrative modes at their disposal. We simply cannot speak about the past without a plot. The plot manifests itself in all discourses of history, realistic or speculative, which is why White can conclude that there is no history which is not at the same time a philosophy of history. The plot of history is not in a correspondence relationship with the past. The plot is a formalization of a poetic insight of the historian or philosopher. Such a formalization of a poetic insight can also be called a discourse which would make the plot its "family" or category of similar discourses on a comparative level. The following claim made by White that we cannot know by way of absolute proof which mode of history is the most realistic in the sense of being the closest to the nature of the real past is based on the same understanding of method and research as Richard Rorty's, to which I referred earlier. The consequence is that realistic writings of history have a rhetorical style which is realism and this realism is grounded in a choice of style/mode that is not dictated by the past or generally reality as it really is. Consequently, the choices of style/mode of history which figure in historical discourses reflect ethical or aesthetical views of the ones who produce or re-produce a particular historical discourse. The choices do not reflect epistemologies of truth but epistemologies of knowledge often purported to be the truth. Scientific writings of history, thus, have no higher claim to truth than other modes of history. The predominance of certain modes of history in academia reflects only ethical or aesthetical choices which have become conventions of procedure among professional historians.[19] Accordingly, I do not in the

---

18. White 1973: XI-XII.
19. To avoid misunderstandings, I should stress that this perspective does not make it possible to say anything about the past. Firstly, there are only a limited

present essays value the historical discourses of professional historians as representing real history any more than other categories of historical discourses. Therefore, the present essays can be conceptualized as an inquiry into the modes, ethics and aesthetics of historical discourses in Israel in the 1990s; an inquiry that is critical towards transcendental truth-claims of both "new" and "old" historians alike.

To my mind, there are two aspects of Hayden White's philosophy of history towards which relevant criticism can be directed. The first is concerned with what he calls the modes of history. White defines these modes as archetypical narrative plots following Northrop Frye's *The Anatomy of Criticism* (1957). The plots of Romance, Comedy, Tragedy and Satire consequently become the structural possibilities presented to historian or others within which histories can be cast.[20] This seems a somewhat limited field of narrative options and Frye's taxonomy cannot be said to the only one available. The second is the question whether archetypical plots can be identified at all. White himself touches upon this criticism by arguing that he is aware that there might be other basic plots such as the epic and that in each history several plots can be represented at the same time in different aspects of the history. Still, White argues that every history must have a meta-plot for it to be coherent and aspire to be a history.[21] Furthermore, White considers history a restricted art form that has normally only one aim which is to inform about the past in a commonsensical way. More advanced art forms cannot be categorized only by means of an analysis of emplotment.[22] I find that White's use of a notion of archetypical plots is too rigid as a general understanding of narrative while I have no doubts regarding its heuristic value when it comes to history. I have generally refrained from generalizations based

---

      number of things that can be said about a thing for it to be that particular thing. Secondly, facts are facts as singular statements but they can be contextualized in a number of ways through which they get to mean something. It is this contextualization that is a reflection of how history-in-general purportedly is. The facts are irrelevant to us, they are not even facts to anything in a meaningful way, before being contextualized. Furthermore, for a discourse to be coherent it logically establishes what is true and what is not. The point is that truth is established by way of discourse thus truth is contextual not transcendental.

20. White 1973: 7.
21. Ibid. 8, note 6.
22. Ibid.

on the notion of archetypical plots in the present studies but I use the literary categories of Tragedy, Comedy, Satire and Epic when it seems appropriate regarding the understanding of given historical discourse.

Secondly, we should be critical of White's statement that we have the choice between the different modes of emplotment. This might be true in an ideal situation. We must question, though, whether this possible choice really is a choice and how possible it is. Firstly, the choice between interpretive strategies only exists when history has been revealed as ethical or aesthetical statements instead of statements about how the past really is in a transcendental sense, and even then it is doubtful whether we have a choice or not. If we are under the impression that the sources of the past pass messages to us for us to interpret then we have no choice apart from going with the interpretation that successfully claims to be the correct interpretation. Reason then dictates our choice of mode of history within a communicative community guided by the rules of reason. Even when history has been revealed as ethical or aesthetical statements, some statements will succeed in achieving the status of some sort of commonsense which makes the choice of another mode of historical explanation an oppositional choice. Another way of phrasing it would be that even though we realize that formally speaking White is right, and all historians did, we probably would not find a proliferation of different types of histories. Thus, we can agree with White that historical discourses are ethical and/or aesthetical statements, and that our differentiations between them are ethical and aesthetical differentiations, but the statements and differentiations are contextual themselves; they are not just free but stand in relation to other discourses and structures of the social domain. The only possible mode in which to write a history like White, following his taxonomy, is in an ironic mode informed by a critical, counter-historical perspective.[23] Far from reflecting choices of interpretive strategies, historical discourses reflect ethical and aesthetical discourses that dominate or struggle in a given social domain and radical criticism is the only means by which we can enable just the awareness of the possibility of a free choice. Where White thinks that the awareness of the poetic basis of historical discourse gives us choice of interpretive strategies, I claim that this awareness is highly conditional and based

---

23. Irony is the trope of which Satire is the fictional form.

on criticism of history, knowledge and commonsense. According, in the present essays I will not argue as though the texts are reflections of open and individual choices between different ethics and aesthetics but as though the historical discourses reflect both private and public projects and concerns that crystallize in relationships to other discourses of the social domain.[24]

Through his studies of modern, realistic writings of history, White develops a broad concept of the historical imagination. The historical imagination is constituted by all the attributes of a particular historical discourse. In this sense, it is a meta-concept that is intended to capture the structural and discursive contents of a historical discourse under a name. Thus, it enables me to use the concept of, for example, the Zionist historical imagination. The concept of the historical imagination as a unification of all the attributes of a historical discourse is justified by a definition of the central attributes of a historical discourse. We have touched upon the plot as the narrative structure of a historical discourse but beside the plot White defines other modes that characterize a historical discourse. These are the modes of argument and the modes of ideological implication. White argues that apart from the mode of emplotment, histories also can be conceptualized by their use of a formal argument through which

---

24. The distinction between public and private is a complex one and an important philosophical discussion within such a theoretical perspective as mine. Within critical theory and the discourse theory of Ernesto Laclau and Chantal Mouffé there are no a priori private discourses; that would imply the existence of an "originative subject". Richard Rorty, though, makes this distinction contextually as something that occurs in Western, affluent, literate societies where private self-creation projects and public, political projects do not have to be the same. Basically, it means that Rorty thinks that in Western, rich, societies people can pursue their private projects of beliefs and identities without thinking that the same projects would be beneficial if applied generally. Thus, there is created a difference between a person's discourse for self-creation and -explanation and the type of discourse the same person supports and reproduces in the public realm. This is obviously in opposition to the Kantian imperative and is caused by the fact that many needs and desires of most people in the West are not and cannot be a matter of public policy. Affluence has solved or reduced many of the basic private problems that could translate into public projects through welfare and general high standards of living for the majority of the population. I consider Israel to be on the periphery of this type of Western society and thus displaying some of the cultural signs of such a society. I will discuss this in some detail in context in the essay *History and Irony*. Laclau & Mouffe 1985: 114-122, Rorty 1989: 73-95.

the specific events of the history can be explained following certain rules of argument. In opposition to the indirect historical explanation of the plot, the formal argument is explicit. White operates with four types of formal argument which are the Formist, Organicist, Mechanistic, and Contextualist historical arguments.[25] These types of formal arguments are to be considered the rules by which the explicit argument of the historical discourse is conducted. The mode of ideological implication is based on the idea that there to every plot and formal argument are connected certain ideological implications. White following Karl Mannheim's *Ideology and Utopia* (1946) identifies four types of meta-ideologies that can be singled out as implications of the plots and arguments of a historical discourse.[26] These are Anarchism, Conservatism, Radicalism and Liberalism.[27] These meta-ideologies are all responsible in as much as they aspire to reason, science and realism. They are committed to public discussion with other systems that also have claims to reason, science and realism. Accordingly, they are conscious of the coherence of their arguments in a way which totalitarianism is not. This does not mean, however, that these ideologies have not got a totalitarian potential. They are committed to the victory over the competing systems but

---

25. Very roughly put, the characteristics of each are: The Formist have completed a historical argument when the studied sets of objects have been identified in all their specificity. The focus is on the uniqueness of the events, objects and agents of the historical situation. The Organicist attempts to place the particularities of a historical situation as components of a synthetic historical process. The specific components of history are components of a whole which is qualitatively different from the individual parts. These wholes are at all times greater than their components. Organicism is the historical argument of nationalism. The Mechanist is also integrative but reductive more than synthetic. Focus is on the laws that govern the historical processes. Both individual components and larger classes in the historical situation are subjected to processes that dictate an outcome. The Mechanist searches for the causal relationships between things in the historical situation. The Mechanistic perspective is usually attributed to Marxism. The Contextualist represents a functional historical argument. The Contextualist and the Formist share an interest in the specificities of the historical situation but the Contextualist wants to explain these things by way of the functional relationships to other things in the specific historical situation. Contextualists have a problem with narrating the grand narratives because their arguments are tied to the contexts of different historical situations. White 1973: 1-42.
26. White 1973: 22-29.
27. Very roughly put, the main characteristics of these types are: Conservatism

in absence of absolute power they represent meta-ideological positions that are responsible towards criticism, facts, and conventional criteria for logic and coherence.[28] White develops a correspondence scheme in which the mode of emplotment, the mode of argument and the mode of ideological explanation together constitute a historical imagination. Examples of it could be that a history cast as a Comedy will most likely make use of an Organicist argument and have a Conservative ideological implication while a Satiric history will make use of a contextual argument and have a liberal ideological implication. In these present essays, I will not apply such a correspondence scheme to my material but I have explained it in order to account for the theory behind the use of a concept such as the historical imagination. Thus, a historical imagination is the combination of the ways we plot history, the ways we argue it, and the ways in which this reflects our ideological disposition.

The final aspect of Hayden White's philosophy of history that I will pay particular attention to is his theory of tropes. In the present essays I frequently apply the names of the classical tropes such as metaphor, metonymy, synecdoche and irony in ways which might seem a little unusual. The use of the tropes in these present studies is inspired by White's theory of the tropes as not only local figures of speech but as a sort of

---

and Liberalism generally conceive of society as natural and healthy but Conservatism tends to view society as a sort of biology while Liberalism views it as a mechanism. Both are very sceptical towards programmatic, rapid, changes of society. Conservatism understands history as a historical evolution and its natural structure as utopia. Liberalism imagines the possibility of the optimization of the mechanism to perfection in a remote future. Thus, the utopian condition is remote to Liberalism which discourages revolution in the same manner as Conservatism's view that the natural conditions of society are the best we can hope for. In opposition, Anarchism and Radicalism are based on the wish for rapid transformation of the structural relationships of society. Anarchism conceives of society as sick and unnatural and hopes for its change into a real community. Nature is conceived as something that society has disrupted and society has accordingly forced an unnatural condition on people. The utopia of Anarchism is to an extent transcendental in as much as it can only be achieved when people break with society and establish another reality. Radicalism conceives of utopia as imminent. Radicalism works for the implementation of the utopian society as soon as possible. White 1973: 22-25.

28. White considers meta-ideologies such as Fascism, Apocalypticism, Mysticism and Animism beyond the responsible ideologies and therefore they are not in consideration as implications for responsible historical discourses. White 1973: 23, note 12.

poetical foundation for discourse and Richard Rorty's distinction between Ironism and Metaphysicism.[29] In White's conception of the tropes, they do not only apply to overtly figurative language such as poetry. Realistic writings such as science or history are equally figurative; something which has only been disguised by a terminologically disciplined schematization of the words, concepts and discourses applied in these fields which makes them seem perfectly rational and "un-metaphorical". White insists that any thought about an object and the words used to represent this object necessarily needs figurative discourse for the object to become intelligible.[30] The tropes themselves have the same implications as in classical rhetoric. They are all types of metaphor. The classical metaphor is representational in the sense that it uses the understanding of one thing to represent another. Metonymy is reductionist because it makes a part represent other parts. Synecdoche is integrative because it makes a part represent the quality of a whole. Irony is negational in as much as it is doubtful towards the ability of any figure of speech to capture the true essence of something. The tropological perspective is not directed at the analysis of sentences that are metonymical or ironic but at the texts in their totality as extended metonymies or ironies. White thinks of the trope as both an initiator of discourse in the sense of a verbalization of the poetic insight that is the point of departure for our speaking of things and as a more comprehensive poetics that reflects a world-view.[31] Therefore any discourse is begun with a trope that is a reflection of our pre-discursive and pre-logical dispositions and any discourse that, for example, makes universal propositions is an extended synecdoche and any discourse that accounts for singular existential statements (historical facts) is an extended metonymy. Central to White's argument is that the move between the universal and the particular in any academic text is a tropological shift. The point is that it is not the objects of the discourse that define the tropological mode but the trope that makes the objects of the discourse constitute a universal or a particular statement.[32] The

---

29. Rorty's position is explained in detail in the essay *History and Irony* and will not be accounted for here.
30. White 1973: 33, note 13.
31. White 1978: 1-3.
32. It should be noted that White's pre-cursors in using a similar understanding of tropes are classical structuralists such as Claude Levi-Strauss in anthropology, Roman Jakobson in linguistics, and Jacques Lacan in psychoanalysis.

use of the tropes thus arranges the objects, structures, and contexts in different relationships and in different meanings. White uses the example of the difference between metonymy and synecdoche to illustrate this central point. Metonymical reductions are characterized by the extrinsic relationship between the parts in it. Metonymy provides a difference between phenomena in a part-part relationship. Synecdoche creates an intrinsic relationship between the parts in it. Qualities are shared. Synecdoche can construe two parts into a whole that is qualitatively different than the parts.[33] White's tropology accordingly represents both the most specific and most general aspect of his philosophy of history namely that language, its elements and structures is what constitutes the organization of the past and its meaning. In these present essays, I go into different levels of detail with the tropes of the discourses I discuss but generally I use the names of the tropes as indicative of the character of a text in its totality following White and Rorty while I mainly in the essay *History and Irony* discuss irony as a world-view in connection to Israeli historical discourses of the 1990s.

Discourse and Society

In the following, I will account for my use of the concept of discourse. This is obviously connected to the above, which already has shed some light on the understanding of discourse and language expressed in these studies. The aspect that this far has avoided explanation is the complex relationship between discourse and society, or re-phrased discourse and the world. I claim throughout these essays a relationship between the historical discourses of 1990s Israel, other discourses of the social domain and what I usually call socio-economic configurations. I have throughout refrained from categorically defining a direct correspondence relationship between what is said about history and how the social domain is configured. A common misunderstanding goes that discourse is only about mental or imaginative capacities. The real is something other than discourse.[34] I will argue that the real is indeed not only language but things

---

33. White 1973: 35.
34. Some theories of discourse make a distinction between discourse and non-discourse, or the real, as though there is a representational relationship between discourse and the real. Discourse thus becomes the human distortion of the real. This is for example the discourse theory of Norman Fairclough called

of the real are elements of discourse and thus signs to be interpreted. I will in the following attempt to explain this relationship inspired by the discourse theory of Ernesto Laclau and Chantal Mouffe. This line of argument is not explored explicitly in these studies as the focus is on the historical discourses themselves but the understandings derived from this line of argument anyhow permeate these present essays.

In their *Hegemony and Socialist Strategy; Towards a Radical Democratic Politics* (1985) Laclau and Mouffe criticize Marxist interpretive strategies and their aspiration to categorically capture the structural essence of History. They claim that it is impossible to capture a mechanical logic behind social configurations and social developments but far from rejecting the Marxist tradition, they attempt to re-describe central aspects of this tradition in a manner they define as post-Marxist.[35] The cornerstones of the post-Marxist interpretive strategy are the concept of hegemony derived from Antonio Gramsci and their development of the concept of discourse. Both concepts appear central to the terminology of these present studies. I will not here pretend to do full justice to the complex criticism of Marxism and the full layout of the theory of the social of Laclau and Mouffe. As mentioned earlier the foundation of this criticism is the rejection of the stable concepts of Marxist theory such as class, base and superstructure and the idea that these categories define an essence of the social that can be a point of departure for defining any laws of history and social development. Laclau and Mouffe's logic is relational which means that if, say, the economy is what determines class and superstructure essentially, the economy would have to be a self-enclosed system. It is not. The elements of the social exist in a relational relationship to each other of which none is the exclusively determinative base. Accordingly, we cannot fixate absolutely whether changes in the Israeli economy led to new social discourses or vice versa because both are elements in the discursive field where the changes took place. This leads us to the definitions of concepts that are central in this regard.

---

    critical discourse analysis (Fairclough 1995). Foucault also operates with a distinction between the discursive and the non-discursive though not as part of a schematization of the relationship between discourse and the real. See Laclau and Mouffe's comments on Foucault. Laclau and Mouffe 1985: 105-6 and notes 13, 14 p. 145.
35. Laclau and Mouffe 1985: 4.

Firstly, it is appropriate to explain the reason for the impossibility of fixity in the analysis of the social and in this regard the concept of overdetermination is important. Overdetermination is a concept that has been imported to the social sciences from psychoanalysis and linguistics. It means that there to a thing, word or symbol are multiple possible meanings; every thing, word or symbol is overdetermined regarding what it can possibly signify. There is an infinite surplus of signifiers in relation to the signified. Everything in the social domain lacks an ultimate literality that can reduce things to particles in a law of the social and hence the social constitutes itself as a symbolic order as much as the psyche or language.[36] The radical and profound consequence of overdetermination and the understanding of the social as a symbolic order is that society and social agents lack any essence. The regularity of society and social agents is only caused by the relative and temporary fixation which follows the establishment of a specific social order.[37] Fixations such as a Zionist historical imagination accompany a certain social order which is itself a relative stabilization of meanings of the symbolic order that society is. The Zionist historical imagination thus stands in a differential relationship to other discourses of the social order which is why it makes sense as the temporal dimension of this particular symbolic order known as Israeli society.

Discourse itself is the result of articulations where articulations are the practice that establishes a relation between elements so that their identity is modified.[38] Every relation alters the identity of the elements involved and discourse is the structured totality resulting from the practice of articulation. Discourses are never stable or completely fixed because of overdetermination and accordingly there is constantly a surplus of meaning. The surplus of meaning is the reason why the field of Jewish and Israeli history is an arena for a struggle over fixations, identities, no matter how realistically historians attempt to represent the past.[39] What counts as the realistic version of Jewish and Israeli history is a result of a differential relationship to other relative stabilizations that make a symbolic social order. As such Jewish and Israeli history is a field of discursivity

---

36. Laclau and Mouffe 1985: 97-98.
37. Ibid. 98.
38. Ibid. 105.
39. Meaning that realism is impossible except as a particular style.

in which certain elements are pointed out to be the symbolic moments of the imagination of the temporal dimension of a name.[40]

Hegemony is what accounts for the duration of certain stabilizations over longer periods of time. If there existed a direct correspondence relationship between signifiers and the signified and meanings were essentially stable, that would be the end of hegemony. Hegemony is the creation of larger social and political spaces that are constituted by relational identities. Within our field, Zionism as a social and political space is such a hegemonic formation. Hegemony creates meaningful relations between discourses through the exclusion of alternative signifiers and therefore hegemony always exists in a social field of antagonisms. It creates the frontier between positions. The frontier is at the same time the limits of the meaningful discourse that constitutes a certain hegemonic formation as an identifiable social and political identity. The impossibility of controlling the multiple meanings of things has the consequence that hegemony is also only relatively stable. New meanings are constantly incorporated or excluded from the hegemonic formation. Hegemony and frontiers are internal elements of the social itself. This is obviously a logic of negativity. The relative stability of identities within the social such as certain histories or collective identities is secured through the exclusion or domestication of alternative signification. As the social and social agents lack any essence, the social cannot be defined positively and society as a structured totality in general becomes an impossible concept.

Phrased within the particular terminology of Laclau and Mouffe, the political, social and historical spaces of Israeli society of the 1990s were at the point of an organic crisis:

> "A conjuncture where there is a generalized weakening of the relational system defining the identities of a given social and political space, and where, as a result there is a proliferation of floating elements, is what we will call following Gramsci, a conjuncture of organic crisis. It does not emerge from a single point, but as the result of an overdetermination of circumstances; and it reveals itself not only in a proliferation of antagonisms but also in a generalized crisis of social identities."[41]

---

40. The concept of the field of discursivity is explained in Laclau and Mouffé 1985: 111.
41. Laclau and Mouffe 1985: 136.

I will not hesitate to state that we in Israel in the 1990s witnessed a proliferation of floating elements that were not integrated in Zionist discourse. I consider the overdetermination of circumstances in Israel in the 1990s a matter of fact resulting in a proliferation of antagonisms such as the debates over the new historians and post-Zionism, new historical discourses, literary and philosophical discourses which articulate the elements of the Jewish-Israeli discursive field to constitute identities incommensurable with Zionism and its historical discourse. In these present essays I do not follow Laclau and Mouffe's terminology as a method of analysis but my recurrent use of the concepts of discourse and hegemony is philosophically constituted within their theory of discourse. As mentioned earlier, I make claims to a complex relation between what I usually term the socio-economic configurations/developments of Israeli society and the proliferation of new historical discourses in the Jewish-Israeli social domain. Nothing can constitute itself outside discursive conditions and therefore discourse is also of a material character. Changing socio-economic conditions is therefore nothing more than a heuristic concept for appreciation of the inter-relatedness of meaningful articulations about the social domain. The new sociological descriptions of Israeli society of the 1990s stand in a differential relationship with at least some of the changing historical discourses while all of the critical approaches are part of the crisis of Zionist hegemony feeding on and fed by the proliferation of floating elements. I will not go as far as stating that these studies will show a new hegemony rising but they engage in the discourses of the memory struggle that pose a challenge to Zionist hegemony. These discourses do not emerge from the same position, as we will see, but they are part in constituting a field of antagonisms over the meaning of Jewish-Israeli history. As all discourses aspire to hegemony, these new historical discourses are suggestive with regard to a Jewish ethnoscape after Zionism.

Discourses of Israeli State and Citizenship

In any regard, the 1990s can be considered a quite special decade in the history of Israel. Many of the significant political and social developments of Israeli society in the 1990s naturally have a long history but the economic and social reforms that began in the mid-80s and the Palestinian uprising, the Intifadah, from 1987 must be among the most important instigators of the developments of the 1990s. Furthermore came the profound changes in international politics both on a universal and regional level after 1990. The breakdown of communism led to changes in the international world order that influenced Middle Eastern balances of power. Israel's close ally USA established a virtual international, economic and military hegemony which presented Israel with hitherto unknown possibilities to secure itself in the Middle East by peaceful means. The breakdown of communism furthermore led to a mass exodus of Russian Jews to Israel which radically changed Israeli demography and accordingly the political landscape. The most remarkable change, though, came in the wake of the first Gulf war in 1991. Israel and the Palestinians began negotiating a settlement of the conflict which in 1993 led to the Declaration of Principles; a document that attested to the mutual recognition of Israelis and Palestinians and to their rightful claims to a homeland, peace and security. To a large extent, this document became a yardstick for all political developments internally in Israel and between Israel and the Palestinians until the Camp David negations in 2000. The Declaration of Principles was both the symbol of a new historical situation, a significant moment of an Israeli, liberal, utopian discourse, and a very concrete dividing line in Israeli politics and culture of the 1990s. The Declaration of Principles as an axis of public discourse was at one and the same time a historical opening towards post-colonial Zionism and a historical breakdown of the instrumental rationality of Zionism.[42]

According to sociologists Gershon Shafir and Yoav Peled in their *Being Israeli; the Dynamics of Multiple Citizenship* (2002) Israeli history consists of the struggle between three discourses of state and citizenship. These discourses are colonialism, ethno-nationalism and democracy.[43] Shafir and Peled argue that these discourses at the same time exclude each other and presuppose each other in the Israeli context. They intermingle in the political programs of political parties, popular movements, and in state institutions and because of their oppositional nature they constitute the primary dividing lines that produce the dynamics of Israeli historical development. The movements of these discourses are effectively the yardstick for a periodization of Israeli history. Zionism, the pre-state Jewish

---

42. Feldt 2003.
43. Shafir & Peled 2002: 2.

community in Palestine and Israel itself are placed within the heritage of European colonialism. Zionist colonialism belongs to the category of "pure settlement colonialism" which is characterized by the colonization of a territory and the settlement of an immigrant population that is clearly defined in advance often with the aim of establishing a "new society".[44] Shafir and Peled state that a colonialism that at the same time involves colonization of a territory, meaning territorial dispossession of a native population and import of an immigrant population, has very far reaching consequences for the natives compared to other types of colonialism and therefore the resulting conflicts are much more deep seated and intransigent.[45] Accordingly, the conflict between Israel and the Palestinians is much more than just a dispute over land. It is a colonial/anti-colonial conflict through which both collectives produce and re-produce their collective identity and telos.

The institutional backbone of Zionist colonialism is what is conventionally named Labor Zionism.[46] Labor Zionism established the Jewish immigrant community in Palestine as a mobilized political and institutional force from the beginning of the so-called Second Aliyah (second larger wave of immigration from approximately 1904-1914). From the 1920s, the Labor institutions led by the organization of Hebrew workers in Eretz Israel, the Histadrut, controlled all the important institutions,

---

44. Zionist apologetics have it that Zionism is not a type of colonialism because it did not spring of a mother-country, sought to establish an empire and wished to control the natives. This is of course nonsense. A colonial society is any society established through the combination, to various degrees, of military control, colonization, and the exploitation of native populations and their territorial dispossession, justified by claims of paramount right or superior culture (Shafir 1996: 193). Zionism is a national, colonial project which sought to create a pure Jewish-national colony and for that purpose Palestine was colonized and re-populated with Jews. Shafir and Peled 2002: 37.
45. Ibid. 37.
46. Shafir and Peled prefer the term Labor Settlement Movement, justifiably so, because the strain of Zionism which established and controlled the development of the Jewish immigrant community in Palestine was primarily concerned with settlement. To achieve this end a Labor ideology was the best ideological vehicle. See also Sternhell 1999 for a comprehensive analysis of role of the Labor ideology in colonizing Palestine. Sternhell shows how nationalist and colonialist priorities dominated the worldview of the Labor movement and how the quasi-socialist and egalitarian ideology served a clear military, economic and regime purpose under the paradigm of pure settlement colonialism.

the economy, cultural and political life in general. From the 1930s, the Labor movement also controlled the international Zionist institutions most importantly the World Zionist Organization (WZO) and the Jewish Agency (JA), which was the key body of Zionist diplomacy concerning the relationship between the Zionists of Palestine and the British mandatory power. JA was mandated by the League of Nations to represent the Zionists and it gradually became a Zionist government of Palestine despite the existence of directly elected organs for that purpose. Labor Zionism controlled politics and institutions of Zionism and Israel until the landslide elections of 1977. Its discourse of state and citizenship was one of colonialism and communitarian republicanism.[47]

The republican discourse of Labor Zionist colonialism has fostered the key civic virtues that function as icons of the moral purposes of the Zionist community and as the ideal characteristics of each individual member of this community. The civic virtues generate a moral community and accordingly the community is not only for the individual members as a procurer of equal rights and duties. The community is the identity of the members on a collective and also to a large degree on an individual level. Shafir and Peled identify "pioneering" as the key civic virtue of the pre-state Jewish community. Pioneering is characterized by social and personal sacrifice, physical labor, agricultural settlement and military defense and is incarnated in the young, manly, Zionist who conquers the land with shovels and guns.[48] This virtue is typical for Labor Zionist republicanism but with the establishment of Israel in 1948 the movement had to change into a state and its institutions. This transformation was spearheaded by David Ben-Gurion and his invention of the civic virtue of "statism" (mamlachtiut). Statism was basically a transformation of the virtue of pioneering from being in the service of a process of colonization into being in the service of state building and collective action directed by a narrow elite. Statism represents the pioneering virtue of an established state and as such it represented the

---

47. Republicanism is one of the dominating discourses of state and citizenship in Israel. The others are ethno-nationalism and liberalism. Republicanism, or alternatively communitarianism, contends that society is a moral community which should foster certain civic virtues, or values. These civic virtues are, in this view, the basis of the community's existence and the basis of membership. Shafir and Peled 2002: 5.
48. Shafir & Peled 2002: 42-43.

key civic virtue of Israeli republicanism until the gradual weakening of Labor Zionism from 1967.[49]

The re-opening of the frontier in 1967 with the conquest and beginning colonization of the occupied territories was the first major challenge to the hegemony of Labor republicanism. From alternative institutional frameworks such as the religious sprang an ethno-nationalist colonialism which in the 1970s was led by the settler NGO *Gush Emunim* (The Block of the Faithful). The ethno-nationalist colonialism challenged republican colonialism and thereby the statist hegemony over civic virtues. At the same time, Labor was challenged by a liberal-economic discourse which also participated in the colonization of the occupied territories but in a way that eventually led to the undermining of the power to mobilize any collectivist civic virtue. Most settlers in the occupied territories simply went there to improve their individual lifestyles. Thus, the major drive for settlement was defined by cheap housing not pioneering in either its republican or ethno-nationalist variant.[50] We now see the contours of an Israeli history structured by the struggle between republicanism, ethno-nationalism and liberalism.

By the 1990s, Labor Zionism had lost its hegemony over the discourses of Israeli state and citizenship and was internally split between the traditional republicanism and liberalism. The reforms of economy and public sector to control inflation and initiate economic growth from the middle of the 1980s finally undermined Labor's statist ethos and its institutional foundation in the Histadrut and other state subsidized public organizations and companies.[51] Liberal economic discourse was a demand from the logic of economic growth and not the least globalization. In the early 1990s the liberalists of Labor took over the leadership of Histadrut and instantly reduced it from an enormous incorporation regime to a regular federation of trade unions. The eruption of the Intifadah in 1987 developed into a vehicle of liberalization simply because continued conflict

---

49. Ibid. 18-19. To define key civic virtues does not in any way imply that a society is free of political and cultural conflicts. Labor Zionism was dominating but not in an exclusive manner though it managed to generalize its key virtues to count for both right and left of Israeli political spectrum. The sector of Israeli society which was not influenced by pioneering to a similar degree was naturally the orthodox-religious sector.
50. Ibid. 159-183.
51. See Grinberg & Shafir 2000 and Shalev 2000.

in the occupied territories was a serious hindrance for the much wanted economic growth and liberalization. The policies of colonialism were, thus, gradually articulated in economic terms instead of republican or ethno-nationalist and therefore Palestinian political rights and claims were seen through an increasingly pragmatic prism.

Israel in the 1990s
The increased power of a liberal discourse on state, citizenship and economy caused a shift in both the spectrum of Israeli politics and in the social configurations of Israeli society. The republican colonial discourse of traditional Labor Zionism was replaced by a struggle between the ethno-nationalist colonialism of the Likud block and the liberal sections of the Labor movement.[52] The civic virtues of traditional Zionism had gradually been replaced by a more heterogeneous system of values and internal struggles. One of the costs of the loss of hegemony of Labor was the effective incorporation regime constituted of the welfare state and its normalizing educational and social project. The massive influx of Russian (and Ethiopian) immigrants significantly contributed to the dissolution of the previous incorporation regime which did not have capacity to integrate such a number of immigrants in the manner of the earlier waves of immigration.[53] The Zionist civic virtues were in the 1990s under pressure from conflicting tendencies of the entire social domain. The colonial policies of the occupied territories pressured the wanted economic liberalization and following democratic discourses, immigration contributed to the historization of Zionist values or made them representative of only one segment of the Israeli population, and liberalization and globalization generally undermined Zionist communitarianism.[54] The 1990s presented a variety of changes on the local, regional and global level that dislocated traditional Zionist discourse and

---

52. The Labor movement includes parties such as the leftist Meretz (formed 1992) and groups such as Shinui and Democratic Movement for Change before their dissolution, redefinition or integration into other parties. Shinui and DMC were integrated into other groups at the end of the 1980s and early 1990s but Shinui was reborn in 1997 as a more populist, anti-clerical party under the leadership of Tommy Lapid and eventually joined Ariel Sharon's rightist government after the elections of 2003. Shafir and Peled 2002: 213-230.
53. Ibid. 308-334.
54. See also Tom Segev's book *Elvis in Jerusalem* (2002).

this brought about new articulations of identity, history and society concerned with all the floating elements incommensurable with traditional Zionist discourse. The Zionist civic virtues ceased being self-evident and commonsensical to increasingly more Israelis and this development itself established Zionism as a historical phenomenon instead of a universal representation of the real.

In 1992 a new Labor government came into power under the leadership of veterans Yitzhak Rabin and Shimon Peres. This government was highly sensitive to the challenges of the Intifadah, the Russian immigrants and economic growth. The former government of Yitzhak Shamir seemed to lack initiatives to deal with the challenges that could bring Israel out of the worsening security situation and economic stalemate and the Rabin-Peres government offered a "new deal" of which the key issues were stability in the occupied territories, liberalization of the economy and increased integration into globalized economics. These issues were perceived to be decisive for obtaining economic growth and thereby the capacity to deal with both the Russian immigrants and the redefined global and regional order of security politics. Basically, Rabin and Peres' views on Zionism and the conflict had not changed but they shared a perception of the situation as unviable and under the pressure of both the Bush administration in the USA and the business community in Israel, they decided to go into negotiations with the Palestinians with the purpose of acquiring a stability that would serve as the foundation for a reform of Israeli society.[55] This was by no means a consensual line of policy. It was through and through an elite project and perspective which was understood to be in the best interests of Israel in the long run in economic terms. To domestic enterprises and to many "average Israelis", liberalization, opening up for globalization and opting for a compromise on the conflict, could be equalized with a national disaster. It would simply mean the turning away from a society build on institutions of collective solidarity to a liberal society build on institutions of competition. In this respect, solidarity is the togetherness fostered by shared virtues, identities and histories while competition is a contractual relationship without an intrinsic identity. With the policies of the Rabin-Peres government, the political divisions in Israel were decisively made

---

55. Shafir & Peled 2002: 252-259, 335-348.

up of localist forces united by the discourse of ethno-nationalism and globalist forces united by a liberal-democratic discourse. The traditional Labor Zionist republicanism had been confined to the background.

Here we take Labor republicanism as an expression of a national type of community and as a structurally integrated socio-cultural unit while ethno-nationalism and liberalism appear to be the dominating tendencies of the period of the gradual weakening of the national socio-cultural unit from the end of the 1960s until present times.[56] In the Israeli context, these developments have led to new sociological categorizations of Israeli society that take into account the process of globalization and the re-orientation it has caused of Israelis' relationships and conceptions of their state. In the effort to re-describe Israeli society in the 1990s with a focus on social categories and globalization dynamics, Israeli sociologist Uri Ram has been at the forefront. Inspired by classical sociology's dichotomies such as *Gemeinschaft-Gesellschaft* (Tönnies), *Mechanic-Organic* (Durkheim) and *Traditional-Rational* (Weber), Uri Ram transplants the sociological concepts of the great transition to modernity of 19th and early 20th century to a similar great transition to post-modernity of the end of the 20th century.

In Uri Ram's perspective, the present great transition consists of the development of a new *Gesellschaft* defined as the global capitalist community of both economy and culture.[57] The process that leads to the new *Gesellschaft* is the process of globalization. The earlier great transition in 19th and early 20th century was characterized by a similar development only then the new *Gesellschaft* was the modern nation-state. Following Tönnies, Ram defines the *Gesellschaft* as a contractual relationship while the *Gemeinschaft* is a traditional, emotional, community. Accordingly, the modernizing agent of the previous great transition, the nation-state, is today the traditional, emotional, community while the modernizing agent is globalization. The economic-rationalist-mechanist reason of globalization establishes it as an agent of modernization and development (as growth) while the nation-state and its civic virtues are regulators of this process in defense of the "community". In this relativized conceptualization of classical sociology, the reactionary forces of today

---

56. See Barber 1995 and Bauman 2000 for a general description of the political tendencies of globalization.
57. Ram 1999.

were the modernizing forces of yesterday. Nationalism was the ideological and cultural imagination and discourse of the modern nation-state but today it has transformed into an ideology of an Ancién Regime; a community organized around tradition, emotion, religion and mythical ties. The ideological and cultural discourses of the current process of modernization are liberalism and post-modernism. The nation-state is still the dominating unit of the world system but the process of globalization permeates the integrity of the nation-state as a center for development and culture. The result can be conceptualized as glocalization. Present-day cultural, social and political divisions are placed on a global vs. local spectrum. Politics, culture and identities become increasingly global or local while the nation-state is transformed from an agent of change to the romanticized object of longing and utopia of reactionaries.[58]

In the Israeli context, the above translates into Zionism being the ideological and cultural vehicle of a Jewish "great transformation" of the late 19th early 20th century which transformed Jewish local and traditional religious communities into a rationalized national society in the Israeli nation-state. Zionism was, thus, a vehicle of modernization within the complex of modernization in the West which included the modern phenomena of capitalism and socialism, colonialism and imperialism, and democracy and liberalism. The modernization paradigm of Zionism to a large extent justified its colonization of Palestine through the 20th century while the modernization paradigm of the present great transformation at the turn to the 21st century to a large extent de-legitimizes the practices of colonialism. The economic rationality of globalism simply dismisses the financially irrational colonial tensions and conflicts of Israeli society which in the 1990s seemed as the most anachronistic aspect of Israeli society. The colonial project of Zionism can no longer make claims to any universal Israeli values and it is primarily the elites that reject Zionist values just as it was the elites that endorsed these same values during the previous transformation. Upper middle class, educated Israelis and the intellectuals are by and large at the globalist end of the spectrum while the poorer and least educated strata of Israeli society are afraid of this development and therefore adhere to the traditional values of Zionism.[59]

---

58. Ibid. 325-26.
59. Surely, anti-globalism and nationalism also have intellectual prophets in Israel like anywhere else in the West and globalist intellectuals are also critical

The economic and social transitions of Israel after the economic stabilization plans of the 1980s implemented by the national unity government after the 1984 elections led to what Ram calls a "bourgeois revolution".[60] The collectivist Labor Zionist institutions were systematically cut down and successive governments sponsored private initiatives and liberalization to accommodate the private sector which, as mentioned, in 1994 brought about the transformation of the Histadrut into a regular federation of trade unions. The middle class created by liberalization and the "bourgeois revolution" is the generally speaking the locus of globalism and a liberal, pragmatic, worldview in Israel.

Ram distinguishes a number of identities that characterize respectively the localists and the globalists of Israel in the 1990s. The localists conceive of their identity as Jewish before Israeli and they support the idea that Israeli citizenship is defined by ethnicity. Spatially and temporally, they identify with *Eretz Israel* and Jewish collective roots in ancient Israel. Culturally, they are particularistic and conceive of the Jews as a chosen people either in religious terms or as particularly singled out by anti-Semitism.[61] The globalists believe in civic citizenship and conceive of their identity as Israeli before Jewish. They relate to the state of Israel, the present and the near future. Culturally, they are universalistic and

---

    of aspects of the process of globalization such as diminishing welfare, social rights and the lack of control of international corporations and capital. The term globalist does not necessarily entail that the social categories identified by it find everything that happens in the process of globalization positive. In this sense, many anti-globalization movements are in fact globalist rather than localist/nationalist in their worldview. They are just critical of the present shape of the process of globalization and often find their support in alternative youth cultures that are very critical of nationalism also. Such youth movements of course also exist in Israel and are regularly portrayed in the media.

60. Ram 1999: 332.
61. Uri Ram uses only the national-religious sense of the "chosen people" theme to define the localist position. I have expanded it with a secularist version that most often employs anti-Semitism as evidence for the particular position and situation of the Jews. In this version, the world is essentially hostile to the Jews and therefore any criticism of (or attack on) Israel's semi-theocratic system and ethnic hierarchy is anti-Semitic. In some respects, Ram's use of the term the "chosen people" is problematic because there are of course many ways to interpret the "chosen people" theme in both Jewish theology and secular identity politics. In fact, as we will see, the "chosen people" theme is also present in the texts of some of the more radical proponents of post-nationalist discourse.

conceive of Jewishness as a completely normal identity.[62] This sociology of identity does not capture all the variations and hybrids of Israeli identity in the 1990s but it presents a basic outline of orientations and discourses struggling in the Israeli arena. As we will see in the present essays, the post-nationalist discourses of history and identity in Israel in the 1990s actually transcend the schematization provided by Uri Ram. Some of these discourses are indeed engaged in an effort to re-capture a Jewishness beyond both the Jewishness and Israeliness of the Israeli political and social spectrum.[63]

Uri Ram's sociology of Israel in the 1990s shares many of basic points of Shafir and Peled's sociology but it focuses on establishing a sociology of identity and knowledge. The dominating identities of Israel in the 1990s are thus oriented along a new axis which itself is defined by the erosion of the power of the nation-state as an agent of modernization. The axis that appears in the process of globalization goes between the global *Gesellschaft* and the local/national *Gemeinschaft* and it radically alters the social and political composition of Israeli society in terms of economy, politics and culture. The nationalist Zionist discourse has lost its hegemony because the nation-state in the new great transformation no longer is the locus of the modernizing forces. New localist and globalist discourses struggle over memory and identity and Uri Ram chooses the terms "neo-Zionist" and "post-Zionist" to capture the positions at the respective ends of the axis.[64] The cultural changes are primarily our concern here and particularly the way these changes influence perceptions of Jewish history and identity.[65] As a heuristic model, we here accept Uri Ram's description of

---

62. Ram 1999: 334, figure 4.
63. We find examples of this particularly in the essays *History and Irony* and *Re-placing History and Identity*.
64. Ram 1999: 337. I take the terms "neo-Zionist" and "post-Zionist" to imply positions of identity politics in a social setting which is itself post-national. Hence, the terms need not imply new ideologies as many elements of so-called neo-Zionist and post-Zionist discourses have existed throughout the history of Zionism. I consider neo-Zionist and post-Zionist discourses in ideological terms to be basically the same as traditional revisionist or national-religious Zionism and left-wing, spiritual Zionism and in some cases anti-Zionism, respectively.
65. Uri Ram has on a previous occasion contributed with a sociology specifically of the debates over the new historians in Israel. His analysis of the historians' debate evolves along the same lines as described above. The historians' debate is on the surface conducted as an academic dispute but obviously there are

the changes of Israeli constitutions of identity, history and knowledge as a development inseparable from the changes brought on Israeli society by liberalization, globalization and conflict. In the broadest terms, we consider the analogy of the "great transformation" to economic globalization and cultural postmodernization to be an appropriate imagery of the cultural tendencies of Israeli society in the 1990s.

The historical momentum achieved with the Declaration of Principles in 1993 lasted effectively only until 1995 when Israeli Prime Minister Rabin was assassinated. The assassination of Rabin threw Israel into a political turmoil and at the same time the Palestinian public grew increasingly dissatisfied with the way the peace process turned out for them. After the initial euphoria they did not experience the boost in living standards, political freedoms and freedom from colonization that was expected.[66] The extreme asymmetry of intentions and experiences of the peace process between Israelis and Palestinians gradually reproduced the traditional insurmountable obstacles to a solution to the conflict such as history, religion and identity. Palestinian terror inside Israel from 1996 places a heavy pressure on the globalist strata of Israeli society and they can be considered attacks on the very foundation of the possibility of a liberal political discourse in Israel. Terror is also, though, an extremely destructive counter-attack against the continued colonization of Palestine which did not come to a halt during the period of liberalization. Liberal economic discourse might have undermined the collectivist values of colonization but the civic and societal dimension of liberalist discourse lacked far behind the economic in power. A way to put it is that the Israelis experienced the economic benefits of liberalization and globalization through the 1990s as a result of the Declaration of Principles while the Palestinians did not come significantly closer to their political goal of freedom from colonization.

---

strong contextual currents which relate to the changing configurations of Israeli society. The historians also divide themselves along the axis of localism vs. globalism. The localists among historians consider national history essential to collective knowledge and values, and they consider it "true", while the globalists consider national history mythological and oppressive. Ram 1998.

66. See Amira Hass' book *Drinking the Sea at Gaza* (1999). Hass reports in detail on the experience of the Palestinians during the first years of the peace process.

In 2000 Israeli Prime Minister Ehud Barak from Labor attempted to create a final settlement of the conflict. This attempt failed and brwought about the rise of a second Palestinian Intifadah and the dissolution of any strongly organized, politically weighty expression of liberal political discourse in Israel such as the Labor party was between 1992 and 1995. The 1990s not only ended chronologically in 2000, it also ended as a period when the historical opportunity of breaking with the century old logic of colonialism and counter-violence was felt as a possibility. Hence, we in these present essays consider the 1990s a historical period characterized by massive changes of Israeli society. These changes can appropriately be described as the policies of economic liberalization, the immigration of about one million Russians and Ethiopians and the signing of the Declaration of Principles in 1993. An integrated aspect of the changes of Israeli society during the 1990s was the inception of a significant struggle over memory and identity. This struggle was occasionally popular such as the debates over the new historians and the *Tekumah* series in 1998 but it was also a subtle struggle integrated in Jewish-Israeli literature and philosophy. The waning of Zionist hegemony on discourses of identity and knowledge brought about a proliferation of alternative discourses which we tentatively will define as post-nationalist.

Post-Nationalist Discourse on Israeli History:

Readings of the New Historians

In 1987-88 the so-called New Israeli Historians published their historical presentations of various aspects of the 1948 war for Palestine. Benny Morris, Avi Shlaim and Ilan Pappé had had the opportunity to consult previously closed archives in Israel, USA and Britain when writing their works and accordingly their works were anticipated to disclose truly new information on the establishment of Israel in 1948, the creation of the Palestinian refugee problem and Zionist-Arab relations. The historical presentations of the new historians did present previously unknown historical data from the period through reference to documents, protocols and transcripts that earlier historians did not have the opportunity to frequent. In line with the arguments of this essay, which basically holds that meaningful and perceptible history is "in text" not in the past itself, I will in the following present a series of readings of the new historians' by now classic works. The readings will engage in the textual level of the historical presentations of the new historians in order to disclose the textual and discursive innovations of the new historians. I will argue that discursive, imaginative and tropological aspects of the new historians' historical presentations constitute a different, or new, history. A history that breaks with the national imagination of Jewish-Israeli history and establishes a new historical imagination in a dialectical relationship with a new historical situation.

The Ghost of 1948; Benny Morris and the Palestinian Refugee Problem
The 1948 war, the Israeli War of Independence, has in the nationalist Jewish-Israeli history a unique position and meaning. In terms of *real-*

politik the war consolidated the United Nations decision to partition Palestine but with major changes. Palestine was divided between Israel and Jordan and up to 700.000 Palestinians became refugees. Israel was established as an internationally recognized democratic Jewish state. Thus, from a Jewish-Israeli nationalist perspective there are fundamental reasons for the position of the 1948 war. More interesting, though, for the perspective of this essay is the position and meaning of the 1948 war in nationalist historiography as a motif. In the most elementary sense all histories need motifs to indicate beginnings and ends, turns and developments, and accordingly motifs in a historical presentation point to ideological and conceptual figurations informing the text. As a motif in nationalist Jewish-Israeli historiography the 1948 war marks an inaugural and definitive event in a positive and transcendental sense. The impact of the 1948 war was perceived as decisive for every Jew as indicated by the proper names "The Jewish People" or "The Jewish Nation" and metaphorically figured as e.g. the "Rebirth" or the "Return to History" of the Jewish People.[67] The new historiography crystallizing in the late 1980s took issue with the 1948 war as an Israeli myth of creation and turned the focus away from the Jewish nation-building aspects of the war and directed it at the effects of the war and the effects of Jewish policy and national identity making on the Palestinian population and on the region as a socio-political entity. The Jewish polity and ideology, Zionism, became re-interpreted as a European, modern, national and colonial movement which should be understood in context with 19th and early 20th century European understandings and attitudes towards native peoples of the extra-European imperial world order. This marks a significant shift in historical outlook from the Zionist historical imagination at work in nationalist Jewish-Israeli historiography, which ultimately perceived Zionism and the 1948 War as a process of liberation of the Jews from European, anti-Semitic, and historical oppression. Furthermore, nationalist Jewish-Israeli historiography in both its Marxist and liberal strings perceived nationalism as a modern, liberating, natural, force representing a democratic strive for freedom in opposition to the parochial patterns of organization in Arab Palestine.[68] The new historio-

---

67. Kimmerling 1995, Ram 1998.
68. Kimmerling 1995, Raz-Krakotzkin 2004.

graphy effectively sets a new agenda for history in the Israeli context in its critical detachment from Jewish-Israeli national memory and its focus on the effects of the nation-building enterprise on the immediate "others", the Palestinians.

In this respect Benny Morris has delivered the most significant contribution to the re-setting of the historical agenda in Israel with his book *The Making of the Palestinian Refugee Problem, 1947-1949*. To Benny Morris and the other new historians the 1948 war is as important as in nationalist historiography but in a double meaning as both a constitutive national myth and a decisive socio-political event and for both reasons deserving critical investigation more than commemorative celebration. The change in historical outlook presented in the new historiography will not in this essay be appreciated as having occurred at random through the individual historian's discovery of historical sources in themselves telling a new "story". Instead the change in historical outlook will be appreciated at the level of discourse and tropological analysis in recognition of the relation between certain discourses and tropes and corresponding ideological and social configurations. We shall in the following read Benny Morris' historical presentation of the event of the Palestinian refugee problem as a text and as such a discursive construction of meaning.

Discourse and Tropes in Benny Morris

Contrary to nationalist Jewish-Israeli historiography Benny Morris sets in his *The Birth of the Palestinian Refugee Problem* time and space coordinates for his historical presentation that do not depend on the collective or individual subjects inhabiting or acting in the designated time-space. Morris sets his time-space coordinates to Palestine 1947-1949 and devotes only very little text to a presentation of events occurring prior to his time-space. The histories of the Jewish People, Zionism or the Palestinians and Palestinian nationalism are not invoked to give direction or purpose to his historical discourse. Apparently, it still seemed impossible for Morris to avoid a historical introduction all together and begin his presentation *in medias res* which indeed would have given his study a phenomenological character instead of a historical. Morris avoids the collective histories and self-representations of Zionism and Palestinian nationalism and thereby any genealogical positioning of the actors at play in the time-space of Palestine, 1947-1949.

In the following we will read Benny Morris' *The Birth of the Palestinian Refugee Problem* with a view to his historical discourse and the tropes used in this discourse to give meaning to the historical events highlighted by Morris. The tropological analysis will unfold on two levels. One inspired by Hayden White's thinking on tropology in historical discourse, and tropes and discourses' reference to certain general ideological figures, and a second level on which the argument will be extended. On this second level, the concept of the trope will be expanded and we will attempt to read what in history usually is named the historical contexts as a kind of trope. The attempt is based on the equivalence between the function of the trope in discourse and the function of the historical context for historical understanding. As the trope initiates and transfers a pre-discursive and pre-logical meaning or direction to a discourse so the historical contexts invoked by the historian or others to give meaning to historical events initiates and transfers a meaning and direction to the historical understanding. Though this contextual meaning is not pre-logical it is not epistemologically or empirically grounded in the sense that other contexts are equally possible and it therefore resembles the imaginative and poetic act of troping in discourse. There is no originality in the claim that historical events have different meanings when read through different contexts. Most historians would agree with such a line of argument. The reading of the historical contexts as tropes claims legitimacy on a different level, namely the level of philosophy of history. Historians might agree to the claim that different contexts for a historical event give different meanings but in most cases they will also agree that some contexts are truer or better than others in a scientific or methodological sense. Such a pretension is based on the view that historical method can provide a road between the object of study and the historian which can be evaluated with regard to its truthfulness in a transcendental, not discursive, sense. Not only classical positivism holds this view but also hermeneutical approaches, which take into account tradition, discourse and the subjective position of the historian, accept the historical event as an object that through method and reflection can apprehended in itself.[69]

---

69. The hermeneutical perspective on history should not be mistaken for positivism, though. It is concerned with the nature of historical knowledge and con-

To the purposes of this text the introduction of the concept of the trope function in order to emphasize the imaginative, poetic and ultimately ideological nature of the level of creation of meaning in history. At the same time the trope indicates the literary and linguistic figuration of history whereas the traditional historiographic term context indicates an empirically given structure that sets the historical sources and the historical narrative in its proper place regarding what can be made of this or that particular history. History is a many-facetted activity, which operates on many levels, individual and communal. An activity, a practise, and a way of thinking, which creates meaning in collective and individual past-present-future relations in a both biographical and genealogical sense more than an empirical science. At the same time historicity is a condition for meaning. Things, events, names, customs and peoples come into being through difference. The essential difference that creates events and things separated but related to each other is also a difference in time. Before something can be set in relation, differentiated, and come into being, other things, events and concepts always-already exist as preconditions. Precisely because of historicity we cannot gain access to the past as a "once-reality" because the past does not exist beyond the perimeter of current fluctuations of difference, of meaning. The effects of the past we meet are merely ghosts that still have influences and impacts in current discourses.[70] It is in the nature of the ghost not to be the same and still not quite different from what is should represent. When historians attempt to capture the ghost, its origin cannot be entirely established and what is created in writing is a new thing. A new event, which is a contribution to a history of contributions. Thus for our purposes in this essay, we will appreciate the works of the new Israeli historians as a historical event; contributions to the history of contributions which we usually call the history of Zionism and Israel. Furthermore, we will engage in their discourses and the ways the

---

sciousness and does not conceive of history as pure representation. Gadamer did with his hermeneutics seek "the thing in itself" through a hermeneutic consciousness that took into account presuppositions and the history of effects of a historical event. We can say that hermeneutics reject the immediate appearance of a historical event in order to know it. It is basically the opposite strategy than the one employed by classical empiricism. Gadamer 1989: 300-307.
70. Derrida 1973, 1994.

1948 war for Palestine haunts these historical discourses. Discourses that feed and are fed by current social and intellectual fluctuations in Israel and the world at large.

Israel is indeed haunted by the ghost of 1948 as are the Palestinians. The issue of what really happened in 1948 regarding the establishment of Israel and the making of the Palestinian refugee problem has been a recurrent historical and political theme ever since 1948. Ideological rifts and divisions in the Israeli population and the political establishment have been deepened over the issue of 1948 and the Palestinians and to Palestinian nationalist and revolutionary organisations 1948 is something akin to a disaster of creation. Their primordial happiness was destroyed by evil forces and modern Palestinian resistance identity arose. It is interesting to note that the importance of 1948 for Israeli and Palestinian moral and historical discourses seems to be growing steadily over the last many years, but in particular since the end of the 1980s.[71]

***

Initially, I mentioned the fact that Benny Morris' account of the Palestinian refugee problem sets different time-space parametres than most previous accounts of the making of the Palestinian refugee problem and the establishment of Israel. The mainstream Jewish-Israeli historical perspective of these events, as we meet them in the classical literature on the history of Zionism and modern Jewish history, have mapped history in an all together different manner.[72] Laurence J. Silberstein uses in his *The Post-Zionism Debates: Knowledge and Power in Israeli Culture* the phrase "mapping" of the making of history, which is a very precise expression of the power-effect in creating a system and thereby rules of interpretation in line with Silberstein's Foucaultian perspective.[73] My phrase "time-space parametres" resemples Silberstein's mapping but where Silberstein lets the process of mapping conclude the making of a new history, I wish to include other aspects such as tropes and discourses. Thus, the setting of time-space parametres is only one aspect of making a history.

---

71. This importance is part of a struggle about and redefinition of the relationship between Israelis and Palestinians.
72. My perspective on Zionist history resembles that of Myers 1995 and Silberstein 1999.
73. Silberstein 1999: 15-45.

Morris's account of the Palestinian refugee problem has, as its title indicates, as its target the period of the actual war between several Arab states, the Palestinians and Israel, which also is the period where the Palestinians physically fled in huge numbers. The focus is on the period of the unfolding events and not on the preceding political, ideological or other developments in the longer term. As Fernand Braudel pointed out in his article about the *longue durée*, the significance of certain events change according to the time span within which we measure.[74] In short time spans human actions and individual events are significant while in longer time spans systemic and institutional change are significant and in the very long time span natural and environmental developments seem the most noteworthy. This is also the case with Benny Morris's account of the Palestinian refugee problem. The very short time span operated by Morris enhance the importance of the 1948 war and the large number of singular events referred to in his account magnify the scope of the events from 1947 to 1949 on individual life situations and on the absolutely local political-strategic situation. This is in opposition to the classical Jewish-Israeli accounts of the period that operate with much larger time-space parametres where the Jewish-European history is the point of departure for an accounting of the events of 1948.[75] Thus, Morris's setting of time-space parameters to the period of 1947-1949 and the geography of Palestine alone signals a break with conventional "mapping" of the 1948 situation. 1948's position in Jewish-Israeli history is placed, as I have mentioned, in the line of causalities and chronologies of Jewish-European history, not Palestinian. Here again, I wish to stress that Jewish-European history should not be understood in an objectivist manner but as the aforementioned history of contributions that constitute Jewish History.[76] Morris's account ceases to be Jewish history by avoiding the parametres of Jewish history and its teleology and plots and instead becomes a new-history. An important reason for the controversy

---

74. Braudel 1980.
75. This is indeed one of the arguments directed against Morris by Shabtai Teveth. I will furthermore argue that the Zionist historical imagination works within a totality of Jewish History as a history of suffering and displacement which is always present also in lesser and more local historical representations.
76. As Myers and others have shown convincingly, realist Jewish history came into being in the 1800's and Zionist Jewish history much later. These "mappings" are Jewish History. Myers 1995.

over Morris's book is the break with Jewish History in its time-space parameters and its plots and which at the time of its publication made it almost unacceptable to other Jewish-Israeli historians. Shabtai Teveth wrote about the book in Commentary Magazine:

> "If their research is incomplete, Morris and Shlaim also ignore central facts and background material necessary to a proper understanding of the historical scene. It is, for example, impossible to describe Israel's War of Independence, and the flight and expulsion of Palestine's Arabs, without taking into account the tripartite struggle among Jews, Arabs, and the British that had racked the country for the previous three decades. The important landmarks in this struggle were the Arab riots of 1929 and 1936-39, the Peel Plan of 1937, the White Paper of May 1939, and the Land Ordinance of early 1941, the efforts of the Yishuv to increase immigration and settlement, and, beyond all these, the Holocaust. Yet these matters are invoked by our authors, and then just barely, as they were a set of technical specifications. What we have here is not only a case of historical foreshortening but an attempt to disconnect the birth of the state of Israel from the experience and tribulations of the Jewish People at large."[77]

Shabtai Teveth does not argue in detail with Morris over empirical disagreements in his passionate attack on Benny Morris. He attacks Morris' time-space parametres and his "troping" of the events during the 1948 war. Teveth's central point is obviously that it is unacceptable that Morris does not place the suffering of the Jews in Europe as his point of departure for an account of the events in Palestine in 1947-49. Morris leaves the defining element of Jewish-Israeli history post World War II out of his account and therefore Teveth sides him with the enemy; the Palestinians and their political line.[78] The concern for Teveth is the break with what is meant to be Jewish History as a meaningful narrative for the Jewish-Israeli collective. This is not to imply that such a history cannot be critical and investigative, as Morris claims in his *Tikkun* article, but to point to the effect of the kind of narrative told when it comes to the meaning or morality of the historical events treated in the narrative.[79]

---

77. Teveth 1989: 25.
78. Teveth 1989: 24.
79. Morris 1988.

Texts, such as histories, produce effects as much as they should be considered events in themselves and Benny Morris' historical narrative is a different event with a different effect than the narratives that Teveth and others call for and represent.[80]

Benny Morris' article in *Tikkun* in the autumn of 1988 started the whole debate over history of the 1948 war and the Palestinian refugee problem and eventually became the historical firmament of the post-Zionist writings of the 1990s.[81] Morris' article is a frontal attack on the establishment of historians in Israel who are criticized for being uncritical and overtly ideological in their positive presentations of Zionist and Israeli goals and actions. To Morris there is a historical explanation to the attitudes of the establishment of historians towards the Zionist movement and Israel and that is that the older historians themselves were the Zionists who had partaken in what they naturally perceived as the great epic of Jewish achievement during the hardest times and harshest conditions. Morris wrote:

> "Israel's old historians, by and large, were not really historians and did not produce real history. In reality, they were chroniclers, and often apologetic, interested chroniclers at that. They did not work from and of a solid body of contemporary documentation and did not normally try to paint a picture that offered the variety of sides of a given historical experience. They worked from interviews and memoirs, and often from memories. They had neither the mindset nor the materials to write real history. // The second factor is the nature of the new historians. Most of them, born around 1948, have matured in a more open, doubting, and self-critical Israel than the pre-1967, pre-1973, and pre-Lebanon War Israel of the old historians. Most of the old historians, indeed, had lived through 1948 as highly committed adult participants in the epic, glorious rebirth of the Jewish commonwealth. They were unable to separate their lives from the events they later recounted, unable to distance themselves from and regard impartially the facts and processes through which they had lived. Most – if asked – will admit as much – and in this, incidentally, they share a common experience with most chronicler-participants in national liberation movements and revolutions in the modern age. The generation

---

80. See also Shapira 1995.
81. Morris 1988.

of nation-builders seldom casts doubt or looks frowningly back upon its handiwork."[82]

The younger historians, who grew up in an Israel well established, naturally inherited the potential for critical historical investigations through experiences such as the Lebanon war. Such events assisted in creating a more open, doubting and self-critical Israel, as Morris puts it. As a commonsensical argument there is a point to be noted in Morris' statement. There is of course a difference between the perception of events having occurred in real time for the older historians and the perception a historian might have of the same events after a generation or more. Morris, rightly so, compares the first generation of Israeli historians to chronicler-participants in other national liberations movements. Morris seems to understand the generational shift as a maturation process towards a better, truer and more balanced-critical understanding of the birth of Israel. An understanding which can include the Palestinian refugee problem. That is why he can proclaim that new Israeli historians have been born who can produce critical and more objective accounts of the formative years of Israel. The Tikkun article's most important contribution to the crystallization of a new historical imagination, though, was the labelling, or branding, of a group of Israeli historians as the New Historians and their writings as the New Historiography. It does not seem as if Morris had an ideological programme in mind but rather the setting of a demarcation line between chronicler-historians and real, academic and critical historians. The phrase "the new historians" became a very powerful concept during the 1990s in the so-called post-Zionism debates way beyond the content and polemics of the actual books of the new historians. The new historians became the discursive locus for a new critical intellectual tendency, post-Zionism, in Israel and what we examine in this text is the deeper structure of the historical imagination reflected in this tendency.

***

When reading Benny Morris' *The Birth of the Palestinian Refugee Problem, 1947-1949* one is struck with its precision, detail, pragmatism and not the

---

82. Morris 1988. The text has been reprinted in Morris's *1948 and After* (1990). I quote from the 1990 version p. 6-7.

least the absence of emotional outburst and pathos that often characterize histories written of such events. Zionist histories have naturally made emphasis of the suffering, will to live and resolve of the Zionists and have taken in the obvious symbolism of the creation of Israel after the Holocaust. Such pathos is absent in Morris' presentation of the 1948 war also when it comes to descriptions of pressure and violence inflicted on the Palestinians. The general terminology used by Morris is also guided by an effort to be neutral which is why almost no popular or metaphorical names are used to describe events. The Israeli Independence war becomes the 1948 war and so forth. The implicit and contextual meaning inherent in the proper names such as the Israeli Independence War is of a great deal of importance regarding the matter of defining what sort of history is being told. The proper names designate and position the protagonists and identify the motifs such as beginnings, scene of action and end. When we consider the works of the critics of Morris and the new historians, we see that their choice of proper names and protagonists, such as the Jewish People, and sequences, time-space parametres, creates a very different meaning derived from the same sets of facts used by both the new historians and their critics.

As initially mentioned, Benny Morris structures his history of the making of the Palestinian refugee problem differently than traditional Jewish-Israeli history. Morris sets the time-space parametres of his narrative narrowly to the period of the actual action, 1947-1949. The pre-history of the war goes back only to around 1900 and does not include European Jewish history. It is also important to mention that it does not include Arab-Palestinian history before that time either. In an Israeli context Morris epitomizes what Furet has called problem-oriented history.[83] The problem to be solved is the reason for the Palestinian refugee problem. Morris sets out in a metonymical mode:

---

83. Furet 2001. The term problem-oriented is used by Furet to point to the difference between classical narrative history and the "scientification" of history. To Furet, problem-oriented means a history that sets out to solve a problem, not to narrate a biography or collective biography. Problem-oriented history borrows from sociology and therefore does not look to the singular unique events but to the comparable events. Problem-oriented history sets out to prove a thesis and is therefore compelled to apply theories of argumentation, at least a minimum, to be academic. I find problem-oriented history a good term to point to the difference between Zionist history and new history.

> This study sets out to describe the birth of the Palestinian refugee problem which, along with the establishment of the State of Israel, was the major political consequence of the 1948 war. It will examine how and why, over December 1947 to September 1949, some 600.000-760.000 Palestinian Arabs became refugees and why they remained refugees in the immidiate post-war period.[84]

The task of the study is to provide cause-effect answers to the Palestinian refugee problem and the central question for Morris is the classical "what really happened". After clarifying the problem at hand, Morris continues to explain the highly ideological disagreements between Israel and the Arab states over the issue of the Palestinians. The fate of the Palestinians provides the Arab states with an ideological weapon against Israel and the same Palestinians single Israel out as the most civilized and just nation of the Middle East. It all depends on whether the Palestinians fled voluntarily or if they were expelled. It seems as if Morris' intention was to find the reality behind the ideologies and pass a judgement as to what in fact happened during the 1948 war.[85] On the surface, the study has no interest in the collective histories of the Jews or the Palestinians.

The Birth of the Palestinian Refugee Problem, 1947-1949 begins with a short presentation of the background for the actual action. The background consists of a very brief history of Zionist and Palestinian political developments since around 1900 and, most importantly, two sets of rules for interpretation. The key to the lessons drawn from the study's investigations is found in the background chapter.

The brief history that Morris presents begins with the commencing Zionist immigration at the end of the 19th century. The important events are the First World War and the Balfour-Declaration, which committed the British on a rather contradictory policy, namely the promise to support a Jewish national home in Palestine and safeguarding Arab Palestinian rights and at the same time under the mandate from the League of Nations to prepare the population for self-government. The goals were not compatible, especially as the Palestinians were increasingly dissatisfied with the Jewish immigration to the land. Violence between the two populations erupted frequently and from the beginning of the 1930s an atmosphere of general distrust and outright hatred prevailed between

---

84. Morris 1987: 1.
85. Ibid: 1.

Jews and Palestinians. From 1936 with the Palestinian uprising against the British and the Zionists, the situation was very tense as also Jewish groups began to be on the offensive. The British had to come up with a plan for restoring order especially with a situation in Europe rapidly deteriorating. The Peel commission of 1937 recommended a partition of Palestine in 3 sectors, a small Jewish, a larger Arab and a British sector including Jerusalem and the port of Jaffa. The commission's suggestions were debated but rejected by the Palestinians, who would not accept partition. Instead, the British chose to appease the Palestinians and the Arab states by issuing a White Paper in 1939 which severely restricted Jewish immigration to the land. This decision was disastrous for the Zionist and for Jews trying to escape from Europe and accordingly it radicalized the Zionist efforts to achieve a solution in Palestine. In 1942, the Zionists for the first time officially demanded a Jewish state in Palestine and they began preparing to wage war for it.

The situation in Palestine after World War II proved untenable for the British and they laid the case for the UN. Over the summer 1947 the United Nations' Special Committee on Palestine (UNSCOP) visited Palestine and interviewed political and religious leaders on both sides. The Zionists favoured partition and the Palestinians rejected it. On 27th of November the UN decided to partition Palestine in two states and to keep Jerusalem and Bethlehem an international zone. With the decision to partition Palestine violence erupted between the Jewish and Palestinian populations of Palestine. It had the characters of a civil war and the British mandatory power did as little as possible to prevent the fighting. It declared that its government over Palestine would cease on May 15th 1948. Until then its efforts would be directed at a controlled evacuation of Palestine.[86]

Morris makes one statement in opposition of the traditional position in his presentation of the background for the Palestinian refugee problem and that is the claim that the *Yishuv*[87] was superior to the Palestinians militarily and administratively.[88] The issue of the military and political balance has been debated heavily since the new historians and Morris

---

86. The above is based on Morris 1987: 4-7. It shows us that Morris' narrative by its wording is within the consensus of what happened up to the 1948 war.
87. Hebrew for "settlement". Is the common proper name for the Zionist-Jewish population of Palestine from 1882 to 1948.
88. Morris 1987: 7.

was the first to suggest that the *Yishuv* was the strong part right from the beginning. Otherwise, Morris presents us with a short history that does not in itself contain any hints at how and why things developed as they did during the war.

The rest of the background chapter is dedicated to a sociological description of the two societies and to an analysis of the state of the notion of a population transfer meaning a voluntary or forced expulsion of the Palestinians from the territory of the Jewish state. We shall call this analysis an ideology analysis. Previously, it was suggested that establishing a historical context should be considered a "tropological" move because the context imposes a structure linked to a specific formation of meaning. Only certain meanings can arise from certain structures and we will therefore now look at contexts in Morris.

In his background chapter, Benny Morris provides us with categorical descriptions of both Arab and Jewish society in mandatory Palestine. In the following, we will consider these descriptions, in combination with the structures of Morris' historical narrative, the rules of interpretation of the historical event which eventually define the type of history written and the types of conclusions possible with the type of history.[89]

Palestinian society since around 1900 is described as a traditional Middle Eastern society. Modernization had only begun in the urban areas and among the larger and wealthier urban families. The majority of the population were peasants or day workers living at a very low level of income and low level of modernization. Politically, the Palestinians were organized in families and clans, not in parties in the modern sense of the term. Parties did exist but exercised only a very limited influence and only on the relatively modernized urban upper class. Collective political action was not a factor of any importance until the Zionist movement began colonizing Palestine. When collective political action did occur, it was directed by local village and clan interests, not by more abstract political notions or remote loyalties. Modern political ideologies such as nationalism were not an important factor in Palestine among the Arab

---

89. Foucault argues in his *Nietzsche, Genealogy, History* that what should be interesting in a genuine historical study are the rules of interpretation at a given social historical scene, i.e. the discursive formation by which "the historical", "the social", "the true", "the objective" are engaged in at a certain time or time span. I share this interest and use the phrase "the rules of interpretation" as directed by Foucault 1977: 151.

population until the struggle against Zionism intensified during the 1930s. In course of the conflict with the Zionists, two families set the political agenda in Arab Palestine and with this development modern Palestinian nationalism became a uniting force. Still, Arab Palestine had after World War II no effective and coordinated national leadership, no collective organizations on egalitarian and democratic basis and no bureaucratic apparatus for effective and systematic integration of the population. Palestine had from 1900 to 1947 become the national territory of the Palestinians but only as an ideology not as an organizing principle. Organization among the Palestinians was basically pre-modern.[90]

In opposition to a poorly organized Palestinian society, Morris finds a very well organized Jewish society. The *Yishuv* had tight and consensual political organizations, egalitarian and democratic institutions and its leadership enjoyed broad legitimacy in Jewish society. The level of modernization of Jewish society in Palestine was much higher than in the Arab society and the Jewish organizations were able to integrate their political goals to a vision of statehood. Nationalism was a moving force from the outset of the Zionist organizations in Palestine. The Zionists were preparing for statehood and had therefore established a number of democratic and bureaucratic institutions that could function independently of the mandatory power almost immediately after a British withdrawal. Morris makes special mention of the Jewish militias, especially the *Haganah*[91], because of their professional and competent leadership who managed to organize an effective military force out of very limited means. In Morris' view, the *Haganah* was the main advantage of the Zionists to a degree that its significant numerical inferiority vis-à-vis the Palestinian and Arab militias did not prevent it from being a superior front organization for the *Yishuv* in the expected armed struggle for Palestine.[92] No Palestinian or Arab organization had full control over their militias and no possibility for an effectively organized effort against the Zionists.[93]

Morris establishes time-space parametres, Palestine roughly from 1900 to 1950, collective actors with distinct and different social and organizational habita and he also finds a motivational factor, namely a

---

90. Morris 1987: 7-23.
91. Defence in Hebrew.
92. Morris 1987: 22.
93. Ibid: 23.

particular notion of transfer in the political discourse of the Zionists. The notion of transfer in *Yishuv* thinking as developed by Morris is based on the existence of a number of committees under the leadership of the *Yishuv* dealing with population issues, among other things. Morris also reminds us that the Peel commission of 1937 touched upon the transfer issue when it recommended a partition of Palestine and that possibly encouraged Zionist thinking on the issue.[94] Morris creates the impression that Zionist politics had an undercurrent of transfer thinking deliberately held out of public debate due to its controversial character. This undercurrent permeated the Zionist mainstream, who knew well that transfer was a sensitive issue in international opinion, especially after World War II. Transfer was debated in these committees as a solution to the problematic reality of a Jewish majority of only 60% but it never came to any decision making because it would jeopardize the outcome of the UNSCOP commission and eventually the final UN decision regarding the partition of Palestine.

Morris draws extensively on the papers of Yosef Weitz, who was director of Jewish National Fund's Lands Department. Weitz is placed by Morris as a central person in the bureaucracy of the *Yishuv* and Morris therefore assumes that Weitz's very positive position on the transfer question expresses the prevailing mood in the Zionist administration. In Weitz's papers it appears as if a transfer of the Palestinian population was a key issue in Zionist politics from around 1940 onwards and thus widely supported by the leadership. Transfer was thought of both in terms of various schemes for voluntary population transfers and forced expulsions.[95] In other words, the population composition of the Jewish state was so problematic that the leadership considered population as one of the most pressing issues to be dealt with.

In summary, Morris finds one structural model by which to explain the outcome of the 1948 war, the constitution of Jewish and Palestinian society, and an ideology analysis that explains the motivation among the Jewish politicians and armed forces to expel the Palestinians in huge numbers. The Jewish society was structurally and politically superior to the Palestinian and that facilitated the swift dissolution of Palestinian society. At the same time, Jewish political thinking in the period involved

---

94. Ibid: 26.
95. Ibid: 27p.

a notion of transfer of the Palestinian population and that provided the ideological background for the positive acceptance, and also for the active encouragement, of the Palestinian exodus. The outcome of the 1948 war, and the birth of the Palestinian refugee problem, was pre-scripted by a strong and devoted Jewish society and the notion of transfer of the Palestinians in *Yishuv* thinking pushed this solution forward when the opportunity came.

When we consider Morris's structure of explanation, as above, his ironic and famous conclusion is strikingly out of the line of argument. Morris concludes that "[T]he Palestinian refugee problem was born of war, not by design, Jewish or Arab."[96] Morris also concludes that there were no orders issued to expel the Palestinian population and there were no encouragements issued by the Arab leaders for the Palestinians to flee.[97] The exodus occurred due to the chaos, fear and violence of war, and not due to a structural mechanism and ideological motivation. Morris conclusion has been widely cited and debated. Especially historians Walid Khalidi and Nur Masalha have paid attention to the discrepancy between Morris's text and his conclusion.[98] Khalidi argues that Morris does not take the full consequences of his argument and his narrative which, following its logic, would make the term "ethnic cleansing" suitable for the conclusion. Morris does not conclude anything categorically and that does create an interpretive tension between his rules of interpretation and the meaning he wishes his readers to derive from the text.

In a way, Morris breaks his own logic but as Hayden White has pointed out, tension can exist between the layers of a historical text and Benny Morris in his conclusion shifts from the metonymical, reductionist analysis of his text to an ironic negational conclusion.[99] A conclusion that has irritated critics of Morris, not only the aforementioned Khalidi but also Anita Shapira.[100] In my view, Morris has laid the foundation of a new Jewish-Israeli history in his setting of time-space parametres, new rules of interpretation, and an overall contextualist, metonymical historiographical style. In Morris, the whole object of knowledge, the Palestin-

---

96. Morris 1987: 286.
97. Ibid: 286 pp.
98. Khalidi 1988, Masalha 1991.
99. White 1973: 29.
100. Shapira 1995.

ian refugee problem and the 1948 war, is *pre*figured differently than in traditional Jewish-Israeli historiography.[101] The time-space parametres, rules of interpretation and historiographical style are prefigurations constitutive to the realistic discourse that purports to be a representation and explanation of what really happened during the 1948 war. In the new history of Morris, the operating time and space is Palestinian, the Zionist were the stronger part and had to that fact an ethnocentric ideology. At the same time, Morris' contextualist, metonymical style corresponds to a liberal ideology.

There is No History, only Historians: Ilan Pappé

Ilan Pappé was a member of the triumvirate mentioned by Morris in his *Tikkun* article and from the beginning one of the new historians. His work *Britain and the Arab-Israeli Conflict* (1988) initially brought him into the ranks of the new historians, but here I have chosen to analyze his *The Making of the Arab-Israeli Conflict 1947-1951* from 1992. This choice is due to the latter work's pretension to give an account of the 1948 war in an integrative manner and also due to its integration of the new history of Benny Morris and Avi Shlaim. Therefore, *The Making of the Arab-Israeli Conflict 1947-1951* is the first comprehensive, integrative account of the 1948 war in the new historiographical style and thus deserves attention.

Since the beginning of the 1990s, Ilan Pappé has been engaged in Israeli and international public debates with a much higher frequency than the other new historians and he has come forward as the foremost advocate for new history after Morris' initial article in *Tikkun*. Pappé's engagement is in many instances overtly political and he is active on the leftwing of Israeli politics on the united Jewish-Arab, post-Marxist list named *Hadash* (Hebrew for New). This is mentioned because, as I see it, it is an integrated feature of Pappé's perception of his historical work and imagination. It should also be noticed that Pappé's public engagement has created a certain distance between Morris and Pappé regarding their understandings of history where Morris occupies a tradi-

---

101. Prefigured meaning outside the realm of the academic as it is conceived in realistic historiography and "plotted" before the actual analytical treatment of the events.

tionalist, positivist position and Pappé a relativist position in debates.[102] But as my reading of Ilan Pappé's work will show, these differences has no influence on the similarity of their work at the level of text and the discursive construction of meaning in the text.

In August 1993, Ilan Pappé was interviewed to the Israeli daily *Yedioth Aharonot* under the heading *There is no history, only historians*. In the interview Pappé expressed the view that historians are no matter what sort of objectivity they argue with engaged in the problems and dilemmas of the present and that it is impossible to see history beyond present time conditions. This perspective makes it more relevant for historians to either achieve consensus over controversial issues or to approach history with a multitude of perspectives. Pappé favours a multi-perspectivist history where emphasis and focus in the narrative shift between the different positions inhabiting both the historical and present field.[103]

The problem that comes to mind regarding an analysis of Ilan Pappé as a historian who has played a key role in shaping a new historical imagination in Israel concerns his public role as an intellectual in radical opposition to mainstream Israeli politics. Pappé has on many occasions spoken out in opposition to Israeli policies and also written more theoretical texts in which he has argued for a "postmodernist" perspective placing ideology over fact in history.[104] For our purposes here, Pappé the historian will be separated from Pappé the public figure though this, as mentioned, probably runs contrary to his own perception of history and politics. There is simply no connection between his theorizations of history, as they appear in various interviews and articles, and his historical writings. Pappé makes the same positivist truth claims as Benny Morris and the Zionist historians in both his methodology and historiographical style. Thus, the controversies over Pappé in the Israeli public sphere, and also in university politics, will not be considered.[105]

---

102. On several occasions there have been quite heated debates between the new historians, not so much over what happened historically as over what to do about it. The difference between the new historians has been explicated sociologically by Uri Ram 1998.
103. Pappé 1993.
104. Pappé 1997a.
105. For a short discussion of the political implications of post-Zionism see Feldt 2001.

A War Decided in Advance: Ilan Pappé and 1948

Contrary to Benny Morris, Ilan Pappé is more ambivalent towards the task he sets himself in *The Making of the Arab-Israeli Conflict, 1947-1951*. He does not as straightforwardly start out to solve the problems of what really happened during the 1948 and yet still claim that, by reference to newly opened archives, we are approaching more correct or truer knowledge of the 1948 war. A knowledge that challenges the very foundations of Israeli collective memory and also political discourse. Pappé states that: "The aim of this book is first to present the reader with a new history of the war of 1948 and: The newly available material has served to demolish many myths and misconceptions – to the extent that one scholar considered it sufficient for his account of the war simply to enumerate one shattered myth after another".[106] Thus, to Pappé, the task of his work is not only to solve a historical problem but also to line out a new history of the creation of Israel and the Arab-Israeli conflict. The necessity of a new history is set by the facts extracted from the archives and by the ongoing Arab-Israeli conflict. Pappé thereby closely resembles Morris in his statement of intentions and in his positioning as an historian above and detached from the Zionism of previous Israeli historians.

Before addressing Pappé's historical discourse, it should be mentioned that Pappé's account does not deal with military details or events on the battlefield. This perspective is deliberately left out by Pappé because it, according to Pappé, belongs to micro-history and therefore cannot cast light on the important political questions. It is worth mentioning because Zionist histories of 1948 often emphasize the heroic battles, will, resolve and suffering of the Jewish fighters and therefore evade the larger picture of conquest of the prospected Palestinian state. Pappé, like Morris, distances himself from the traditional account of a heroic struggle for freedom by setting other parametres. The preferred parametres for Pappé are political and, according to Pappé, diplomatic because it is in these aspects of the Arab-Israeli contest over Palestine that we can decide who really had the power and international goodwill.[107] As we saw in the case

---

106. Pappé 1992: VIII. The mentioned scholar is Simha Flapan who wrote *The Birth of Israel; Myths and Realities* (1987). It must be noted that it is questionable whether Flapan's book can be called scholarly when considering its highly political tone.
107. Pappé 1992: VIII.

of Benny Morris, Ilan Pappé also writes problem-oriented history and not particularistic history as if he had followed only the Jews through the events of 1948.

Ilan Pappé sets his historical scene with time-space parametres similar to those applied by Benny Morris, namely Palestine from about 1900 to about 1950. The context is exclusively Palestinian even though the account focuses on international diplomacy regarding Palestine. The central subject through time and space of the account is not a Jewish collective subject but it is a scene upon which two key actors struggle for power and dominance influenced by a newly formed international organizations such as The League of Nations and after World War II The United Nations but also the dominant colonial power in the area, Great Britain. This historical scene is in Pappé's historical imagination first and foremost a Palestinian scene, not an Eretz Israeli scene, onto which the Zionists are foreign intruders as is the British mandatory rule. As we saw in the case of Benny Morris, Ilan Pappé chooses to give a very short introduction to Zionism. The introduction depicts Zionism as a Jewish national movement originating in Eastern Europe with close affinity to European nationalism and colonialism.[108] The traditional Zionist historical understanding of Zionism as a Jewish renaissance movement that aimed at restoring Jewish existence in its primordial homeland and freeing the Jews from anti-Semitism is not considered by Pappé as a legitimate plot for the history of Palestine and the 1948 war.[109]

Ilan Pappé considers the diplomatic battle for Palestine to be the most important factor that determined the outcome of the 1948 war. He argues that the Zionists had the superior position in the negotiations and debates that led to the decision in the UN to partition Palestine, and that that decision in it-self was a victory for the Zionists and also signed the fate of the Palestinians as there was no support in the Arab world for partition. The Zionists had unhindered access to influence

---

108. Pappé 1992: 1-15.
109. Zionism has three basic historical plots. 1. The strive for political freedom or collective self-determination, which can be derived from Theodor Herzl 2. The organic unification of Jewish culture and Jewish politics, which can be derived from Ahad Ha'am 3. The desperate fight for Jewish collective survival, which is a right-wing revisionist plot developed from the 1920s. In all three plots, aspects of the other plots figure in lesser degrees.

the members of UNSCOP[110] because the Palestinian and Arab leaders had decided not to cooperate with the UN regarding any solution that did not mean complete Arab control over Palestine. According to Pappé, this opportunity was met by the Zionists in a very planned and professional manner that impressed most of the members of UNSCOP. At the same time the Holocaust also created something akin to a moral imperative to support the Zionists in their quest for a Jewish homeland even though it went against other political principles. This was especially evident in the conflict between the pro-Arab attitude of the American state department and the pro-Zionist attitude of the White House. The officials of the State Department generally followed the advice of their Middle East experts and the White House followed what seemed politically and morally necessary at the time.[111] Pappé also points out that the two superpowers, the USSR and the USA, in the course of 1947 came to agree on the establishment of a Jewish state in Palestine. The effect of this surprising agreement was that both important blocks in the UN were sure to vote for the partition of Palestine.[112] The odds were much in favour of the Zionists when it came to the vote in the UN on November 29, 1947.

In a telling passage, Pappé gives insight to his view on proper history when he dwells on the very common speculations on the motifs of the Zionists to accept the partition plan. Pappé finds three different motifs which give meaning in very different histories. The first motif is Zionist and it says that the Zionists accepted the partition plan as a compromise to end hostilities in the land. The second is idealistic saying that the Zionists accepted the partition plan because they supported it and they would work for upholding it. The third possible motif is anti-Zionist and it says that the Zionists only accepted the partition plan as a tactical step before opportunities came for further territorial expansion. None of the motifs can be established as the single cause for the Zionist acceptance of the partition plan. Pappé finds such speculations useless, though so intriguing that he lets us know that he finds the third motif likely.[113] Instead, Pappé suggests that historians ought to study the effect of each

---

110. United Nations Special Committee on Palestine established in May 1947 to investigate for the UN the possiblities for a solution to the Palestine problem.
111. Pappé 1992: 16-46.
112. Ibid: 16-46.
113. Ibid: 45.

battle, such as the diplomatic, on the larger conflict between Zionists and Palestinians and not waste energy on speculations. The interesting question is not why the Zionists accepted the partition plan but whether the Jews of Palestine faced annihilation or not in the 1948 war. Here Pappé's conclusion is clear: When international diplomacy, economy, politics, infrastructure, military capacity and so on are considered, the Jews in Palestine did not face annihilation. Pappé sums up that the Zionists had the skills to win the war and the Palestinians had not.[114]

The above is one of Pappé's most direct and conscious efforts to draw a line between Zionist history and new history. Zionist history is concerned with the collective subject of the Jews and their historical course from exile to redemption while the new history is problem-oriented. It is oriented, in Pappé's case, towards the material and political conditions that created the known outcome of the 1948 war, namely the establishment of Israel and the creation of the Palestinian refugee problem. Baruch Kimmerling remarks that Zionist history is oriented towards the intentions of the Zionist movement and the central politicians as reflected in official papers, and not the consequences.[115] This observation is similar to Pappé's. Zionist history is basically re-productive. It rearticulates and reinforces a Zionist historical discourse and it does not alter the historical and perceptual animosity between Israelis and Palestinians. The new history investigates the power-effects of the involved parties on each other, and does not record whether the parties had noble intentions before engaging in the conflict. In the Israeli case, such histories becomes highly controversial when dealing with the 1948 war because in Zionist histories and public Israeli mythology, Israel fought the 1948 war as a war of survival in which Israel was the weak and threatened part. The term power-effect is not meant to indicate that the new history written by Morris or Pappé is inspired by Michel Foucault's perspective on history. Rather it indicates that the new historians, such as Pappé, investigate the consequences of adopted policies and structural settings on the actors on a historical scene within a certain time to answer specific historical questions such as why did Israel win the war and why did so many Palestinians leave Palestine. They are particularly interested in analyzing the consequences of Zionist policies towards the Palestinians, which should be ascribed to importance of 1948

---

114. Ibid: 46.
115. Kimmerling 1995: 56.

and the conflict in Israeli history. They deal with the recurrent ghost of 1948 that occupies such a central position in every legitimate Israeli historical and political discourse.

***

In the course of his book Ilan Pappé delivers an account that integrates, and in some sense incarnates, the essences of the new history. His primary contribution is the diplomatic battle, as mentioned earlier, and the ability to write a complete new history of the 1948 war.[116] The works of Benny Morris and Avi Shlaim are relied upon when it comes to the account of the Palestinian civil war, the exodus of the Palestinians and Zionist relations to the Arab world, but Pappé also integrates the works of a number of Palestinian and Arab scholars, which in the very politicized academic environment in Israel is quite unheard of. It reflects Pappé's idea of history as a present-time activity that has both a very political and educational significance to it. Palestinian and Arab historians' narratives are placed in an equal relationship with Israeli.[117] Pappé makes one significant contribution to Morris' version of the making of the Palestinian refugee problem in his account. He supports Khalidi, Masalha and others in their critique of Morris' conclusion. Pappé does believe that the Zionists and later the Israelis conducted a policy of ethnic cleansing against the Palestinians and he also believes that Morris has written the best documentation of it though Morris does not make this conclusion.[118]

In the final paragraphs of his book, Pappé sums up the conclusions of a non-Zionist history. The war of 1948 was decided in advance in the corridors of the UN and in public world opinion. The Palestinian and Arab position was a factor of very limited importance in the international political climate after WWII, which was underlined by poor leadership and diplomatic skills among Palestinian and Arab leaders. The two superpowers and public world opinion supported the Zionists' cause and the Holocaust made it impossible to voice a moral protest on

---

116. Morris attempted the same with the entire history of Zionist presence in Palestine in his *Righteous Victims* (2000).
117. Pappé has participated in several projects with Palestinian historians and he has engaged in the debate over how to "bridge the narratives", a process that he supports. (Unpublished working papers).
118. Pappé 1992: 89-99.

behalf of the Palestinians. At the same time there existed an understanding between Israel, Transjordan and Great Britain that a partition of Palestine that would involve the creation of a Palestinian Arab state was undesirable. Israel had obvious strategic interests in disregarding the UN partition resolution (181) as had Transjordan while Britain did not favour partition at all, but supported Transjordan as an ally in its claims for as much of Palestine as possible. Every negotiation and peace plan after the 1948 war failed due to Israel's unwillingness to withdraw from the conquered territories and unwillingness to allow the return of the refugees. Israel held the position that the partition plan could not be implemented retroactively and immediately began to integrate the new territories in the state. Finally, Pappé stresses the importance of 1948 for the present situation between Israelis and Palestinians.[119] The present condition that Pappé wishes to create a historical relation for is primarily the situation of the Palestinian refugees in the West Bank and Gaza but also the Palestinian diaspora. The international diplomacy in the 1940s and the establishment of Israel are the historical origins of the Palestinian suffering today. Ilan Pappé's account is still an Israeli history but intentions and idealism are set aside and the narrative portrays the power-effects and the realpolitik of statemaking but with clear empathy for the Palestinian situation today.[120]

***

Ilan Pappé's history of the 1948 war operates with the same time-space parameters as Benny Morris', Palestine approximately 1900-1950, and he writes in the same metonymical, realistic style as Morris. The aim of Pappé's historical presentation is to give cause-effect answers to historical problems such as why did Israel win the 1948 war. Pappé's intention with the account was directly to provide a new comprehensive history of the 1948 war in which the perspectives and conclusions of the new historians were completely integrated to a more or less full narrative. As we saw in the case of Benny Morris, Pappé does not attach any significance regarding

---

119. Morris does the same in his article in *Tikkun* (1988) which points to a not insignificant political, oppositional awareness in their works. This awareness surely has been a vehicle for the production of a new history but also a sign of the dwindling power of the Zionist regime of truth.
120. Pappé 1992: 271-273.

the meaning or morale of the history of 1948 war to Jewish history prior to 1900. The birth of Zionism in Europe as a Jewish national rennaissance and a rebellion against both Jewish tradition and gentile anti-Semitism does not infuse Zionist political strategy and political goals, and finally the victory in the 1948 war, with any particular meaning that goes beyond mere realpolitik. The Zionist narrative of a struggle for liberation is, in Ilan Pappé's and Benny Morris' writings, ideology and should be analyzed as such. Thus, the Zionist historical imagination, its tragic and comic plots, its teleology and latent messianism is rejected all together and replaced by a metonymical and occasionally ironic, liberal history composed of "dead end streets" as historian Anita Shapira has phrased it in her critical evaluation of the new historians.[121] Shapira explicitly notes that Israeli history before the new historians had some meaning and direction, and some sort of vision of history. History itself as a human activity is being trivialized by the new historians since they have no vision. They compose histories of dead end streets, they change the great human comedy to a non-story in which irony makes human vision and greatness impossible.[122] Benny Morris and Ilan Pappé use a realistic, metonymical style when they analyze and narrate the individual historical events and they set out to solve problems and indeed to undermine the nationalist history of Israel of which these problems are part. Morris is clearly not an ironist but his highly contextual, metonymical style, and disregard of the collective histories of Israelis and Palestinians has fostered a new history. Pappé on the other hand is an ironist though he writes the same type of history as Morris. It is when the individual historical events are combined to an account, a narrative, in Pappé's meta-texts that irony becomes visible as the dominant trope. There is basic doubt as to whether truth can be obtained and, from a Zionist perspective, some suggestions in the new history even border on catachresis.

The Collusion

Avi Shlaim, who has made a very significant contribution to the new history, will only be analysed shortly because his main arguments have

---

121. Shapira 1995: 28.
122. Shapira 1995: 28.

already been presented and they develop along the structures as elaborated upon previously. We will refer to Shlaim's work *The Politics of Partition* (1990, 1998). It is a condensed and revised version of his study *Collusion across the Jordan* (1988). The first has been chosen because it represents the core version of Shlaim's contribution to the new history and it contains some passages that take into account the debate over the new historians which of course can not be found the 1988 edition. The 1988 edition is highly empirical but also highly polemical. Shlaim did like Morris and Pappé conduct research in the Israeli State Archives, among other central documentation centers, in the 1980s and had access to the same previously classified materials from the period around the 1948 war. In the preface to the book, Shlaim explains his way into the subject of Zionist-Arab relations as a matter of experience. He researched and planned for another study but came across documents that influenced him deeply on a personal level. He found out that the knowledge he was brought up with in Israel was wrong and almost nothing but propaganda and that disturbed him so much that he had to change subject and write a history over the new documents.[123] Shlaim readily admits that his work was carried by a great deal of indignation particularly over Israel's actions but also over the actions of King Abdullah of Jordan[124] who did not act out of any sense of pan-Arab loyalty or sympathy for the Palestinians. Shlaim's introduction is quite interesting due to the fact that it reflects openly over his personal motivations and is attentive to the criticism that he met with the publication of *Collusion across the Jordan* in 1988. Remarkably, he altered the title of the book due to criticism of the term "collusion" and opted for less value-laden terms. The most important revision that Shlaim made in the 1990 version regards the moral evaluation of the actors of the 1948 war. As mentioned, Shlaim was driven by a degree of indignation which led to a negative portrayal of both Zionists and King Abdullah and an overt victimization of the Palestinians. Shlaim changed this perspective in recognition of the rules of realpolitik and in particular regarding the evaluation of Abdullah, he turned about and in the 1990 version Abdullah is a pragmatic leader with a sense for moderation and compromise. This does not in any way

---

123. Shlaim 1998: VII.
124. Jordan was established in 1946 when Abdullah became king. Between 1921-46 the area was named Transjordan and Abdullah had the title of emir.

affect the presentation of the historical sources but only the meanings and conclusions drawn from them.[125] Thus, Shlaim's 1990 version represents, like Pappé's *The Making of the Arab-Israeli Conflict*, an integrated and evaluated condensation of new history.

Avi Shlaim's major contribution to the new history is in the re-evaluation of the status of the confrontation between the Zionists and the surrounding Arab states, in particular Jordan. Zionist histories often depict the conflict as an existential confrontation between a united and strong Arab world and a weak, defensive Jewish state. Israel was indeed attacked by the surrounding Arab states but Shlaim argues throughout his work that the Arab states were internally divided and not very devoted to liberating Palestine. The Arab states did not succeed in mobilizing for a decisive battle with the Zionists and in this respect Abdullah of Jordan played a significant part. Shlaim shows how the Zionists had friendly contacts to Abdullah for a number of years before the war for Palestine and that Abdullah was quite open minded about Jewish political presence in the region which he believed could benefit the entire region. Abdullah suggested that the Zionists accepted self-rule in an expanded "Semitic" kingdom reigned by himself. When the Zionists rejected this proposal, Abdullah came to the conclusion that the Zionists were too strong and wilful to be defeated and he opted for "an understanding" between the parties. At the same time Abdullah was commander of the united Arab front against the Zionists. Shlaim suggests that Abdullah betrayed his Arab allies by not engaging the Arab Legion[126] unconditionally in the war and not following the master plans. Instead, Abdullah relied on his understanding with the Zionists. The understanding included, according to Shlaim, military restraint in case of war and a sharing of the Palestine mandate between the Zionists and Abdullah.[127] These conclusions initially led to Shlaim's evaluation that a "collusion" had taken place between the Zionists and Abdullah against the Palestinians. In the larger picture of new history, this presentation of Zionist-Arab relations around 1948 add significant strength and coherence to the claims made by Benny Morris and Ilan Pappé. The Zionists figure as a decisive and strong power in the making of the post-1948 political and structural situation of Palestine/

---

125. Shlaim 1998: VII-XVI.
126. British trained and equipped Jordanian army.
127. For this see in particular chapters 1, 2, 4, 8, 11, 12 of Shlaim 1998.

Israel. Driven by a powerful national ideology and under the protection of Great Britain and after WWII the superpowers, the Zionists won the battle for legitimacy and built a society prepared for independence and eventually armed struggle. The Zionists drove the Palestinians out in the course of the 1948 war and managed to increase the territory of the prospected Jewish state in tacit understanding with Jordan. The Arab states were divided, weak and competing among themselves which in the final analysis makes the Zionists the strongest actor on the Palestinian scene. This is a figuration of a new history of the 1948 war in the Israeli historical context in sharp contrast to Zionist history.

Considered as a discourse, Avi Shlaim's history of Arab-Zionist relations evolves along the same structure as we have seen previously in the cases of Morris and Pappé. The time-space coordinates are about 1900 to about 1950 in Palestine. No regard is given to particularistic moralities of modern Jewish history and the Zionist historical imagination. The account is problem-oriented, as we saw it with Morris and Pappé, and the central problem experienced by Shlaim is basically the same, namely how did the Zionists manage to win the war for Palestine. Shlaim also refrains from the metaphorical proper names given to historical events in Zionist history and he uses a metonomycal, reductionist style to narrate and elaborate the chosen source materials. The master trope of the historical presentation by Shlaim is irony which comes to light when we consider his meta-text and speculations over the vocation of historians. Shlaim's history contains all the elements of satire. The actors are manipulative, scheming against each other and the situation at the end is not much better than at the beginning. There is no historical lesson to learn or no human or divine comedy to give hope for the natural progress of history. Opportunities are lost in *The Politics of Partition,* not won. Shlaim and the other new historians see the existing body of literature on the 1948 war in both its academic and popular versions as a "fabric of myths"[128] that has proliferated due to the highly mobilized national-patriotic agendas of both Israel, the Palestinians and the Arab states. The strength of the myths has different reasons. Among the Palestinians and the Arab states the reason is primarily mobilization of citizens against Israel and in Israel the reason is reaffirmation of a "manifest Zionist destiny".[129]

---

128. Rogan and Shlaim 2001: 2.
129. Ibid: 2.

Apart from the inevitable teleology of a history in which the end is the most obviously known factor, Shlaim refutes the national-patriotic plots as legitimate for a history of Israel and the Arab-Israeli conflict and replace them with a satiric plot.

Final Comments

Since the publication of the first works of the new historians, there has been a considerable public debate in Israel and in the international media which I have only superficially touched upon. Still, there is reason to mention in passing that Benny Morris, who has delivered the most detailed and path breaking new history, has publicly denounced the political and intellectual tendency, post-Zionism, that his work has meant very much to. We saw previously that Morris' history among the new historians' can be singled out as the account least overtly sympathetic to the Palestinians and their political quests in the present. Morris has in the Israeli and international press, since the outbreak of violence in 2000, several times claimed that the Palestinians are to blame for the violence and that the Palestinian leadership only recognize Israel as a practical arrangement.[130] At the same time, Morris has evaluated his works of history in the light of his present political opinions and defends his conclusions from the end of the 1980s in fact several of the most critical issues are being reinforced in Morris' update to *The Birth of the Palestinian Refugee Problem*.[131] Morris believes that the actions of the Israeli forces during the 1948 war were more or less justified, and definitely necessary, and that many readers of his books do not have the same moral detachment that he has when he writes them. Morris declares in the interview that he is a Zionist, which he has always been, but that he is misunderstood by many of his readers. He can write about Israeli massacres and expulsions of Palestinians and still support the outcome of the war because terrible things happen during war and many of them were necessary, for example

---

130. Morris and Shlaim debated Morris' apparent change of mind in *The Guardian* in February 21 and 22 2002.
131. In an interview to the Israeli daily *Ha'aretz* on January 9, 2004, Morris explains how he has found more cases of Israeli atrocities during the 1948 war in his continued work in the archives.

the expulsion of the Palestinians.[132] Obviously, the interview with Morris has provoked debate but the reason it is mentioned here is to point to the fact that the new history is not the expression of a united position or ideology. It is a tendency that generates changes and is itself generated by socio-political changes in the longer term. There can be drawn different moral conclusions from the new history, which we have seen in the public appearances of Morris under the current outbreak of violence between Israel and the Palestinians, but the Zionism of Morris is not a Zionism embedded in traditional Zionist historical imagination. Rather, it is liberal and pragmatic in its assessments of the rules of real-politik and in its un-idealistic assessment of the alternatives to the outcome of the 1948 war, which by Morris is considered far worse. Morris' personal and political evaluation of the current historical situation as reflected in the media does not involve a re-articulation of the visions of the Zionist historical imagination but Morris distances himself from the side of the post-nationalist spectrum that he most frequently has been associated with. The effects of the historical presentations of the new historians considered as events are not controlled by the historians but enter a much wider discursive field than the academic-historical because of the position of the events of 1948 in collective Israeli historical discourses and because of socio-cultural changes. That the new history has become the discursive locus for an intellectual-political tendency such as post-Zionism does not necessarily imply that the new historians should be considered post-Zionist.

***

Previously, it was suggested that Jacques Derrida's notion of history as a sort of "haunting" of current discourses and fluctuations of meaning by past events is an appropriate metaphor for the significance of the 1948 war in Israeli and also Palestinian history. Derrida most explicitly developed this line of thought in relation to the positions of Karl Marx in European history and he named his investigation a "hauntology".[133] Marx and Marxism are many things in innumerable settings. Every new scientific, or other, exploration of the phenomenon is an addition to

---

132. Ibid.
133. Derrida 1994.

the hauntology of Marx, not a reduction that closes us in on what the phenomenon "really is". The 1948 war that led to the establishment of Israel and the Palestinian refugee problem has such a significant position in Israeli historical and political discourses that we can consider the 1948 war as a ghost that haunts current Israeli discourses of historical, political and existential legitimization. With the new historians, new texts were added to the Israeli "hauntology" of 1948. The new Israeli historians provided us at the end of the 1980s with a forceful and consistent refiguration of the 1948 war which in the 1990s amounted to something like a national reckoning in the context of 1948's renewed significance as a central aspect of the Israeli-Palestinian peace negotiations between 1993 and 2000. The dominant discourse of "peace-making and liberalization", as Shafir and Peled has phrased it, provided the broad sociocultural background of legitimacy to a post-nationalist Israeli history.[134] The new history gave knowledge and thereby strength to a new vision of the historical relations between the Zionists and the Palestinians in which the 1948 war figures just as prominently as in Zionist history but embedded in a new discourse.

At the level of discourse the new historians created a new place, or a new historical scene, for Zionist-Jewish history. In the new history, Zionist-Jewish history is confined to Palestine from 1900 which is an alteration of the time-space coordinates of traditional Zionist history. Zionist history generally operates from a European context of Jewish national renaissance, anti-Semitism and ultimately the Holocaust that are all aspects that must be included in a proper and legitimate history of the 1948 war from a Zionist perspective. Critical or not, such histories operate the same historical imagination as Zionist ideology whereas the time-space coordinates of new history give prominence only to actors and actions on the Palestinian historical scene. When the Zionist historical legitimizations are left out of the presentations, the entire history looses meaning and direction and gains new ones. The new history relies on a different plot for the historical account of Zionist-Jewish history in Palestine and the 1948 war and if we apply Hayden White's correspondence scheme that explicates relations between certain tropes, narrative plots and ideologies, we see that the new historians' satirical plots and

---

134. Shafir and Peled 2000.

use of the meta-trope irony corresponds with a liberal ideology.[135] As elaborated on previously, the implementation of certain tropes is basically a pre-discursive and pre-logical operation. The same is the case with the choice of contexts for the historical study, which is both pre-discursive and pre-empirical. We can thus state that the new history is *pre*-figured differently than Zionist history and with its consistency taken under consideration, it constitutes a new Israeli historical imagination, which is post-nationalist. In White's *Tropic of Discourse* pre-figuration is considered a fundamentally poetic act for the historian indicating some individual randomness in the application of meta-historical visions.[136] This seems not to be the case when we consider the correspondence between the historical figures of the new history and other socio-cultural developments in Israel during the 1990s. Instead, it seems that the new history's figuration of Zionist-Jewish history functions in a dialectic relationship with wider discourses of legitimization in Israel related to socio-political changes. Such a new pre-figuration of Zionist-Jewish history as placed in a Palestinian time-space invariably alters the patterns of meaning that are related to basic questions of right and wrong in a historical perspective between Israelis and Palestinians. Placed in a Palestinian time-space it is harder to imagine the Zionists on a mission for rescuing the Jews from persecution than conceiving the Zionists as European colonialists.

In Israel in the 1990s, Zionism was not generally conceived of as a European colonization movement but the new historians and the debates over their writings helped to facilitate an Israeli non-Zionist history of Zionism to function as an intellectual opposition to a previous cultural paradigm. This non-Zionist history, the new history, was set in a problem-oriented, metonymical (Morris), ironic (Pappé and Shlaim) style and the post-nationalist liberals in Israel and in Jewish environments abroad by and large adopted it. The histories of the new historians are not only explorations of the past but also symptoms of the present they are written within. There is no doubt that the new historians' works themselves are historical signs of beginning changes of Israeli cultural patterns and as cultural discourses, the new historians' works should be considered the historical meta-narrative of the period of liberalization, globalization and peacemaking in the 1990s. There is no place for public legitimacy for a

---

135. White 1973: 29.
136. White 1978: 1-4.

post-nationalist history if not there is a legitimate public discourse that does not hold the national imagination high – if not there is an erosion of national culture that gives way for a post-nationalist tendency.

History and Irony

In Works of Orly Castel-Bloom and Etgar Keret

Introduction

History is not only what we find in history books or in a museum. History is also a way of thinking, and a discourse, which operates in practically all textual presentations of human and social relations. The relations in texts between past, present and future, and differences between individuals and things that come into shape because of a process of historicizing, can only be constructed in discourse and therefore are historical relations cast in discursive plots that make use of different tropes to introduce arguments and meanings to the text. In the field of literature, history has given names to entire genres and history is in many literary presentations a highly significant element of the construction of meaning. Historical imaginations in the most prosaic sense develop out of historical novels, poems and children's books and the figures of history in such texts do not necessarily differ from the figures in academic history but they reach a far wider audience. The relations between history, literature and configurations of society are complex but history and literature must be said to belong to the same category of speculative and theoretical productions of meaning and truth, which develop in a dialectical relationship with society's socio-economic configurations. The disciplinary conventions of literature, however, are different than those of history and therefore history itself can be symbolized in a variety of ways which it cannot in academic history because it in its modern type ultimately is conceived as a realistic discourse. Accordingly, literature does not have to be realistic, such as a historical novel, to theorize or speculate over history and to construct a more or less explicit historical imagination. Most theorists of history and probably many historians recognize the proximity in origin between modern history and the modern realistic novel. Put crudely, we can say that history is still anchored in 19th century positivism while modern literature has developed vividly in many directions.

Hayden White's philosophy of history is directly based on the equivalence between realistic literature and history which enables White to read works of history inspired by Northrop Frye's theory of archetypical plots in literature. There is also the possibility of reading history in literature but that requires a different strategy while still accepting the basic outline of analysis given by White. In order to engage in the historical imagination of Israeli literary texts, a complementary reading of Michel Foucault's thinking on history, the body and the author will be presented. The complementary reading of Foucault serves as both a theoretical key and a special focus on embodiments of history. Furthermore, Foucault's perspective of history has had what seems as a powerful influence on White's philosophy but it is not occupied with forms of history.[137] Instead, it is philosophically and critically concerned with historicizing concepts, knowledge and rules of interpretation, and with suggesting alternative modes of historicizing such as archaeology and genealogy. Foucault offers perspectives on the manifestations of history as an embodiment of personal experiences that can be articulated through different discourses, both academic and artistic.[138] The discursively articulated embodiment of personal experiences can be characterized as both a recognition of the individuality and the contingency of imaginations of history and a recognition of history's formal and nominal existence as a discourse controlled by rules. When we turn to presenting Israeli literary texts in the following, the Foucaultian perspective is an important tool to understanding and describing the individual literary presentation of history and the discourse that represents it at the level of society.

---

137. Primarily Foucault's critique of historical discourse and its truth-claims have influenced White. White 1987: 104-141.
138. A central guide to Foucault's understanding of history is the text *Nietzsche, Genealogy, History* (Foucault 1977).

The Israeli Literary Tradition and Zionist History

> "The coming into being of the notion of "author" constitutes the privileged moment of *individualization* in the history of ideas, knowledge, literature, philosophy, and the sciences. Even today, when we reconstruct the history of a concept, literary genre, or school of philosophy, such categories seem relatively weak, secondary, and superimposed scansions in comparison with the solid and fundamental unit of the author and the work.
>
> Writing unfolds like a game that invariably goes beyond its own rules and transgresses its limits. In writing, the point is not to manifest or exalt the act of writing, nor is it to pin a subject within language; it is rather a question of creating a space into which the writing subject constantly disappears".[139]

The concept and function of the author and the work is not connected to the individual habita of the writer of texts but related to the meaning, position and use of the name of an author and her work as an icon of certain meanings and positions. The author and the work step into wider discourses as icons with numerous more or less defined meanings and morals attached, but the author also creates a mental, social and historical space that claims its independent existence over the dispositions of the author. In this double sense, artistic utterance can be individualized, as an icon of certain meanings and positions, and privatized as a personal uttering in a negative sense and at the same time it may be understood as a recognizable meta-discourse on collective terms. Much of Zionist-Jewish and Israeli literature in the first generations of Modern Hebrew writing resembles the traditional understanding of the Greek epic in as much as it was conceived and received as a collective enterprise. In its shaping of Modern Hebrew and its articulations of modernistic and national Jewish sentiments and narratives, it collectivized Zionist history and identity and created the collective Zionist "I", a hero, who kept on living in the epic as an icon even after death. This epic is a constructive, community building effort, which basically is a rise from death or an avoidance of death.[140]

---

139. Foucault 1979: 141-142.
140. I am here discussing the type and function of Israeli literature in a wide and discourse social field not in a strict literary sense. In a strictly literary sense,

Zionist and Israeli writers have played an instrumental part in shaping the Zionist historical imagination by plotting the Tragedies and Comedies of a national Jewish renaissance and inventing the Zionist persona-hero figured as a fighter, soldier, pioneer, farmer or mythological avenger. The function of the author was that of a culture politician and ideologue who most often worked in close cooperation and affinity with the political leaders of the Zionist institutions and the political editors of newspapers and periodicals, and most often within the Labor Zionist movement. The boundaries transgressed with these writings were the boundaries of Diasporic Judaism and the space created was a Zionist and territorial space.[141]

Modern Hebrew writing has a close connection to Zionist history. It was shaped in the same period and in the same social and cultural environment of the Jewish Enlightenment (Haskalah) and the post-Enlightenment period. In this period, influenced by both secularist rationalism and German romanticism and idealism, the dominant perceptions of Judaism, Jewish identity and Jewish history were fragmented into several mutually exclusive tendencies. The cause was primarily the socio-economic changes of post-Napoleonic Europe, which for the Jewish populations meant a virtual destruction of traditional patterns of organization, community status and not the least the traditional sources of legitimacy.[142] As for the rest of Europe, modernity transformed not only the institutional and economic foundations of the European societies but also society's discourses on identity, legitimacy and history.[143] As Yerach Gover notes, practically all Jewish writing prior to the Jewish Enlightenment was theological and embedded in the discourses of Jewish

---

Israeli literature is surely much more varied and not only figured as epics. Hebrew literature has been written about in a historical perspective by many writers of which the works of Gershon Shaked must be considered canonical.

141. For a somewhat similar perspective see Wisse 2000: 323-348. The conventional perspective on the Hebrew canon is laid out by Gershon Shaked in his monumental *Hebrew Narrative Fiction 1889-1980* (1977-1993).
142. Sorkin 1987, Meyer 1967, Katz 1986.
143. As Uri Ram and Zygmunt Bauman suggest, modernity changed the rules of argumentation and created a new *Gesellschaft*, namely the nation, and thereby turned the previous Gesellshaft of religion and tradition into a new *Gemeinschaft*, a local and emotional affiliation. Ram 1999, Bauman 2000.

cosmology and the changes of the beginning of the 19th century changed this characteristic radically.[144]

Hebrew writers such as J.H. Brenner, H.N. Bialik, Ahad Ha'am, M.J. Berdichevsky, S. Tchernichovsky and S.Y. Agnon invented the new language of Jewish modernity while they were inventing Modern Hebrew discourses on social identities and historical identities in their fiction and ideological essays. Many of the works of the above mentioned writers can be considered pre-Zionist because they are modernist, influenced by nationalist sentiments, and express models of Jewish existence that can be incorporated in Zionist ideology and Israeli national life. These writers drew many of the normative and moral boundaries of modern Jewish social and historical identities. The Zionist renaissance literature created a secular, moral Jewish historical subject and a community of moral subjects brought together by primordial, organic and historical determinants. While the pre-modern Jewish communities were knit together by theology and a cosmic, circular, historical imagination, the new secular and national community were connected by way of "blood" and a basically organic, and teleological history.

Though there are detailed and conventional ways in which to divide modern Hebrew writing into periods, it suffices to note that the first real challenge to the hegemonic discourses of Modern Hebrew writing came with the mass immigration of the 1940s and 1950s of Jews from the Arab countries who in many cases had no relation to Zionism and the social configurations which gave birth to it.[145] The demographic and social ruptures of the huge waves of immigration did not in the longer term change the social and historical discourses of Hebrew writing but it did create an internal oppositional literature. Yerach Gover shows, however, how this internal opposition, which also includes non-immigrant writers such as A.B. Yehoshua, Amos Oz and Yoram Kaniuk, does not fundamentally challenge the hegemonic discourses of Hebrew writing because they accept the Zionist meta-narrative, and the historical plots, but they are concerned with the continued morality of the Zionist moral subject.[146] They accept,

---

144. Gover 1994: 22-23. As for history, Yerushalmi 1989 shows how Jewish writings of history until about 1820 were also fully embedded in Jewish cosmology and chains of rabbinical authority.
145. With this rough periodization, I follow Gover 1994: 24-25.
146. Ibid.

and in fact even reinforce, the Zionist persona-hero and re-enforce the boundaries, in spite of their criticism of e.g. the treatment of Arab Jews or their criticism of the occupation since 1967 of the West Bank, Gaza and East-Jerusalem. They have a contract with the state: they are society's moral intellectuals but they do not create a new language, a new discourse on Jewish-Zionist history and identity. The division between a pre-state literature and a post-state, and the challenges posed to Hebrew writing and Zionism by the demographic and cultural changes of immigration, was successfully overcome and hegemony was re-established until around 1990 when new authors gradually replaced older icons.[147]

Hebrew Writing and History
Previously, it was mentioned that Hebrew writing has a close connection to Zionist history because both were the offspring of the same changed conditions of 19th century Europe and belong to the same tendency of Jewish existence that followed the civil and economic revolutions. Modern Hebrew writing broke with theology and created the narratives of Jewish modernity, while the creation of modern Jewish history in the same period re-enforced the new realistic and rationalistic discourses by means of scientific history inspired by contemporary German history.[148]

Just as Hebrew writers prior to the establishment of the Zionist movement can be considered pre-Zionist because of their occupation with what later became Zionist sentiments and their easy retrospect integration in Zionist discourses, the founding of modern Jewish history with *Wissenschaft des Judenthums* in the 1820s can be considered pre-Zionist.[149] The

---

147. 1977 is often considered the moment when the unified Zionist imagination was challenged by the defeat of Labour Zionism in the elections. This is correct to the degree that Labor Zionism's historical, social and political vision to a large extent controlled society, but 1977 did not lead to new boundaries for Jewish-Zionist identity and history or opened up for new alternative discourses.
148. Yerushalmi 1989, Myers 1995, Meyer 1967.
149. A somewhat bold statement because *Wissenschaft des Judenthums* also produced non-Zionist Jewish historians such as Dubnow, and reformists such as Geiger. The term pre-Zionist should be understood in the sense of the creation of a singular, chronological, and secular Jewish history, which in effect frames the discourse of a Jewish social and historical body (a collective subject). Such a figuration of Jewish history can easily be integrated retrospectively in Zionism.

histories of Wolf, Zunz, Jost, Graetz and the other *wissenschaftliche* historians of the 19th century broke with theology and compiled Jewish history according to contemporary scientific criteria, but more importantly for this context, they created the Jew as a modern historical subject, whose identity did not gain legitimacy from God but history. Their concern was the same as the writers of Hebrew fiction, namely the re-invention of Jewish history and identity in a secular and rationalistic language. By the end of the 19th century Jewish history developed into Zionist history, became an ally of the Zionist movement and was institutionalized in Palestine from 1924-25 with the establishment of the Hebrew University in a similar movement as Hebrew writing.[150]

History in the canon of Modern Hebrew writing is present as an overall narrative frame, which means as a typical relation between past, present and future that serves as a realistic model for Jewish-Zionist experience. This is evidenced in the highly epic and allegorical quality of Modern Hebrew writing which raises collective concerns to the forefront of the texts in a specified cultural-ethnic setting. The epic quality can make the texts embrace the collective subject in the story of the individual protagonist. The texts become models for identification and sources of direct social knowledge of self and society, while the allegorical quality as an extended metaphor creates a direct resemblance between text and society, or history.[151] These texts very often construct a total history in each narrative, which is one of the implications of both epic and allegory, and thereby they imitate, or reproduce, the same totality as Zionist history, namely the specific Jewish historical and social experience.

A total history is a history that encompasses and integrates both the individual events and experiences and an identified, nominal, metaphysical history. In this case it would be events and experiences that have a meaning in a Zionist discourse which are integrated, or encompassed,

---

150. Myers 1995: 74-108. There are a few notable exceptions among historians such as Simon Dubnow who wasn't a regular Zionist and still wrote some of pioneering works of Jewish history in the period of the establishment of Zionism and settlement in Palestine.
151. Israeli literary criticism often focuses on an allegorical reading. The texts must be an image of society, and preferably a constructive image. Society, the collective identity, or the conflict becomes the topics of discussion between writers and their critics through allegory and the expectation of such. I will discuss this further when engaging in Orly Castel-Bloom's writing.

in a history specifically identified as Jewish. Collective histories, such as Jewish histories, are necessarily metaphysical as they follow a collective subject through time and space, a subject that is more than just a congregation of people with a Jewish self-identity. The essence of meaning is not in the individual problem-solving of the fictive protagonists in literature but in metaphysical laws governing Jewish history. Even prominent critical writers such as A.B. Yehoshua and Amos Oz, fall in this category of literature that encompasses a total history. Such writers might be critical towards the history proposed by Ben-Zion Dinur or other founding fathers of Zionist history, but they nevertheless accept the same ethnic boundaries, historical paradigm, and the teleology of Jewish history in Zionism.[152]

An effect of history's total presence in much Hebrew writing is that the writing becomes overtly political. Epics of Zionism and allegories of the political or moral situation of Zionism or Israel exist in abundance and they provide both the edifice of Zionism and often harsh criticism of Israel's treatment of the Palestinians or criticism of the military culture. But the dominating presence of the totality of the Jewish-Zionist experience not only serves to re-enforce the state's contract with the intellectuals about criticism within common boundaries, but also the ideological aspects of ethnic-communal boundaries and the tropes and plots of total history. This total history is paradigmatic nationalistic, realistic and exclusive.

In the canon of Modern Hebrew writing, the course of modern Jewish history is the principle on which the experiences of the individual protagonists are based. This means that the principle form, the typical past-present-future relation, is embedded in the *telos* and the utopian imagination of Zionism. Higher laws of history and Jewish existence are governing the perspective on the present reality and that reduces the individuals inhabiting Modern Hebrew writing to agents in opposition to creators of lesser utopias where the casts and plots of Zionism might be

---

152. These writers do in fact show the dissonances of the total history of Zionism in many of their novels or short stories but the stories themselves are constituted and dominated by the same total history at the same time as they are about that total history or total experience of Zionism. Their protagonists are often trapped in the structure and logic of Zionism but moral and existential priorities leave other utopian options out of the question.

challenged. On the surface, it could seem as if there is a healthy dialectic between structure and agency, or between history and individuality, in Modern Hebrew writing but the structure, the *telos* of Zionist history, is dominant to a degree that the relation stops being dialectic and instead becomes totalistic.[153] There is no doubt that the conflict between Israel and the Palestinians has led to a reinforcement of the dominance of total history in Modern Hebrew writing. Violence directed at the collective identity of Israelis and Zionists in fact increase the internal ethnic and communal violence to the effect that the structures of total history, and its presence at the level of experience in the texts, will be continued in spite of social fragmentation. There is no truly universal and individualistic dimension to the canon of Modern Hebrew writing but there is a strong body of texts that has created a national, ethnic-communal discourse of experience, which becomes the icon, or language, of authentic Jewish-Zionist life.

History in the canon of Modern Hebrew writing is Zionist history and Modern Hebrew writing reflects this history in its epic and allegorical qualities and its embedment in a specified ethnic-communal setting, a setting that is the prime concern of the texts. Most texts in the canon of Modern Hebrew writing encompass a total history. This means that Zionism's historical order becomes also the narrative order. The specific ethnic-communal history exists as a precondition for the situation of the texts and in the present moment of the texts, an icon of Jewish-Zionist experience is presented. At the level of discourse, the plots of history presented in the canon of Modern Hebrew writing are the same as the ones dominating in Zionist history, namely Comedy and Tragedy. Hebrew writing, of course, makes use of different plots but the underlying historical order on which the present moment of the texts is based is cast as Comedy or Tragedy.[154] On trajectories of Modern Jewish history a body of canonical texts established the discourses of potential and possible Jewish-Zionist experience, and thereby also the boundaries of legitimacy. The canonical authors and their works stand out in the Israeli arena as

---

153. Gover observes that the dominant *telos* of Zionism has a mobilizing effect that enables people to cope with the pain of conflict and violence and still be enthusiastic on behalf of the Zionist utopia. Gover 1994: 31.
154. White 1973: 1-42. In these pages White presents a typology of historical writings based on classical theory of plots and tropes.

openings into the authentic dilemmas of Israeli sociality, but they are mere examples of the limits of discourse and the social experience of ethnic nationalism, Zionism.[155]

Satire and Irony in the 1990s

A number of Israeli writers rose to prominence in the 1990s, writers who in common understanding has been categorized as "untraditional" or even "post-Zionist". These writers to some extent rejected the yoke of the Israeli author, which places a burden of political correctness and even superior political and existential knowledge on the shoulders of the author. The new writings should not be read as an insight into authentic Israeli sociality but should be read as individual utterances, moral lessons, or even ethics. The texts are not allegories or realistic expressions of the Jewish-Zionist experience. It is curious to note that the new writers entered the literary scene at the same time as the new historians published their works, under the Palestinian uprising from 1987-93, and their popularity reached high points in the middle of the 1990s under the peace process between Israel and the Palestinians. Though these events are not related in a linear way, it seems that there from about 1990 existed an arena for a potential change of the discourses of history and experience. As Judith Winther remarks, it seemed as if a door had opened through which texts entered that did not describe, criticize or even deal with Zionism. They were beside or beyond Zionism.[156]

Orly Castel-Bloom's Dolly City

> The genealogist needs history to dispel the chimeras of the origin, somewhat in the manner of the pious philosopher who needs a doctor to exorcise the shadow of his soul. He must be able to recognize the events of history, its jolts, its surprises, its unsteady victories

---

155. I must note that my re-description of the Modern Hebrew canon follows the same structure as Simon Halkin's classic from 1950 *Modern Hebrew Literature* (see his introduction and e.g. p. 73). There is one crucial difference though. Halkin thinks that the modern Hebrew canon mirrors the historical forces that Zionism represents, while my perspective understands the modern Hebrew canon as an active discursive shaper of experiences and histories that are Zionist.
156. Winther 2003: 119.

and unpalatable defeats – the basis of all beginnings, atavisms, and heredities. Similarly, he must be able to diagnose the illnesses of the body, its conditions of weakness and strength, its breakdown and resistances, to be in a position to judge philosophical discourse. History is the concrete body of a development, with its moments of intensity, its lapses, its extended periods of feverish agitation, its fainting spells; and only a metaphysician would seek its soul in the distant ideality of the origin.[157]

Orly Castel-Bloom's *Dolly City* is a text that fundamentally disturbs the boundaries, historical imagination, and moralities of the discourses of the Israeli experience. Castel-Bloom as an author-name is generally perceived by critics and academics as an expression of radical feminism with its intense rebellion against perceived masculine and violent categories of language and tradition and against a "gender-mapping" of the world of human relations that have naturalized women in certain positions. Castel-Bloom's protagonist in *Dolly City* is Foucault's genealogist, understood as a feminist, who exorcises and dispels the culturally and historically stigmatized female soul through violent and deconstructive operations of the body's faults and diseases. As in Foucault's understanding, history is a concrete body of a development, which metaphysicians investigate to explore the origins of things, on which the genealogist operates in order to be able to diagnose its philosophical discourse. Violence is done both when things are held in perceived natural origins, be it women, history, tradition, and when the body is operated on, but in operation it is revealed that nothing is natural. The whole, closed, integrated body is a synecdoche that covers a vision of a corporate, organic, unity in the likeness of nature and produces a sense of identity, which doctor Dolly surgically dissembles.[158] But unlike Foucault's genealogist, who apparently, and illogically, is able to stand outside the historical body, Dolly cannot diagnose the problem. She is embedded in the same vision of unity and her deconstructive effort is schizophrenic and paranoid.

* * *

---

157. Foucault 1977: 144-5.
158. Hoffman 2000: 2. Hoffman shortly discusses this perspective on the body in her general discussion of embodiments.

Dolly City takes place in a city, and sometimes in what seems a country, named Dolly, and it follows the life of a female doctor named Dolly. Doctor Dolly lives in an apartment on floor 37 in a 400-story tower. The apartment has an operation room where Dolly performs medical experiments on rats and other guinea pigs. Surgery seems to be both an obsession and to have a therapeutic value for doctor Dolly. The narrative begins with the death of Dolly's gold fish and her dog. The gold fish is cut into tiny strips, seasoned and eaten by Dolly who contemplates her activity as an analogy to ancient ritual practises. "In the very ancient times, in the land of Canaan, righteous men would sacrifice bigger animals than these to God. When they cut up a lamb, they would be left with big, bloody, significant pieces in their hands, and their covenant would mean something".[159] Afterwards, Dolly takes the life of her sick dog in an act of mercy killing and then calls up a guy who disposes of dead pets for money. Dolly insists on participating in the burial of the dog to the disliking of the pet-disposer. He informs her that he buries the pets in the sand dunes by the beach. Everything goes peacefully until the man begins to mutilate the dead dog, chopping it into peaces and throwing the peaces into the grave. Dolly goes crazy and forces the pitchfork from the man and kills him with it in a rage. She feels good about her self and drives off in his car only to discover that a newborn baby is on the backseat. The baby is in a terrible state, blue, with a hole in its stomach so it's possible to see into the interior of the body. Dolly brings the baby home, sews him up, sedates him and her self under a great impulse to execute him, and finally gives him the name "Son".

Dolly takes Son to heart with the energy of an all-controlling Mother. She is sick with concern for him and she measures his well-being with meticulous, scientific precision, puts the data into computer-models, and pumps him full of inoculations for all kinds of diseases. In fear of infections, she destroys her laboratory with all the guinea pigs and germ samples that she had collected, and sterilizes her self. Son's safety becomes her prime concern and she starts to do medical examinations on him with obsessive energy. Dolly suspects a heart problem with Son and she begins a history of surgery on Son just to check if everything inside him is in order. This is how she finds out that Son has only got one kidney. The quest for a kidney for Son leads her to Germany: "An

---

159. Castel-Bloom 1997: 11 (English version), 1992: 9 (Hebrew version).

Arab baby – they hate us; we hate them. I'll kidnap an Arab baby, remove his kidney, and transplant it in to the body of my only son. But then I frowned. Everyone knows that you can't mess with Arabs; even talking to them is dangerous and if you turn your back on them, you're dead. And then I sat down and thought about the history of mankind. Of all the people that ever lived, who were the most swinish – which of them had broken all the records? The answer was clear".[160]

In Germany Dolly finds an orphanage where she can obtain a kidney for Son. She kills most of the German babies at the orphanage with a feeling of historical irony. Her Jewish son lives, the German babies die.

Dolly continues her obsessive controlling behaviour towards Son while he grows up. For some time he is literally glued to her back so she can have both her hands free and still control Son. In this period, Dolly is in a completely paranoid state seeing cancerous diseases everywhere and having fantasies about tumours developing in her surroundings. She constantly feels that surgery is the proper treatment for all the concerted illnesses springing up around her. She and Son live from day to day until finally her sister who recognises the serious state of both Son and Dolly takes Son away from Dolly. Son goes to live in a home for battered children and Dolly is periodically submitted to mental hospitals.

Six years pass before Dolly looks up Son now 13 years of age. Son wants to join the army, the marines, and he leaves Dolly in a mental institution and goes off to fight sea battles. At the end of the novel, Son returns from the sea and only sees Dolly briefly. Son submits her to an institution for the elderly where she, after a number of years, learns from a newspaper that a young weirdo has attempted to highjack a plane from the national Israeli airline named B.OFF. Dolly comments: "I was worried about the boy but not hysterical. I knew that, after everything I'd done to him, a bullet or a knife in the back was nothing he couldn't cope with".[161]

* * *

Dolly City is not a coherent allegory of life in either Tel Aviv or Israel though that would be a reading that invites itself to readers who are accustomed to the Israeli literary canon and its critics. Rather, *Dolly City* is

---

160. Castel-Bloom 1997: 51 (English version), 1992: 33 (Hebrew version).
161. Castel-Bloom 1997: 182 (English version), 1992: 123 (Hebrew version).

a schizophrenic and paranoid fable about a mother and her son, which dissembles most conventional categories of time, space, sequence, and not the least human relations. It is the fact that neither Dolly, Son or Dolly City metaphorically represent anything in a reality of modern Israel as reflected by conventional representations of the Jewish experience, and thereby rejects the discourses of Zionist history and Jewish experience, but still is a densely packed text with metaphors concerning the individual relation between time, space and experience, that makes *Dolly City* a disruptive event. *Dolly City* could have taken place anywhere but in spite of such contingency, local conditions influence both bodies and experiences of the protagonists. These conditions are clearly Jewish-Israeli as expressed by Dolly's psychologist: "There are names for things. There are identities".[162]

Dolly's situation and her fears concerning Son have names, identities and histories in common with many other human relations in the Israeli context. The fear of death and the fear of loss due to the on-going war with the Palestinians create an identity as "bereaved parent" or "orphan" between diverse individuals that Dolly refuses to recognize.[163] Normality as an orchestrated, logical, coherent, historical narrative that gives places, individual and collective identities to people does not exist for Dolly and she experiences things without any normalizing effect from the discourses of the Jewish experience. Instead, we witness a schizophrenic and paranoid identity constructed out of a multitude of layers of significance that have no order or chronology. Historical tribal rites, orgiastic killings, and blood revenge inaugurate historical identity for Dolly and individual identity is built up by the Mother-Son dialectic to which the doctor title that Dolly identifies with is also connected. The historical and emotional identity markers are not logically organised or explained as natural but they affect the individual, Dolly, who without integration in the hegemonic discourse of Jewish experience displays the contingency and arbitrariness of identity. The world is cancerous,

---

162. Castel-Bloom 1997: 147/1992:98.
163. It should be said that in *Dolly City* there are no Palestinians but "Arabs" appear as both a frightening enemy and as some sort of historical yardstick for the status of the Israeli self: "Yes, that's the generation gap for you, I reflected. My mother spits on the Arabs, I look them straight in the eye, and one day my son will lick their arses." Castel-Bloom 1997: 132/1992: 89.

sick, and hostile, but at the same time Dolly is fragmented, paranoid and thus not an icon of stability in a sick world.

This is the effect when we read *Dolly City* with an understanding of history and identity as something logical and objective in it self, and exterior to the original self, but again *Dolly City* shows that nothing is natural, or original, and that history and identity first and foremost are inscribed in the body of the individual. The body is the real historical map:

> "I took a knife and began cutting here and there. I drew a map of the Land of Israel – as I remembered it from the biblical period – on his back, and marked in all those Philistine towns like Gath and Ashkelon, and with the blade of the knife I etched the Sea of Galilee and the Jordan River which empties out into the Dead Sea that goes on evaporating for ever.
>
> Drops of blood began welling up in the river beds cutting across the country. The sight of the map of Israel amateurishly sketched on my son's back gave me a *frisson* of delight. At long last I felt that I was cutting into the living flesh. My baby screamed in pain but I stood firm. When I had finished marking all the points my neglected education succeeded in pulling out of the creaking drawers of my mind, I went back to being what I am – a doctor – and I disinfected and dressed the cuts, and sewed them up where necessary.
>
> I contemplated the carved-up back: it was the map of the Land of Israel; nobody could mistake it."[164]

With violence Dolly physically inscribes herself and Son in the Land of Israel, Son's blood runs in its rivers and history becomes embodied in their lives in the appearance of a biblical map. Not only is the drawing of the Land of Israel on Son's back an inscription in a nominal history, it is also a mark of identity that changes in the course of time and conditions. When Son is taken from Dolly she is told that she can have him back when she returns to the '67 borders.[165] One of the first things Dolly does when she meets Son again is to look at his back: "The map was amazingly accurate and up-to-date; someone had gone over all the lines and expanded them according to the child's growth. I examined

---

164. Castel-Bloom 1997: 44/1992: 29.
165. This passage could be considered a political comment from Castel-Bloom but has other implications as well.

the map. One thing stood out – he had returned to the '67 borders. It was beyond belief".[166]

History in *Dolly City* is individually inscribed as scars on the human body and becomes as such private and only raised into generalizations and commonality by the identities shaped by the discourses of the real, normality, tradition and power. All violent conventions that Dolly, the doctor-surgeon-genealogist, is disrupting by her surgical operations on the historical body, Son, and her schizophrenic and paranoid mental capacities. She is ultimately only successful as an exhibition of the violent impulses of history, identity and discourse, not as a heroine because she fails and is finally submitted to an institution by her own object of control, the masculine Son.[167] History has no order or logic that does not stem from the individual and therefore the individual embodiment of history and the social discourses, the rules of interpretation, are the sources of history itself. Furthermore, Dolly's genealogical and deconstructive efforts against domination fail to build her self as a full and coherent identity. She finds in surgery that the body is only a machine with changeable and reparable parts and that there is nothing natural and original to be recovered. The imaginary historical and social coherence is dissolved in *Dolly City* but truth, sanity or normality is not the result of the dissolution.[168]

The historical imagination in a text such as *Dolly City* is built up around a different concept of history than what previously was called the canon of Modern Hebrew writing, and its principal form is not constituted as a realistic, logical or teleological past-present-future relation. Castel-Bloom's discourse in *Dolly City* envisions history as lines, scars and parts on the individual body and mind, and thereby contributes to a privatisation of history on basis of a concept of history resembling Foucault's concept of history as a body of a development.

---

166. Castel-Bloom 1997: 132/1992: 89.
167. Deborah A. Starr also notes the same development in the text, which is of high importance in a feminist reading. Dolly has a fatherless son, a unique opportunity to break masculine control, but in spite of all her efforts Son manages to break free, and even to alter the map on his back, and places Dolly out of influence in an institution. Dolly's violent project of liberation is defeated. Starr 2000: 232.
168. Adi Ophir discusses the moral lessons of this type of texts, and is quite concerned, and its relevance in the project of Israeli society post-Zionism. Ophir 2001: 202-22.

Dolly City, then, is not a Zionist text in as much as it does not deal with, interpret or lay out a Jewish experience but a human, motherly, female experience in which history, identity and discourses are defining contingencies; factors that violently shape physical and mental existence. The narrative forms or plots to explain or embed history and identity are not coherent, chronological, structures but more different lines and plateaus without beginning or end; something which might better be caught up in the concept of the rhizome as applied by in the philosophy of Gilles Deleuze and Félix Guattari.[169]

Previously, it was suggested that history, when understood in context of embodiments, is synecdochic when envisioned as a full and coherent body; a corporate unity. This is the tropology of Zionist history which Castel-Bloom's discourse disrupts with its exhibition of the historical body as a body of changeable fragments and lines without coherent structure; an irony.

The Liberal Ironist – Etgar Keret

> "I use "ironist" to name the sort of person who faces up to the contingency of his or her own most central beliefs and desires – someone sufficiently historicist and nominalist to have abandoned the idea that those beliefs and desires refer back to something beyond the reach of time and chance. Liberal ironists are people who include among these ungroundable desires their own hope that suffering will be diminished, that the humiliation of human beings by other human beings may cease."[170]

---

169. Deleuze and Guattari 1989: 21-22. "Unlike a structure, which is defined by a set of points and positions, the rhizome is made only of lines; lines of segmentarity and stratification as its dimensions; and the line of flight or deterriorialization as the maximum dimension after which the multiplicity undergoes metamorphosis, changes in nature". Deleuze and Guattari continues to explain the difference between discourses that operates with origins, unities and continuities, and "rhizomatic" discourses that operates by variation, expansion, conquest, capture and offshoots. "Rhizomatic" discourse's method is "mapping" as opposed to "tracing", something that likens Castel-Bloom's discourse to Deleuze and Guattari's rhizome. Laurence J. Silberstein also borrows this concept from Deleuze and Guattari in his *Mapping Jewish Identities*. Silberstein (ed.) 2000.
170. Rorty 1999: xv.

Richard Rorty defines the liberal ironist as a person who is aware of the contingencies that defines her identities and who realizes that these identities and their histories can be historicized. The implication of historicization is that identities and histories have no foundation; they are given by time and chance.[171] Somewhere else Rorty writes that an ironist is someone who constantly doubts her final vocabulary because other final vocabularies are appealing and their attraction display the contingency of her own final vocabulary.[172] A liberal ironist is a pragmatist and an anti-revolutionary because violence, suffering, and humiliation are the worst things we do.

In the 1990s, one of Israel's most popular, notorious and appealing writer was Etgar Keret whose humorous, yet melancholic, absurd, but familiar, short stories gained a wide readership particularly among the younger generations, while the older generations debated Keret's negative influence on both literary culture and society as such. Keret is Rorty's liberal ironist. He is very aware of the coincidence of his Israeliness, his existence (his parents are survivors of the Holocaust) and the contingencies of his beliefs (his sister is an ultra-orthodox and his brother is heading the Israeli legalize marihuana movement). He would any day prefer a "peace of the suckers" to a "peace of the brave" because he cannot relate to such things as historical justice or metahistorical truths that some people are willing to die for. The cruelty inflicted on human beings is far worse than the loss of territory or historical visions.[173]

Etgar Keret debuted in 1992 as a comic strip writer and published a year later his first collection of short stories. His preferred style is the satiric and absurd short story or the comic strip but he has also published children's books. Besides his writing Keret teaches at the Tel Aviv Uni-

---

171. Rorty uses historicization the same way Foucault uses genealogy; that is in opposition to history. History is concerned with origins, unities and structures and historicization (genealogy) is concerned with the *Herkunft* of ideas, discourses and histories. Thus, historicization does not establish the solid foundation for a belief but display its involvement in certain discourses, patterns of organisation and mere coincidence.
172. Rorty 1999: 73. A final vocabulary is the sets of words that can describe our ideals, hopes, beliefs. It is the sets of words that are final because if tested their users have no non-circular argumentative recourse. Rorty mentions words such as "true", "beautiful", "God", "the Revolution", "professional standards", and "decency".
173. Interview with Keret in *Ha'aretz* May 15, 2002.

versity's film and media department. As an author-name, Keret can be regarded as a writer of the post-modern, American type, defined by an ironic, easy going style without points of reference or adoptions from Israeli or European high culture and a close affinity to American popular culture as it is portrayed in American films.[174] To the Israeli critic and the older generations of Israeli intellectuals, Keret represents increased americanization, postmodern irony but also an indirect rebellion against the established values such as Zionism.

Keret's preferred heroes are often anti-heroes because of the history of heroism as a violent and idealistic ideology which often involves cruelty against others and solid metaphysical convictions. The protagonists are anti-heroes, meaning every day people or absurd characters whose relations and interactions are coincidental, irrational and absurd, but still very human, normal and loyal. The normal-absurd dichotomy is often dissolved to show the absurd in the normal and vice versa. This works as an opposition to heroism (idealism), rationalism and in opposition to the metaphysics of Israeliness in general.[175] To Keret, according to an interview, Israeliness is "hummus ahla", which is a mass produced commercial brand of hummus. It is not really good, not spicy, but everyone can eat it and it is easy to spread on bread. It is a "quick fix". Culture is not really authentic, it is a mass product for mass consumption, while authenticity is private and related to specific experiences and human

---

174. If there is a European high culture reference in Keret's works it would be Franz Kafka, whose absurdities could be seen as an inspiration for Keret, I would suggest.
175. By metaphysics I mean a thinking that searches for the intrinsic nature of things, the natural condition of things, and truth in the sense of the most correct description of reality. Richard Rorty writes of the metaphysician: "Metaphysicians think that human beings by nature desire to know. They think this because the vocabulary that they have inherited, their common sense, provides them with a picture of knowledge as a relation between human beings and "reality," and the idea that we have a need and a duty to enter into this relation. It also tells us that "reality," if properly asked, will help us determine what our final vocabulary should be. So metaphysicians believe that there are, out here in the world, real essences which it is our duty to discover and which are disposed to assist in their own discovery. They do not believe that anything can be made to look good or bad by being redescribed – or, if they do, they deplore this fact and cling to the idea that reality will help us resist such seductions". Rorty 1999: 75. In opposition to the metaphysician Rorty puts the ironist.

relations that just happens to be Israeli.[176] Keret's anti-heroes and his perspective on culture are representative of a popularized view of what post-Zionism is. An upper-middle class, well-educated, pragmatist elite with liberal and materialistic values inspired by American culture and fostered by the economic growth of the 1990s as well as the Oslo process and globalisation. Cosmopolitans whose culture is more "Western" in a universal sense than Israeli and whose Israeliness is tied to experience, friends and family more than history, nation, religion and ideology.[177] Compared to the imaginations of shared identities and shared historical destiny of the canon of Modern Hebrew writing and its cultural particularism, Keret's stories and sense of history and identity are private and ironism makes him resistant to cultural essentialism. Thus, Keret, like Castel-Bloom, creates alternative Israeli discourses which can't be included in the Zionism of the canon of Modern Hebrew writing, though they are cornerstones in the post-modern canon of Hebrew writing as reflected in articles on feminism, embodiments, post-Zionism and historical and literary culture.[178]

In the story about the busdriver who wanted to be God, Keret sets up a discourse that basically evolves around a dichotomy between principles and *Menschlichkeit*. The busdriver initially incarnates principled behaviour and the other protagonist, Eddie, is the person who, also in principle because he suffers from a disease that makes him come inevitably late to everything including the bus, incarnates the all but perfect man guided by wishes, desires and misfortune. The busdriver wanted to be God earlier in his life but since it didn't happen he instead became a busdriver, which was his second preferred career choice. The analogy that invites it-self would be about power but in this story it is the issue of principles versus compassion that is the connection between this particular busdriver and God. The busdriver is a principled man who would any day prefer the common good to the good of the individual:

> "And it wasn't because he was mean that he didn't open the door, because this busdriver didn't have a mean bone in his body; it was

---

176. Interview with Keret in the Israeli daily *Ha'aretz* on May 15, 2002.
177. The post-Zionism Tom Segev describes in his book *Elvis in Jerusalem* (2003) and a cosmopolitan elite of the sort described by Zygmunt Bauman in *Liquid Modernity* (2000).
178. For example in the pages of the journal *Theory and Criticism* which must be considered the leading Israeli critical academic journal about culture.

a matter of ideology. The busdriver's ideology said that if, say, the delay that was caused by opening the door for someone who came late was just under thirty seconds, and if not opening the door meant that this person would wind up losing fifteen minutes of his life, it would still be more fair to society to not open the door, because the thirty seconds would be lost by every single passenger on the bus. And if there were, say, sixty people on the bus who hadn't done anything wrong and had all arrived at the bus stop on time, then together they'd be losing half a hour, which is double fifteen minutes. This was the only reason why he'd never open the door. He knew that the passengers hadn't the slightest idea what his reason was, and that the people running after the bus and signalling him to stop had no idea either. He also knew that most of them thought he was just an SOB, and that personally it would have been much easier for him to let them on and receive their smiles and thanks. Except that when it came to choosing between smiles and thanks on the one hand, and the good of society on the other, this driver knew what is had to be."[179]

The busdriver's principles allow him no mercy on the individual because that would work against the interests of the common good and the interests of the common good are based on a theory of justice. The busdriver is in principle the perfect citizen but confronted with Eddie in a situation where Eddie really needs to catch the bus, the driver remembers when he wanted to be God. Back then he promised himself that he would be merciful and compassionate, if he became God, and he is forced to defy ideology and let Eddie in.

Principles, common good, utilitarian theories of justice are thoroughly ridiculed in Keret's discourse as something quite inhuman or at least misunderstood while the individual action, that breaks with the rationalized idea of good, to do something "irrationally" good is "God-like" in the sense that a person, the busdriver, stops time, plans and rationalities to do something for another person, Eddie. From a rationalist perspective, the busdriver could have argued that his action helped Eddie achieve his goal, getting the girl, but Keret makes sure that this is not the case. Eddie is eventually stood up by the girl, thus, it was to no avail that he ran after the bus in the first place. His effort, will and effect on others did not create any logical improvement of his situation. The outcome

---

179. Keret 2001: 1-2/1998: 7.

of the story is that the busdriver remembers the compassion for Eddie and gives him a sad look in the mirror, which makes it possible for Eddie to bear the burden of his misfortune. Principles and ideology stand in opposition to individuality, compassion and *Menschlichkeit.*

Keret's stories do not unfold in any sort of metahistorical plot and there are rarely any projections of the metaphysics of Modern Jewish history present to shape the fundamental patterns of action and meaning for the protagonists in the stories. The stories are situated in streets, bars, apartments and in Israel but only because of the identifiable objects inhabiting the scenes, the language spoken and concrete actions and patterns of behaviour recognised as Israeli. The stories are not situated in Modern Jewish History and they are not synecdochic in the way that they are meant to represent an icon of the Israeli experience. They are more like little worlds of human experience in which the Israeli reality occasionally intrudes. The ability to create little worlds that do not claim to be representative of any essentialist claim, that are not analogies of life in an ideal sense or claims to be indicative of larger metaphysical questions such as the nature of Israel or Judaism or Jewishness is truly an ironic capacity, as Richard Rorty points out in his readings of Proust and Nabokov.[180] Yet, these descriptions of little worlds of human relations are highly moral stories though not in an idealistic, Kantian, sense of universal morality, but in a sense that more resembles the concept of solidarity. This solidarity between human beings is a morality in opposition to universal or utilitarian theories of justice and in opposition to the power of the commonsensical "right thing to do", as we saw with Keret's busdriver.

In the story entitled *Siren* the protagonist is literally saved by the bell, the siren that symbolizes the commemoration of Israel's fallen soldiers. On Holocaust Day, the protagonist Eli, discovers that Gilad and Sharon have stolen the janitor's, Sholem's, bicycle. Gilad and Sharon are top students, top athletes and going into the best corps of the army and they took the bicycle while they were celebrating that Sharon passed the psychological test before entering the elite army unit. Sholem, the janitor, is a quiet existence who cries on Holocaust Day because he was in a *Sonderkommando*, something that Eli does not know what is. Holocaust Day is described as something trivial and there is no emotion or edifice in the portrayal of

---

180. No comparison between Keret and the mentioned writers is intended. Rorty 1999: 96-122, 141-169.

an orchestrated and meaningless ceremony during which the school's pupils go about their usual business mocking each other and positioning themselves. When Eli meets the crying Sholem on the stairs, he is surprised because he meets real emotion on Holocaust Day.

Eli tells the school headmaster about the theft of Sholem's bicycle in confidence that he is a secret informer but word gets out and Eli, betrayed by Sharon' girlfriend with whom Eli is in love, runs into a beating behind the school by the hands of Sharon and Gilad. As the beating is imminent, the siren for the commemoration of the fallen soldiers sounds and Gilad and Sharon stand still as wax mannequins. Eli is saved and runs home through streets with people standing still:

> "I wanted to get away from there, to run, to raise my hands and protect my face, but the fear paralyzed me. Then suddenly, out of nowhere, there came the wail of the memorial siren. I'd completely forgotten that it was Remembrance Day for the fallen soldier. Mikey [Sharon] and Ron [Gilad] came to attention. I looked at them standing there like shop-window mannequins and suddenly I wasn't afraid anymore. Ron, standing rigidly to attention, eyes closed, holding Mikey's jacket. Looked like an oversized coat hanger. And Mikey, with his murderous look and clenched fists, suddenly looked like a little boy imitating a pose he'd seen in an action movies. I walked to the hole in the fence and passed though it, slowly and quietly, while behind me I heard Mikey hiss, "We're still going to fuck you," but he didn't budge. I walked on home through the streets with all the frozen people looking like wax dummies. The sound of the siren protected me with an invisible shield."[181]

This story has provoked some debate in Israel because it has been taken as a critique of Israel's Holocaust memorial practices and it has also received critique for being ironic towards something that in its nature defies irony, namely the Holocaust. Keret does indeed turn things upside down in identifying the Holocaust memorial as part of the triviality of the system, making it an opposition to emotion and compassion and relating it to power and reproduction of power in the characters of Gilad and Sharon. Furthermore, the very unsympathetic habita of Gilad and Sharon are the favoured competences of the elite army units, something which in Keret's discourse adds to the destabilization of the commonsensical good

---

181. Keret 2001: 82-83/1996:12.

and honourable features of Israeli society. The protagonist, Eli, is on the surface insensitive to the Holocaust Memorial, which bores him, and he does not know what a *Sonderkommando* is. Viewed from the perspective of Zionist discourse, this is evidence of an erosion of a specific Israeli identity construction. In Keret's discourse, however, Eli is the average sensitive boy and the system is the insensitive wall of triviality.

An alliance is formed between the two weaklings of the story, Eli and Sholem. These two anti-heroes are the good, normal people, despite and because of their ridiculousness, and they are both moral individuals, through compassion, in their actions. Eli feels compassion and respect for Sholem because Sholem was in a commando unit (Eli's ignorant association of the word *Sonderkommando*) and because Sholem cried on Holocaust Day. Sholem is compassionate as the only human being in the story who cries on Holocaust Day and he displays something that seems as real emotion based on experience and presumably empathy. In Keret's discourse the two anti-heroes are presented as the only non-wax mannequin persons. This alliance is a moral alliance of the same sort as the one demonstrated by Keret's bus driver. It is a morality that is in opposition to universal morality represented by the system's production of good. It is an individual morality which surfaces in defence of persons subjected to acts of cruelty. It does not stand in for visions of good produced by ideology or a hegemonic system. It is pragmatic and liberal and not judgmental when it comes to general criteria for what is rationally and logically deemed as the good and right thing to do.

In the Israeli context Sharon and Gilad are local heroes and the Holocaust memorial represents a moral and national a priori commemoration, which makes the boyish "borrowing" of Sholem's bicycle not excusable but secondary to the achievement and potential of the boys. Thus, Eli's dilemma becomes that his "snitching" of Sharon and Gilad is in opposition to the idea of the collective good, because he undermines their character by telling about this minor incident, though his snitching normally would be considered the right thing to do. Put colloquially; Eli steps in it by doing the right thing against the wrong people. In creating this setting Keret creates a completely relativistic life experience. The ironist lesson is, in the absence of rules, that the best and most moral decision to opt for is the one that goes against cruelty towards the weak. The ultimate irony of Keret's discourse is that history comes in defence of this decision by Eli. History incarnated by the siren that signals the commemoration of the fallen soldiers provides the possibility of escape and thus the institutionalized memorial ceremonies comes to actually save the persecuted. History is in this story by Keret not characterized by certain time-space parameters of the past but by the institutions of society and the normative cultural patterns, such as memorials, that invoke the past in the reification of the current order of discourse. Keret uses the sensitive issue of Holocaust commemoration, and derived from that also Holocaust education, as the example of a reification of history and morality that stands in opposition to *Menschlichkeit* and thereby rebels against the commonsensical perceptions of the production of good. Liberal compassion and struggle against cruelty do not become reinforced by trivialisation and institutionalisation. It is, in fact, in Keret's discourse the other way around. The individual is threatened by normative culture and the ideologically produced good.

Etgar Keret only uses very few historical references in the discourses of his short stories, of which the story of the siren is one of the clearest, but still his discourses counter-theorize the total history perspectives of the canon of Modern Hebrew writing. In an interview, Keret tells the story of how his parents met and he emphasises the absurdities and contingencies of this happenstance.[182] It seems as if Keret employs this familiar and personal story as a philosophical non-theory for his own dispositions and the plotting of his stories. Keret simply holds history as a series of contingencies that lacks an absolute interpretive key but these contingencies and the personal relations involved in them shape the individual and, furthermore, history acts unequally in different life experiences. Such history cannot be total or be uplifted to a coherent theory of history because none of Keret's uses and non-uses of history, nor his stories, can be taken as an icon of history itself or life itself.

In interviews, both Keret and Castel-Bloom add to the destabilization of the allegorical and epical strategy of reading commonly employed by the Israeli critic by stating, in Keret's case, that he considers his stories highly moral but that he has no desire to control their interpretations by readers.[183] Castel-Bloom equally positions herself as a writer who writes about Israeli experiences but not as an oracle of the totality of the vision of Zionism or Judaism as predecessors such as Amos Oz or

---

182. Interview with Keret in *Ha'aretz* May 15, 2002
183. ibid.

A.B. Yehoshua.[184] They both resist the author-work function associated with Zionism and thus resist to be the window through which we can see the Israeli experience and icons of Modern Jewish history in its totality. Still, both writers contribute with alternative, ironist, discourses that are contingently and nominally Israeli and do not project metaphysical knowledge but very different descriptions of examples of human relations and their historically contingent coming into being. Keret speaks the Rortyan language of liberal hope for less cruelty based on a private ironism and Castel-Bloom speaks the Foucaultian language of radicalism also based on a private ironism.

Human Parts: Castel-Bloom's Return to Realism

Towards the end of this chapter I want to engage in Orly Castel-Bloom's novel, *Human Parts*. This novel is highly significant for a distinction between the types of irony, conceptions of history, and ideas of public action that are displayed in the writings of Etgar Keret and Castel-Bloom. To achieve this distinction is important both for developing the difference between liberal and radical ironism, and the implications of this difference, and it is important for a description of the range of options that face ironist discourse when liberal public metadiscourse is destabilized. As I described in the first essay, the proliferation of the trope of irony and the plot of satire in the redescriptions of Israeli society, history and experience in the 1990s depends on a wider socio-economic public discourse that articulates political, economical and civil options in a way that makes private ironism a legitimate basis of public participation and action. For such participation and action to be accepted as legitimate and reasonable, as we have witnessed it in the 1990s, certain conditions must have changed and new conditions have arisen. I will claim that the new conditions are, in one aspect, due to what Shafir and Peled calls the re-articulation of the conflict between Israel and Palestinians in economic and liberal terms, and, in another aspect, the lessening of Israeli pain and suffering both in connection with conflict related violence and general social conditions.[185] The radical increase in terror against

---

184. Interview with Castel-Bloom in *The New York Times*, June 17, 2002.
185. Shafir and Peled 2000: 1-2.

Israeli civilians since the mid 1990s has increased private fear and pain to a degree which challenge ironism as a basis for public discourse and it is in this connection that I read Castel-Bloom's *Human Parts*. Terrorism and its production of fear do not necessarily eradicate ironism but it emphasizes which kind of ironism that has something to offer public discourse and which that have nothing.

In *Dolly City,* Castel-Bloom uses the body as the physical entity on which mental capacities, dispositions and identities are inscribed. Dolly's obsession with the body and her surgical attempts to diagnose problems of history and identity lead her to seriously disfigure (re-figure) her son. From a feminist perspective this theme is both about control and self-liberation. Dolly wants to control Son and simultaneously liberate herself from the historical and social control of identities but the attempt fails. The genealogical strategy exhibits Dolly as a schizophrenic. The "philosophical discourse", in Foucaultian terms, that Dolly seeks in order to set herself free cannot be found but, as discussed earlier, it is found that nothing is natural or original.

The discourse in *Dolly City* supports Dolly and her controlling and liberating actions to transgress social discourses and it describes the body as a neutral container of replaceable parts that only gets its individuality, contingently, from the history of the particular container. The title of Castel-Bloom's novel *Human Parts* refers to the same understanding of the human body as described above, but this time the trope that initiates the texts is a classical metaphor. Human parts is, simply, a metaphor for the less than full life experiences of the protagonists who try hard to do their best and achieve the full life in love, standard of living, caring for their children, but in spite of their efforts they remain only fragments of their wishes, only human parts. The novel also follows several groups of people who lead their lives in ignorance of each other but still interwoven in the larger fabric of social and personal despair and at this level of society, the title Human Parts refers to the effect of social conditions on the lives of the protagonists. Thirdly, Human Parts refers to terrorism but not directly to the massacres committed by terrorists. Suicide bombings becomes an icon of dissolution, though there does not figure any suicide bombings of decisive effect for the story in the novel, which adds to the internal social dissolution and give a picture of complete hopelessness. Terrorism has the effect that ever fewer parts of the protagonists' lives remain to resemble a human life. In an interview Castel-Bloom states that she supports Ariel Sharon's war against the Palestinians, not because she wants them dead but because they are the enemy and they threaten the possibility of a coherent life in Israel. Castel-Bloom uses her personal fear of terror and her fears for her daughter's safety as an argument for supporting a violent strategy. In her view terrorism simply makes everyday life almost unbearable.[186]

Human Parts is, according to Castel-Bloom, a novel that documents life in Israel during the second Palestinian uprising from 2000 in real time. In another interview Castel-Bloom states that she was shocked by the events after the breakdown of negotiations between Israel and the Palestinian Authority and that she decided to document events.[187] According to her statements, terrorism made her feel an increased belonging to Zionist history and the Israeli reality, which made her reflect over the right to criticism that she and other younger writers have been associated with. Castel-Bloom comes close to thinking of criticism as a welfare phenomenon and, put crudely, feels that reality has caught up with her.[188] Furthermore, Castel-Bloom thinks of *Human Parts* as her most Jewish work and she very consciously shifts her earlier non-ethnocentric style to an exclusively Jewish frame through an application of the Jewish calendar throughout the novel. Each sequence of the novel is dated according to the Jewish calendar, which is a constant reminder of the history that the novel inscribes itself in. The exclusively Jewish periodization adds another meta-historical dimension to the already present apocalypticism of the novel in as much as it situates the events of the novel in the calendar of Jewish cosmology.

History and Irony in *Human Parts*

In Nietzsche, Genealogy, History Foucault writes that:

> "Finally, descent attaches itself to the body. It inscribes itself in the nervous system, in temperament, in the digestive apparatus; it appears in faulty respiration, in improper diets, in the debilitated and prostate body of those whose ancestors committed errors. //

---

186. Interview with Castel-Bloom in *Klassekampen* April 15, 2002, (In Norwegian).
187. Interview with Castel-Bloom in *The Jewish Week* November 26, 2003.
188. ibid.

> The body – and everything that touches it: diet, climate, and soil – is the domain of the *Herkunft*. The body manifests the stigmata of past experiences and also gives rise to desires, failings, and errors. These elements may join in a body where they achieve a sudden expression, but as often, their encounter is an engagement in which they efface each other, where the body becomes the pretext of their insurmountable conflict.
>
> The body is the inscribed surface of events (traced by language and dissolved by ideas), the locus of a dissociated Self (adopting the illusion of a substantial unity), and a volume in perpetual disintegration. Genealogy, as an analysis of descent, is thus situated within the articulation of the body and history. Its task is to expose a body totally imprinted by history and the process of history's destruction of the body."[189]

In these paragraphs Foucault attaches history directly to the human body as both the appearance of descent and the map of events. The body is both the mirror of physical and mental conditions and the inheritances from ancestors. In *Human Parts* we do not find the exposed body, as we found it in *Dolly City*, but we find the physical and social domain of the *Herkunft* of Orly Castel-Bloom's retraction from satire to social realism. The body as the inscribed surface of events from *Dolly City* has disappeared and social domains, imagined in total conjunction with the real, have taken the place of the body as the map of history. The almost "rhizomatic" lines that made up Dolly's descent and the investigation of this descent, which exhibited her as a schizophrenic, have been replaced by a calendar, a circle, which underlines the passage from private to public concerns between the discourses of *Dolly City* and *Human Parts*.[190] The Jewish calendar places Castel-Bloom's discourse in *Human Parts* within a

---

189. Foucault 1977: 147-8.
190. I agree with Richard Rorty's distinction between discourses for private projects and discourses for public conversations (Rorty 1999: 65). It's a very pragmatic perspective which is in complete opposition to the Kantian imperative, traditional epistemology and ideas of non-discursive truth. Discourses for private projects, such as Orly Castel-Bloom's attempt to destabilize normative, cultural, notions of womanhood, motherhood, and their history, can have private effects on others, such as ironism, but they would be destructive to the practicalities and necessary realism of public conversation. On the other hand, ironism is problematic when it comes to public conversation and collective political action, discourses for public conversation, because it is the opposite of common sense.

meta-historical imagination and an imagined community which was both present and absent for Dolly. For Dolly, community and ethnocentrism are unavoidable violences of social existence and this shows that there have been changes in the conditions of the social domains between Dolly and the protagonists of *Human Parts*. In *Human Parts*, Castel-Bloom directs the attention to these domains that have made it imperative for her to document what she perceives as the destruction of society by deteriorating social conditions and terrorism; developments that also force the collective identity to the forefront of her own self-identity. As in Dolly's case there is no escaping the cultural and social inscriptions on the body and the domain of the *Herkunft* for the protagonists of *Human Parts* and not for the author either.[191] Though it might seem odd that Castel-Bloom all of a sudden writes a realistic novel, there is a certain coherence between the failed genealogist Dolly and the private deconstructive, satirical, project, one the one hand, and the description of Israeli society under the second intifada in a realist tone on the other.

The realism of *Human Parts* is more social than realistic. There is an apocalyptic tension between the exceptional winter with snow, frost and hailstones, terrorism, social deterioration, poverty, mysterious diseases (the Saudi flu) and the sketchy social realism setup of characters. We find the beautiful immigrant from Ethiopia, Tasaro, with immigrant-racial problems and the emotionally difficult upper class Adir with serious asthma, who is her boyfriend. We find Boaz and Kati Hallahmi who are poor except for fifteen minutes of fame when Kati was made an example of Israeli poverty by television. Iris is an unemployed single mother who has descended into poverty recently but struggles for the dignity of herself and her children. She is not poor in her own self-understanding but a victim of circumstances and she is also Adir's ex-girlfriend. On the fringe of the setup we find the lonely, late middle aged, Angelica who teaches painting and make up in her apartment and the president of Israel, Reuven Tekoa, who drives around all day to visit funerals and next of kin to terror victims. Angelica gets acquainted with Kati because Kati desperately seeks a way out of her situation. Kati, of course, chooses

---

191. In the discourse of *Human Parts* the utopian option might be America to which there are references most notably at the end where the president speculates on his trip to Harvard to his daughter who studies there. Castel-Bloom 2003: 249/2002: 267.

training as a beautician, which reflects her girlish imagination and her desire to paint reality over with beauty.

In an interview, Castel-Bloom stated that she watched a lot of television in early period of the second intifada and it seems to be reflected in the superficial and sketchy setup of characters, which brings reminiscences of American TV-series or TV-novellas. The characters are stereotypes of typical social debates and social markers in Israel. Racism, conflict, poor social conditions, emotional problems and loneliness are conflict themes in Israel but also in the Ricky Lake Show. In fact, Kati gets the inspiration for her most radical act of liberation, scamming Ido from the Mizrahi Bank for his last money, from a TV-film.[192] All the characters are of the type to be found in a reality show on TV, something which gives the novel a dialectic tension between the informed understanding of the reality show as an artificial reality and the understanding of the reality show as an irony over life.[193] Castel-Bloom's discourse in *Human Parts* invites a perspective that in fact distorts a realist impression of the real but it still claims to be realist by the stylistic suggestion that reality and its inhabitants are indeed as pathetic and superficial as a reality show. The discourse is embedded in the social domains of its production and is therefore part of the sketchy reality.

The previously mentioned apocalyptic tension develops between an almost biblically troubled Israel and the less than heroic and idealist characters inhabiting it. It seems as if the pain, despair and physical violence of the characters are self enforcing traits of the social domain and above it all the world answers with thunder and hailstones and deadly influenzas.[194] Thus, the realism of the discourse is more concerned with a description of the social habitus of Israel under the second intifada than in describing the real in a transcendental sense.

In *Dolly City*, Castel-Bloom investigated the philosophical discourse of womanhood, mother-son relations and identity as a fragmented historical construction made out of conflicting lines of descent. In *Human Parts*,

---

192. Castel-Bloom 2003: 181/2002: 197-198. The film is entitled *Because of a Kiss* with a heroine named Claudia Helena who is Kati's romantic alter ego.
193. Smadar Shiffman of Tel Aviv University noted in *Ha'aretz* that "maybe our reality has turned Castel-Bloomic", which would be why her novel seems realistic. *Ha'aretz* 26.04.02.
194. It would be inappropriate to say God because Castel-Bloom only uses nature/God as a stylistic tool and plays with commonsensical symbolism.

Castel-Bloom does not investigate any longer but creates a real time description of one of the conflicting lines; that of Israel understood as a community which is a central domain of the self. *Human Parts* has not the level of ambition towards freedom and independent self- constitution as *Dolly City*, but its ironism and non-totalizing discourse is as much a basic condition:

> "Doctors were sometimes obliged to amputate parts of the body affected by gangrene due to the cold, and one of them said to the media: "As if what the suicide bombers do to the victims that remain alive after the blast isn't enough, they have to suffer cold and neglect as well."
> That doctor's appearance and hard-hitting words made a favourable impression on the producer of one of the news programs, and he was given a permanent spot at the end of every edition, after the weather forecast. On his spot, the doctor explained to the viewers how to diagnose chilblains and infections as a result of chilblains, and when to rush to the emergency room.
>
> On the night of the 20th of Tevet, a few hours after the publication of the poverty report, the community television channel of Ramle-Lod located the Beit-Halahmi family who lived in the Ganei-Aviv neighbourhood of Lod. The community channel had prepared in advance for the report, and they wanted to scoop the national channels with a touching human story of hardship – relatively refreshing in comparison to the grief and misery caused by the Arab terror."[195]

The fact that Castel-Bloom sets out to create a realist discourse to represent Israeli life conditions under the second Palestinian uprising does not turn this discourse into an idealist or transcendental history of the Israeli-Palestinian turn away from negotiation and into direct conflict. As mentioned, the discourse of *Human Parts* disturbs a realist representation of Israel under the uprising by mixing unnatural weather conditions, described completely realistically, with a Jewish calendar chronology and characters taken out of the reality show of Israeliness. The discourse still legitimately claims to be realistic because it describes the social domain that is constituted of Israeli conditions inhabited by

---

195. Castel-Bloom 2003: 10/2002: 16-17.

Jewish-Israelis who share a sense of community under the myth of a Jewish chronology. The sense of a "we" is under a process of dissolution that does not lead to individual freedom but to the amputation of another human part.

There is no doubt that Castel-Bloom conceives of this dissolution of the normative community as a loss that leads to the further amputation of one of the parts that constitute the "human". The central schism of this development for the ironist and deconstructive discourses that Castel-Bloom usually presents is that the ironist and deconstructive discourses are concerned with self-creation in a rebellion against commonsensical normativity while the human and social dissolution of *Human Parts* is a development towards destruction. Self-creation has in Castel-Bloom's discourses been a violent, destructive act. However, out of the social dissolution and terrorist violence of the lives of *Human Parts* come no individual creativity only a continued spiralling towards complete amputation of the possibility of being an independent person.[196] Social and terrorist violence thus halt the possibilities of self-creation and make an ironist author such as Castel-Bloom attach herself to the communitarian "we" even though this shallow and reality show-like reality contains nothing apart from being the social domain of Castel-Bloom's discourse. It is not that Castel-Bloom has suddenly discovered the eternal, historical or metaphysical values of Judaism and Israeliness.

In contrast to *Dolly City* the historical imagination in *Human Parts* is Jewish as it is connected to specifically Jewish-Israeli experiences, a Jewish calendar and an almost biblical apocalypse of unnatural weather conditions. This difference is not caused by a shift from an ironist to a metaphysical discourse, but caused by a shift of emphasis from a private project of self-creation in *Dolly City* to a description of the process of dehumanization of Israeli society under the second Palestinian uprising. Thus, history is equally contingent and constructed out of conflicting lines of descent but the genealogical project, the strive for freedom and

---

196. Foucault's notion of life as a piece of art comes to mind when considering Castel-Bloom's Dolly. We may consider the characters of *Human Parts* as the opposite, namely kitsch. Kitsch is something tasteless that imitates art, like the reality show imitates reality. Social dissolution and violence cause a radical empowerment of kitsch as relevant public conversation but it also influences the private discourses so that public and private languages become the same.

an authentic language is given up in *Human Parts* under the threat of the destruction of community. The historical symbolism of the Jewish calendar and the unnatural weather conditions do not indicate a new essentialism in Castel-Bloom's discourse, but it serves as simple metaphor for the community, whose myth is hanging, threatening, over their heads. So the Jewish history of *Human Parts* is not a total history that resembles that of the canon of Modern Hebrew writing. It is a reality show that describes the effects of socially and physically violent attacks on the sense of "we"; the line of descent that is constituted of a Jewish historical imagination.

In a very direct manner, this imagination was activated by an increase of the sense of insecurity that Castel-Bloom has talked about in interviews, both social and physical insecurity. There is no idealist or particular historical morality to the Jewish history referred to in *Human Parts* to replace ironism but the distinction between private and public discourses has been dissolved with the effect that the basically private project of liberation from history and culture comes to seem wrong or out of place when the community is under attack.

Castel-Bloom does not directly refer to the effect of terrorism apart from laconic comments such as the fact the number of deaths in an attack can be detected by listening to the radio channels' play lists and the fact that the president Reuven Tekoa does nothing but drive around to funerals and bereaved family of victims. Still, the suicide bombings are significant to the perspective of history as an embodiment that figures so prominently in Castel-Bloom's discourses. In Foucault's words the body is the inscribed surface of events and the locus of the dissociated self and therefore the most basic definition of humanity. Dolly was engaged in refiguring Son but only in the perspective that the body is the map of our selves, while the suicide bombings literally explode the body, the human, in a voluntary act of destruction. This destruction is the absolute opposite of the ironist, self-creative project of Castel-Bloom in all its radical idealism and therefore the suicide bombings produce a fear that challenge the ironist.[197] Suicide bombings become the symbolic

---

197. I must note that I do not find suicide bombings "un-understandable" or "otherworldly", which they certainly are in Castel-Bloom's discourse. As previously noted, Castel-Bloom has a curious relationship towards Arabs and Palestinians. In *Human Parts* there is no reason for the violence apart from violence itself.

antithesis to the investigation of the embodied history of both collective and self that Castel-Bloom embarked on her earlier writings within an ethnocentric setting where suicide bombings are destruction inflicted on the community by "the Other". Thus, history in *Human Parts* is conceived of in the same terms of contingency and irony as in *Dolly City*, in opposition to the metaphysical history of Zionism, but the private project of authenticity is lost because of changes in the social domains. These changes, epitomized by social decay and terrorism, force community concerns to the center of attention.

Final Remarks

The satire and irony of popular Israeli writers of the 1990s such as Orly Castel-Bloom and Etgar Keret decisively breaks with what I called the canon of Modern Hebrew writing. This break has many facets but it is founded in the replacement of a metaphysical meta-discourse with an ironist discourse. The particular perspective that is disturbed most significantly with this turn to ironism is the historical imagination of Jewish-Zionist experience and identity. The total, realistic and teleological historical imagination of Zionist history and Modern Hebrew writing was embedded in, and integral to, the construction of modern Jewish nationhood and it was inseparable from Zionist ideology and more practical, political discourses. The canon of Modern Hebrew writing is the body of texts that reflects legitimate and historical allegories, epics, tragedies and comedies, which with the use of synecdoche as a meta-trope integrate the individual life experiences and scenes portrayed in the texts in the larger fabric of the telos of Jewish-Zionist history. In this respect, the texts of the canon of Modern Hebrew writing are as representational in their perspective of reality as the texts of Zionist history. Such core modern and nationalist consistencies were challenged by writers like Keret and Castel-Bloom whose discourses are anti-representational, anti-foundationalist and ironist.

The Palestinians are the enemy to Castel-Bloom and she is not interested in the fact that suicide bombings have a history. Castel-Bloom's discourses are not politically correct in the way of Yehoshua, Oz, Grossman or other icons of liberal Israeliness which I find very liberating.

The trope of irony that functions as a meta-trope in Castel-Bloom's and Keret's discourses per definition produces criticism of the normative patterns of Israeli identity and public history because it questions the validity of the representational and foundational legitimacy that nationalist identities and realist history are based on.[198] Irony doubts the truth-claims of history, identity and morality and it doubts that knowledge of any sort reflects "the real as it really is". Irony cannot be integrated in the foundationalist and representationalist discourses of Zionist history and the canon of Modern Hebrew writing because that would mean a destabilization of the premises for upholding certain important distinctions such as true-false, history-ideology, legitimate-illegitimate, Zionism-diasporism, that make Zionist history unquestionably real and Modern Hebrew writing an icon of Jewish-Zionist experience.

The social developments of economic growth, massive immigration, globalization of both economy and culture, and not the least the prospective of peace with the Palestinians of the 1990s constituted the social domain of the proliferation of ironist discourses in Israel. These developments has the effect that the nation-state gradually looses it central position for development and culture and then nationalism becomes an ideology of choice and individual acceptance and thereby looses its power as a normative culture.[199] Discourses of liberalization, economic development and international cooperation and integration set the agenda of public conversation with an oppositional challenge from the "new" nationalism. These discourses are as much cultural as they are political and their cultural equivalents are private self-creative discourses such as the ones proposed by Castel-Bloom and Keret.[200]

The historical imagination that shaped both Zionist history and the canon of Modern Hebrew writing occupy the place of a normative culture, lines of identity construction and oppressive binaries such man-woman, Galut-Zion, Jew-Arab, Ashkenazi-Mizrahi, that the self-creative discourses of the 1990s seek to investigate to disclose its philosophical discourse and be liberated from, as we saw it with Castel-Bloom's *Dolly City*. Dolly became an exhibition of the conflicting lines of descent of

---

198. The "method" to achieve the effect of reality, truth and morality is rejected.
199. Bhabha 1990, Bauman 2000.
200. I do not mean to suggest that ironism only occurs under certain social conditions. Nietzsche was also an ironist and he didn't live in a post-modern capitalist

our identities and this exposure of the radical contingency of her life and her powerlessness to achieve anything from the exposure leave her as a schizophrenic. Castel-Bloom does not suggest any truer or better historical imagination as an alternative to the one her protagonist rebels against, which is an impossibility for an ironist who seeks authenticity and to break out of stereotypes and established categories.

Etgar Keret also writes in opposition to normative culture, metaphysical principles, and the reification of the value hierarchy of the hegemonic discourses as reflected in common sense, which his discourses most often rebels against through plays with normal-absurd dichotomies and classical ironies. Eddie and Eli, two typical Keret-protagonists, are anti-heroes when compared to conventional ideologies of heroism but in Keret's discourses they are the heroes because of their weakness, sense of solidarity and *Menschlichheit*. Keret's stories do not aspire to be an icon of Jewish-Israeli experience and every historical and social dimension in his discourses is circumstantial. Keret is Israeli by coincidence (or maybe accident), which he underlines in the *Ha'aretz* interview through the story of how his parents met.[201] His Israeliness is connected to experience and human relations and thereby purely nominal and contingent. History, as we saw it in *Siren*, is the institutional triviality of the Holocaust Memorial Day and its positive contribution to the story is one absolutely not intended by the system.

Keret like Castel-Bloom creates discourses of private projects that are self-creative in opposition to power and common sense but there are also very significant differences between the two types of ironism that manifests itself in their discourses. Keret is, as I suggested when

---

state. I mean conditions under which private projects and self-creation have wide public legitimacy. In Rorty's opinion ironism is only a healthy basis of public conversation in rich, literate democracies because here it is possible, and desirable, to separate private and public discourses. The reason for this possibility is the relative lessening of pain and suffering in such societies (Rorty 1999). This type of society seemed achievable in Israel in the 1990s. Post-marxist discourse theorists such as Ernesto Laclau and Chantal Mouffe accept most of Rorty's assertions except from the private-public distinction, which is a central discussion in this field. Lauclau and Mouffe operate with a much wider concept of "politics" that makes the distinction between private and public discourses impossible. See Mouffe 1997 for discussions with and of Rorty.

201. *Ha'aretz* May 15, 2002.

making him Richard Rorty's liberal ironist, a liberal whose discourses show that cruelty is the worst thing we do. Eli's rescue from a painful and cruel beating becomes a better point for the siren that howls on Memorial Day than the institutionalized and ideological history it represents. I would claim that the overall moral message of Keret's stories is solidarity, which is a relativistic message in opposition to the ethnocentrism of community and ideological principles. Keret's liberal ironism is not an ideology for public conversation but it nevertheless has a non-subversive utopian character that can serve as little anthropologies of *Menschlichkeit*. Thus, Keret's discourses do not work to dissemble the Zionist historical imagination and its discourses of experience but they relativize it, show the contingencies of life and replace principles with solidarity.

Castel-Bloom, on the other hand, is a radical ironist, which I illustrated by reading her in parallel to Foucault's perspective on history. Violence, cruelty and power are integral to her discourses as both oppressive factors that keep e.g. women in historical and traditional roles overarched by masculinity, and as means to break free of oppression to achieve independence. Her discourses seek and advocate fundamental changes. The body is the surface on which history and identity is inscribed and the body's social domains are included in the lines of descent that make an individual. Castel-Bloom disrupts the synecdochic vision of the body as a unity, with Dolly's operations on Son, and instead portrays it as an irony; as conflicting lines of descent made up of replaceable parts. Violence and cruelty are not an ultimate concern in her discourses but self-creation is.

The radicalism of Castel-Bloom's discourses is also the reason for the shift to some sort of social realism in the novel *Human Parts*. When the community that serves as the background for liberating one self from history and tradition comes under attack from internal and external forces, there is no pragmatism in Castel-Bloom's discourse and liberation is needed along collective lines instead. The Arab and the Palestinian are the enemies of the project of freedom in both *Dolly City* and *Human Parts*, and the cruelty inflicted by Israel is not an important concern, only the cruelty inflicted on Israel is. Then it is not surprising that Castel-Bloom turns to community concerns after the level of pain and suffering have increased while Keret's liberal ironism survives due to its fundamental concern for pain and suffering.

The embodied history of Castel-Bloom is only a philosophically and privately relevant alternative to the Zionist, integrative, historical imagination because it enables no liberal hope for less cruelty. It is basically a private search for a new vocabulary and an investigation of old ones. If we uphold the distinction between private and public discourses it cannot be translated between the two if its purpose should be the relative lessening of pain, solidarity or peace. A translation of Castel-Bloom's discourse into public concerns is the reality of *Human Parts*, while Etgar Keret has something to offer public conversation, namely little worlds that can create solidarity.[202]

The perspectives on history and the discourses of experience created in Castel-Bloom and Keret's texts cannot be integrated in the Zionist historical imagination and experience. Their non-totalizing, individualistic and ironist discourses find legitimacy in the historical changes and dynamisms of 1990s Israel. They do not constitute an ideological alternative.

---

202. This is not a judgement of their literary or artistic qualities in general.

Replacing History and Identity: Back to the Diaspora

History and identity in works of
Amnon Raz-Krakotzkin, Daniel and Jonathan Boyarin
and Ilan Gur-Ze'ev

"The image, the imagined, the imaginary – these are all terms which direct us to something critical and new in global cultural processes: *the imagination as a social practise*. No longer mere fantasy (opium for the masses whose real work is elsewhere), no longer simple escape (from a world defined principally by more concrete purposes and structures), no longer elite pastime (thus not relevant to the lives of ordinary people), and no longer mere contemplation (irrelevant for new forms of desire and subjectivity), the imagination has become an organized field of social practises, a form of negotiation between sites of agency ("individuals") and globally defined fields of possibility.[203]

Introduction

In the following, I will draw attention to a number of philosophical discourses that problematize the Zionist territorialization of Jewish identity and the negation of the Diaspora as both a physical and mental category. The agenda of the discourses is at the same time critical scholarly analysis and contentious re-descriptions of Zionist ideology, history, Diaspora, notions of identity and homeland that aim to work within Jewish politics. These discourses are to my mind central, though avant-garde, to both the critical analysis of culture in Israel and the formulation of an imagination of an alternative historical perspective that seeks to appropriate Jewish and Diasporist sentiments. Thus, the discourses presented in the following are conscious of the effects of academic re-description as not only the uncovering of new or hidden meanings of the cultural figurations of

---

203. Appadurai 2003: 29.

Israeli society but also the alternative openings that such re-descriptions produce. Of course, this is not criteria that single out these discourses because no academic text can escape the dilemma of suggestiveness or re-production. Instead, I have singled out these discourses for two different reasons.[204] One reason is that the authors of the texts have published in *Theory and Criticism*, the leading critical academic journal in Israel and a journal dedicated to the work done by such authors, and the second is that I find it possible to read these texts as suggestive precursors of discourses of Jewish history and identity post-territorial Zionism.

If we conceive of nationalism as the ideological and communitarian aspect of modern nation-state formation and as such a historically specific phenomenon then globalization and the fragmented socio-cultural developments under the rubric of post-modernity give rise to new discourses of history and identity for the present moment.[205] It is in this perspective that I read the following authors; as authors who search for and create a new vocabulary for a new historical situation when post-national Jewishness seems to be offering opportunities that exceed the ones offered by Zionism. These opportunities include the possibility of peace making with the Palestinians and a critical reckoning with Zionism's colonial legacy. In a word from Arjun Appadurai these discourses deal with a new Jewish *ethnoscape* relieved of absolutist territorialism.[206]

Zionism has been conceived as a so-called "Return to History" by its ideologues and supporters.[207] The implications of this return to history have been many in discourses of culture, from ideology to art, and have contributed to the radical changes of the Jewish historical imagination in the 20th century. The theme of return to history epitomizes in a number of ways the modernist, nationalist and Zionist historical imagination and its adherent discourses of legitimate life experiences. The return to history is also an icon of the imagery of the *shlilat hagalut's*, negation of the exile,

---

204. I do not claim that these texts are representative of *Theory and Criticism* but they are examples of lines of thinking appropriated by this journal. I do not suggest either that the authors agree on an ideological level but I suggest that they share a basic ironist, post-nationalist position and an affinity for critical philosophy, post-colonial theory, feminism and post-modern cultural studies.
205. Bauman 2000, Ram 1999.
206. Appadurai 2003.
207. Myers 1995 for a critical analysis of the "Return to History". The "Return to History" has been given moral-philosophical legitimacy from a Zionist perspective by philosopher Emil Fackenheim (1978).

forcefulness as a work towards restoring or claiming order, truth, justice and proper categories and interpretive rules after modern nationalist principles; principles whose efficiency is as factual in modern Judaism as Zionism's facts on the ground in Israel. In the most banal sense, Diaspora became the weak and feminine side of all the binaries used to illustrate the masculine and nationalist necessity and goodness of Zionism such as weak-strong, unnatural-natural, passivity-action, Jew-Israeli.

In both symbolic and concrete terms the return to history is closely connected to territory as a mental and physical category. Zionism is a radical territorialization of a Jewish utopia that supplants imaginaries such as religion, longing and hope with land and thus makes the mental and physical territory the same. The mental territory of Judaism is in Zionism seen as bi-product of nationhood, of the primordial unity between people and land. Virtually all the attributes of Judaism developed in relation to Europe and the Arab Middle East are rejected as corrupted due to an unnatural condition of existence. One of the key shapers of Zionist discourse, Ahad Ha'am, who was one of the most apologetic Zionist leaders towards the diasporic culture of Judaism, envisioned the achievement of the rabbis after the Roman conquest of Jerusalem as a national preservation strategy. The rabbis created a spiritual Jewish national identity in the Jewish texts and practice which served to preserve the Jewish national identity until territory could be reclaimed. In Zionism, physical Israel is the body of the Jews and the sole source of a natural culture.[208] This natural culture is both conceived as being a "before" and "after" the unnatural conditions of the Diaspora that the Jews have suffered for almost two millennia. Therefore it is a revolutionary return to the perceived natural order. Israel becomes the living utopia in Zionist ideology.[209] Thus, territorialization has centred the Zionist historical

---

208. A theme most clearly elaborated by Ahad Ha'am in his classic text *Flesh and Spirit* (Ahad Ha'am).
209. See Gover 1994 for an elaboration of the living utopia and the collection *Israel: The First Decade of Independence* for utopianism in Ben-Gurion's political thinking (ed. Troen and Lucas 1995). The idea of living, being, in a living utopia is characteristic to both post-revolutionary radicalism and conservatism. Radicals think of utopia in realistic terms because revolution can bring about utopia and conservatives think of utopia in realistic terms because social organisation is understood as having a "nature" and a "natural order", which only radicals, anarchists and liberalists can disturb. Both archetypes of ideology have a significant totalitarian potential. White 1973: 22-29.

imagination on *Eretz Israel* as a land, in opposition to a dream, and on the remote past when nature was still undisturbed. The Diaspora became a "period", a historical phase, when historical disasters forced Jews to exist exiled from their natural surroundings; the habitat that created them, namely *Eretz Israel*. This dominant line of thinking is explicit in the Israeli declaration of independence. Anti-Semitism, pogroms and ultimately the Holocaust are the historical proofs of both the unity of the Jews as a national body and their unnatural conditions of existence.[210] Diaspora is itself a problem and generative of hatred from other, "natural", peoples who have "hosted" the Jews, to paraphrase Herzl's introduction to *The Jewish State*.[211]

As mentioned, Ahad Ha'am distinguished himself in comparison to other Zionist leaders and ideologues such as Herzl, Nordau, Weizmann, and Ben-Gurion of the formative period of Zionism in as much as he recognized the strength and achievement of rabbinic Judaism, but he also found that the time was ripe for a new line of action that could restore the soul in the body.[212] Herzl and Nordau had no empathy for the ways of life of the European Jews, especially the East-European Jews who epitomized the negative aspects of the subordinate Jewish life. Herzl and Nordau fantasized about making real, honourable men out of the Jewish excuse for a man, and the theatricality of the duel was their chosen example of the chance to be a real man. The Jewish man was a woman; a theme I will elaborate on when discussing the work of Daniel Boyarin. Ahad Ha'am was continuingly concerned with the Jewishness of the Zionist Movement and he believed that the people of Israel would be saved by prophets not diplomats such as Herzl.[213] Nevertheless, the dominant trends in Zionist ideology sought to re-evaluate and transform Judaism, Jewish identity and Jewish history according to dominant present day discourses of nationhood, manliness, honour and power. Only a minor aspect of the Zionist transformation of Jewish culture was about rescuing the Jews from persecution, as a number of studies have shown.[214]

---

210. From Theodor Herzl to Israeli political discourses today anti-Semitism is both destructive and creative in as much as what was wrong with the Jews in Europe is cured by Zionism.
211. Herzl 1896: 14-17.
212. Ahad Ha'am: *Flesh and Spirit*.
213. Zipperstein 1993: 133.
214. Segev 1986, 1993; Zerubavel 1995, Zertal 1998.

The Diaspora and the fate of the European Jews served as the opposite pole of Zionism and in many respects Zionist ideology shared its view on European Jewry with European nationalists and anti-Semites apart from its most biological traits. Cultural and social anti-Semitism and Zionism were more or less in resonance.

The structural foci of Zionism and its construction of a new locus of the Jewish man have a basis in the complex processes of modernity, which is as much a cultural, discursive, transformation as it is a transformation of modes of organisation, governance and production.[215] The ideology of nationalism and its cultural icons developed as the communitarian dimension of the development of the modern European state out of a fascinating and complex mixture of romanticism, Darwinism and rationalist-realist history and social science.[216] In particular German *Sturm und Drang*-type romanticism, German culture and German universities were idealized in Zionism as the model of a true, original and strong national identity. In terms of creating legitimacy and cultural coherence in the modern European states nationalism was an important vehicle that could produce a worship of the state as long as the state produced and re-produced the names and histories of the national community.

The nationalist communitarianism has two important strings of legitimacy that function as membership cards if groups or individuals live up to their requirements. The dominating string in nationalism is combined of ethnicity[217] and a perceived common history defined as a national history, and the more marginal string of republicanism. Jews in Europe were gradually through the 19th century free to participate in public affairs and join the civil religions of the states but the dominating string of legitimacy within nationalism, ethnicity and history, made

---

215. The varied literature on nationalism discusses nationalism's lines of descent in modernity from many perspectives. Gellner 1997, Hobsbawn 1990, Smith 1991, Anderson 1991, and Bhabha 1990 are roughly representative of the different perspectives in this literature. A good overview of "schools" can be found in Smith 1998.
216. See Myers 1995 for the importance of the German universities in building an educational and research culture on Zionist premises.
217. Understood as a combination of cultural practises, religion and race that often define majority populations. Ethnicity is something else when used on minorities. A Christian Lebanese and a Muslim Syrian are part of the same ethnic minority when ethnicity in public and political debates becomes a social category in the West.

Jewish patriotism a "white mask", and thus it widely came to seem false, superficial and speculative to both Jewish patriots and gentiles alike.[218] The nationalist communitarianism that grew increasingly in the course of the 19th century and early 20th century worked against the traditional Jewish patterns of organisation and legitimacy within the European societies, and in this light it is no wonder that a Jewish national movement appeared. Herzl, Ahad Ha'am, Nordau and other Jewish intellectuals reacted against both increased opportunities and increased demands of modernity by mimicking the gentiles. These developments placed Diaspora at the "roots" of the pathology of Judaism that necessitated a radical cure.

It was the strength of the nation as both a location of culture and development in Europe that made Diaspora unviable to Herzl and the Zionists, and also made Zionism the most potent Jewish ideology in defiance of Diaspora through creation of a parallel to European nationalism.[219] Zionist ideologues simply perceived Diaspora as the central component of the pathology of both general social organisation, and specifically of Judaism and the action to be taken was to normalize the Jews along national and territorial lines. This project was naturally impossible in Europe, the social domain of Diaspora, and the conquest of history had to take place in the ancient-utopian homeland.[220]

Diaspora as Non-History
The theme of the return to history has a significant flip-side to it which is that when Zionism is the return to history then Diaspora is non-history. Diaspora is a position in which there is no essential history of the Jews and where the Jews are passive objects for historical developments and wills

---

218. This is probably one of the most dominant themes in Herzl's work. In the play *Das Neue Ghetto* Herzl lets his hero die by the sword with the message that the only way out of the new ghetto is for the Jewish man to learn how to die with honour. Anti-Semites also use this theme of the honourless, two-faced and weak Jew.
219. Bhabha 1990.
220. The well-known debates of the location of the Jewish state before Herzl's death do not change that the logical Jewish territorial homeland would be Palestine. The territorial focus on *Eretz Israel* does not change, either, the fact that Zionism constituted a rejection of Judaism as it had been manifested for centuries in Europe, e.g. Diaspora.

of other nations. In Zionism, history is identified with collective Jewish self-creation as a mirror image of the histories of the great culture nations Germany and Italy but also inspired by the activism of the Bolsheviks in Russia and constructed in defiance of the "weak" self-creations of rabbinic Judaism.[221] History is in Zionist understanding intimately related to ideas of evolution, progress and the power to define the real in terms of territorial and political hegemony. As Robert Young has convincingly argued in *White Mythologies: Writing history and the West* (1990), this perception of history is an integral part of constitutive European discourses that conquered the world in the days of imperialism and colonialism. Alternative strategies of articulating the relation between past-present-future and the metaphysical were deemed non-historical by the European powers and their cultural representatives. Non-historical is a term in relative equivalence with illiterate and uncivilized and non-historical cultures can only be rescued if they are written into history.[222]

Zionism introduces a Jewish history that reproduces the European nationalist and colonialist historical imaginations. The precursors of Zionist history in the *Wissenschaft des Judenthums*-movement introduced the Jew as a historical subject in rationalist-realist terms. The Zionist historians further developed this achievement by territorializing the definition of Judaism into being an organic relationship between a *Volk* and a physical homeland. In my reading, Zionist history is both a product of and a reaction against European colonialism and the Jewish Diaspora is situated in a non-historical "in between" looked upon by both European anti-Semites and Zionists almost the same way. This is not to say, though, that Zionism belonged to a radical fringe of European national ideologies. It didn't and the Zionist construction of a modern Jewish history under a nationalist paradigm is not different from the histories created

---

221. Sternhell 1999: 47-73; Biale 1986: 145-176.
222. Young 1990. Young addresses the problem of history in relation to "otherness" in a series of critical readings of Foucault, Said, Bhabha and Spivak. Young should not be held responsible for my further comments on the implications of this theme. The dilemma of the subaltern is how to come into being, address problems of self-definition or rescue oneself or the collective from destruction under or despite Western hegemony, without adopting/mimicking the hegemonic discourses. Writing others into history is also a colonial enterprise and the problem of history is thus unresolved.

in the contemporary European states; indeed these developments were an inspiration for the Zionists.[223] At the same time, Zionist history was no less "scientific" according to the criteria of the day than German or French history but the Jewish Diaspora was the structural and ideological outcast of modernity's discursive development.[224]

The institutionalized Zionist history of the Hebrew University in Jerusalem from 1924-25 drew a new historical map of Jewish history within a teleological historical imagination that connected the histories of the ancient Israelite kingdoms with Zionism. The vision was that Zionism represented the modern Jewish return to its proper habitat and thus represented the spirit of the proud and independent ancient Israelites. Zionism and the ingathering of the exiles was also to a large extent the end of history in the sense that the utopian *Alt-Neuland* had been achieved. There was no greater goal than Zionism, the exceptions were spiritual Zionists such as Martin Buber, Judah Magnes and Hugo Bergmann, who saw Zionism in more universal terms as movement of solidarity with suppressed peoples everywhere including the Palestinians, and the radical leftists and communists in *Matzpen*. The Jewish Studies and Jewish History departments of the Hebrew University had the explicit agenda of creating education and knowledge that would foster a Jewish national and historical body and establish Jewish ownership of Palestine in concrete and historical terms.[225] As Myers argues, there was no school or censorship of any kind at the young Hebrew University but there was an overall agreement with the political goals of Zionism and general acceptance of a paradigm; of the principal form that Jewish history could be written within.

In Baruch Kimmerling's analysis Zionist and Israeli history as a nation-building strategy operates on two "fronts".[226] History is part of and a weapon in the conflict with the Palestinians over the legitimate

---

223. European humanism and liberalism was also transmitted in the Zionist historical and educational project but there is no basic opposition between humanism and the identification of history with the power to dominate, define the real and write realistically.
224. Bauman's *Modernity and the Holocaust* (1989) argues that the Jews were gradually placed in "non-categories" in Germany, which made it possible to kill an entire population in an operation analogous to weeding a garden.
225. Myers 1995:13-108.
226. Kimmerling 1995: 42.

ownership of the land of Palestine, which is the first "front". The second "front" is directed at alternative Jewish ideologies to Zionism. There is a dual purpose to each of the "fronts": the defeat of the enemy, the Palestinians and the Diasporists, and the build-up of internal legitimacy. The construction of internal legitimacy is both a theory of justice and a theory of truth and knowledge; an epistemology. This means that in the build-up of a national Jewish history that was and is a part of the struggle with the Palestinians, the simultaneous establishment of discourses of legitimacy of Zionism took place in a struggle against the Diaspora as a way of life and as an ideology.

The first historians at the Hebrew University applied several strategies as means to categorize the Diaspora as non-history. Of the seven strategies listed by Kimmerling, two seem especially important for this reading and those would be the application of a certain periodization and the insistence on the antiquity of the essence of the Jewish national character.[227]

In Zionist history a periodization is invented that has dominated modern imaginations of Jewish history ever since and it has so forth been the most significant mapping of Jewish history to be presented. The defining outline of this historical map is provided by the concepts of sovereignty and territory, and its spatial and temporal lines are drawn after an elementary center-periphery model. The primordial incarnation of the Jewish collective body crystallizes in the early periods of what is defined as Jewish sovereignty over a natural territory, which means in the ancient Israelite kingdoms. The culture developed in this historical period contains the genus and nucleus of Judaism and Jewish nationhood. The periods of this historical map that represent icons of Jewish history are the periods when the Israelite kingdoms were the most hegemonic or the most heroic in their attempts to the regain hegemony. The Davidic and Solomonic reigns, the Maccabee rebellions, the Masada stand and the Bar Kochba rebellion are such icons.[228]

---

227. Kimmerling finds seven "strategies" used by Zionist history, which are: 1. Key concepts 2. Periodization 3. Teleological explanations 4. Exceptionalism 5. Boundaries of the examined collectivity 6. Antiquity 7. Intentions vs. consequences. The seven strategies are not exclusive but intermingle to a large extent in the historical productions. Kimmerling 1995: 48-56.
228. A number of studies confirm this presentation of Zionist history see Myers 1995, Kimmerling 1995, Ram 1998.

From the power and heroism of these ancient events, the national spirit of Judaism was formed. This original spirit was defeated by the Romans and the Jewish people were finally and decisively exiled in 70 CE. The following almost two millennia were unproductive. The most fundamental strength of the period was the ability to preserve the identity of the Jewish people despite the severed bond to the homeland. It is interesting to note that considerable efforts were made by one of the founding fathers of Zionist history Ben-Zion Dinur to minimize the Diaspora period.[229] Dinur who worked as a professor of history at the Hebrew University and served as the first minister of education of the Israeli state compiled huge amounts of primary material of the history of the modern settlement in Palestine and thus authorized what was relevant source material. He was also founding editor of the scholarly journal Zion, which to a large extent set the agenda for relevant scholarship.[230] Dinur defined Diaspora as the period between approximately 600 CE and 1600 and his criteria for periodization were the levels of Zionist activity. Dinur proposed that only in 600 CE did Jewish national life in Palestine disappear and that the messianic movements of the early modern period, which led to some immigration to Palestine, were an expression of Zionist activity.[231] It seems obvious that Dinur was engaged in an effort to minimize the Diaspora in order to downgrade its significance for Jewish culture and in order to universalize Zionism within Jewish history. Zionism became in Dinur's presentation of history an inner impulse in Jews at all times in all places. Zionism in Jewish history in a Zionist understanding replaces religion: at all points in time had Zion been the center and Diaspora the periphery.

The other important strategy applied by Zionist historians is the insistence on the antiquity of Judaism. The insistence that the spirit, value and historical core of Judaism were shaped in antiquity in an organic relationship with the territory naturally redefines everything in Judaism

---

229. Kimmerling 1995.
230. *Zion* was established in 1935 and co-edited by Yitzhak Baer, another of the founders of Jewish history at the Hebrew University. In the first issue of *Zion* the criteria for acceptable scholarship were established by Dinur and these criteria clearly reflect the Zionist historical imagination. Kimmerling 1995, Myers 1995.
231. See Dinur 1969. I find that Dinur on both an institutional and personal level is an example of the discourse of history in Zionism.

developed in the Diaspora as unoriginal or unnatural. According to this view, in Diaspora some of the roots of Judaism were preserved but the average Jewish life was by and large corrupted. Zionism undertook an immense historical and educational project which had as one of its most basic lines the deeming of Diaspora as non-historical.

The Jewishness- Israeliness Dilemma

The Diaspora was despite all the Zionist efforts to the contrary identified with Judaism in common understandings of Zionist ideology. The novel periodization and insistence on the antiquity of Judaism by historians did not de-judaize the Diaspora. The Jew, in this way, became more or less the antithesis of the New Jew, the Zionist or Israeli. As previously mentioned, Zionism incorporated many of the stereotypes about Jews and Judaism invented by anti-Semites and this internalization brought about the need for a revolutionary change of the Jew. The Jew had to become somebody else, namely the Israeli.[232]

In the history of Zionist ideology the most radical example of the negation of the Diaspora was that of the so-called Canaanites or Young Hebrews lead by the poet and essayist Yonathan Ratosh. As a political movement the Canaanites had very little impact and had only few followers but as an expression of a cultural discourse and a deep cultural sentiment in Zionism, they touched upon a central issue regarding the transition from religion to nation. That issue was the issue of the difference between Jews and Zionists/Israelis.

Ratosh shaped his thoughts on the men and women that worked for the building of a new national community in Palestine during the 1930s. However, his political and cultural programme for the new nation became public only in the early 1940s, while news of the Holocaust was reaching the Jewish settlement in Palestine. Ratosh advocated a complete break with Judaism and the Diaspora. Jews were believers in a religion who were dispersed over most of the world while the people living in and building a new national community in Palestine were Hebrews. In Ratosh's radically nationalistic imagination, the Hebrews were the descendants of the ancient Canaanites in times before monotheism and Judaism.

---

232. See Boyarin 1997. This work will be discussed in detail in the following.

The homeland of the Hebrews was the entire fertile crescent and the Hebrews were part of a larger Semitic culture and thus in brotherly relations to the descendants of the other peoples of the region. Ratosh envisaged that a Hebrew and Semitic civilisation of the past, before monotheism led to an abstraction of the relationship between people and land, could be re-invigorated. In Ratosh's imagination nationhood was linked to nature and for the cultural expressions of the nation to be real, they had to be the likes of nature religion with its worship of the seasons, the crops and so on. Monotheism is in this line of thought the beginning of the breaking of the organic bond between nation and land.

Yonathan Ratosh and his Canaanite movement took the discourse of the negation of the Diaspora to its logical extreme. This discourse had as its most basic premise that the success of the nation building efforts in Palestine depended on the national culture as well as on the severance of all strings to the Jewish past. Ratosh chose to publish his declaration of the Young Hebrews during the massacre of the European Jews and this stresses the severity of his claim to collective re-creation. Ratosh even rejected the Zionist movement as a Jewish movement for and of the Diaspora, which therefore couldn't contribute to the creation of a Hebrew nation.[233]

The Canaanites took the issue of the dilemma between being Jewish and being Israeli to the end of the continuum and chose to reject all traces of a Jewish heritage. Of course, the Canaanite discourse on Hebrews, Canaan and the fertile crescent is not part of the commonsensical vocabulary of Israeli public conversations but the issue addressed by Ratosh and his followers is central to the Zionist return to history. The negation of the Diaspora was also the negation of Jewish culture and identity as it existed in Europe before World War II. A milder variation of the Canaanite tendency in Israel has dominated (and still does) public and cultural discourses in the sense that Israeliness is figured as more than a variation of Jewishness. Instead the Jewish heritage has

---

233. Ratosh 1944. For a rather positive analysis of the Canaanites see Diamond 1986 and for a more critical see Shavit 1987. See also Hever's very interesting reading of the Canaanites with a focus on their relation to Arabs/Palestinians, Hever 2002. The Canaanites influenced a number of Israeli artists and writers and were sought rehabilitated by Boaz Evron in his book *Jewish State or Israeli Nation?* (1995).

been recognized but only as a cultural and social situation that had to be redeemed by the *Bildung* project of Zionism.[234]

Israel has since the establishment of the state had good relations to all diasporic Jewish communities with the exception of certain orthodox or alternative communities, which might seem odd in the light of the previous. The reason for this relative homogeneity in opinions regarding the state of Israel as a representative of Jewishness, despite Zionism's negative image of the Jew, is due to the fact that Zionism was by far the strongest Jewish ideology to survive the Holocaust. Already before World War II, Zionism in the West had a significant aspect of charity and philanthropy to it that to an extent overtook the communitarian work of the pre-Zionist organisations. Thus, from the point of view of Western Jews, love of Israel, Zionism and living in the Diaspora didn't seem as much a contradiction in terms as it did from the vantage point of the production of Zionist ideology in Palestine and Israel.[235]

Israel is the structural and logical center of Jewish culture after the Holocaust and this has been reinforced by the modern nation-state system and nationalism, which still categorize larger ethnic-religious collectives as diasporic in a negative sense if they do not wield hegemonic power over a territory or live permanently outside a homeland, such as the Kurds, Palestinians, Gypsies and the Jews outside Israel.

Re-Invigorating the Diaspora

In 1990, the journal *Theory and Criticism* was founded by Adi Ophir and Hanan Hever who are, respectively, a philosopher and a literary critic. The explicit agenda for *Theory and Criticism* was the promotion of academic thinking that takes a critical stance towards state hegemony,

---

234. This judgement of mine is not based on a representational reading of Israeli cultural products but on an evaluation of the position of Jewishness in Zionist ideology. The Canaanites can, to my mind, also be read as a way to avoid the binary of Jew vs. Israeli and its consequences for Judaism. The implication is, however, completely Ratoshian, namely that Judaism should be re-described as something all together different than Israeliness by both Jews and Israelis. Zionism would then have to give up claims to Jewishness, which was one of the basic claims of the Canaanites.
235. Berkowitz 1997 explores this theme in detail.

power, violence and national ideologies and cultures. The appropriated thinking was and is critical philosophy, post-Marxism, post-colonialism and feminism inspired by continental post-structuralist philosophers such as Michel Foucault, Gilles Deleuze, Jean-Francois Lyotard, and Jean Baudrillard. As part of its academic agenda the journal is also directed towards criticism of the Israeli state, its ideologies and cultures.[236] The journal has not in anyway as its agenda to re-invigorate Diaspora as a new ideology for Jewish life in the present and future, but the critical approach to Zionism and nationhood in general has opened up for some debate over Diaspora as both an ethically superior mode of both mental and physical existence and exile or exilic consciousness as a critical corrective to nation-state hegemony and cultural normativity.[237] To qualify the debates in *Theory and Criticism* on Diaspora I have read other texts by in particular of Daniel and Jonathan Boyarin, historian Amnon Raz-Krakotzkin and philosopher Ilan Gur-Ze'ev of Haifa University. The latter also develops themes over the notion of homeland and Diaspora as a mental category and as a suggestive peace education for Israelis and Palestinians. In his educational philosophy, Gur-Ze'ev is very concerned with the articulation of the self and the other historically as well as in the structural and cultural contours of post-modernity in opposition to the violence of normativity. The perspectives to be presented are not uniform but at the same time they point to openings towards the diffuse concepts of Israeli post-modernity.

***

---

236. *Theory and Criticism* 1, 1990. Of course, I cannot conceal my own position within the same line of thinking. I find journals such as *Theory and Criticism* very healthy for both scholarship and intellectual conversation. I deliberately choose to engage in texts that I find challenging and inspiring on subjective grounds and I am of course aware that other readers might with equal strength find these texts irrelevant and out of touch with reality. I do not claim to be more "right" in my readings but I intend to re-describe the texts within the larger framework of post-nationalist discourse on Israeli history.
237. As the case was in *Theory and Criticism* 4-5 (1994-5) involving Daniel and Jonathan Boyarin, Amnon Raz-Krakotzkin and Yoav Peled. D. and J. Boyarin are Americans but I have chosen to incorporate their arguments as parts of a Jewish ethnoscape that does not always follow the Israeli state borders. Their discourses both critically feed and are critically fed by Zionism and Israel.

>"'Exile' as the repressed other becomes the critique of a culture of the static and the whole. The stagnant waters and mirrors that reflected an ossified relationship to sacred space are beginning to show ripples and cracks."[238]

Sidra DeKoven Ezrahi suggests in her *Booking Passage. Exile and Homecoming in the Modern Jewish Imagination* (2000) that "exile" is re-entering Jewish literary discourses as a critical approach to the disenchanted normality of the Israeli experience. The notion of exile opens up for utopianism and the re-enchantment of once sacred space. In Ezrahi's understanding, sacred space is dream space, utopian space, fictional space. It is places and spaces that are imaginative but therefore serve to transgress the limits of the possibilities of the real without succumbing to an ideology or aesthetics of the whole. An ideology and aesthetic such as that of Zionism that claims the living utopia, the idea of the whole, bereaves its adherents of sacred space, of the principle of hope and the possibility of leading counter-lives, as remarked by Ezrahi.[239] The changes that Ezrahi tracks in contemporary Israeli (literary) culture do not signify a return to the modern either-or dialectic of exile or homecoming but rather delimit the weak contours of a post-modern cultural hermeneutics in which exile becomes the condition of otherness, the critical and utopian dimension in both minority and majority Jewish cultures. The notion of exile questions categories and borders and thus produces ripples and cracks in the stagnant and violent national culture of Israel.

Ezrahi emphasizes the ripples and cracks that in contemporary Israeli literary culture as developing the contours of a post-modern hermeneutics in which the concrete notions of exile and home are dissolved and re-crystallized as mental categories. But, as I would claim, these are equally detectable in contemporary Israeli philosophy. In the vocabulary of the present essay, it is the plots and tropes of the Israeli historical imagination that are changing.[240]

---

238. Ezrahi 2000: 239.
239. Ibid. 233.
240. In the vocabulary of the present essay the concrete dialectic of exile and home refers to realistic answers to questions such as "what is the true and natural condition of Jewish life?", "what is the real meaning of Jewish history?" and "what is real Jewish identity?" The histories that seek to answer these questions are metonymical and/or synechdochic in their discourses on the real

Hayden White asserted in his classic *Meta-History. The Historical Imagination of 19^h Century Europe,* that there is no history which is not at the same time a philosophy of history.[241] The Israeli historian Amnon Raz-Krakotzkin has in this respect contributed significantly to both a new history of "exile" in Jewish history and to a new philosophy of "exile" in contemporary Israeli philosophy of history. In Raz-Krakotzkin's dissertation from 1996 the notion of exile in Jewish medieval history is sought re-evaluated in comparison to the understanding of exile in Zionist historiography as sketched out by Ben-Zion Dinur.[242]

Dinur perceived virtually every attempt made by Jews in history to immigrate to Palestine as some sort of pre-Zionist activity no matter what the circumstances were. Messianism and apocalypticism are widely recognized as instigating factors for Jewish immigration to Palestine and in Dinur's optics these movements were basically fed by the unique Jewish relation to the physical land of Eretz Israel. Thus, they were movements expressing deep core values of Judaism, i.e. the organic relation to the land, in the same way Zionism expressed such values just in another language shaped by a different time.[243]

Raz-Krakotzkin treats the notion and practise of exile amongst Jews in medieval time as an expression of hope and utopian longing in its own right, not as a political agenda to restore a territorial kingdom of Judaism. Raz-Krakotzkin's primary concern is historiographical in as much his efforts are directed towards a re-evaluation of the relationship between Jews and *Eretz Israel*. Zionism has given an enormous impetus to the Return to History to such a degree that a principle of return has been constructed in Zionist and Israeli history that is an a priori assump-

---

they seek to represent. The post-modern hermeneutics of Ezrahi translates into a basic undecidability on such questions. Realism is a powerful ideology and aesthetics but still just that and the re-crystallization of exile in mental categories signifies the appropriation of the trope of irony in the discourses of Jewish history and identity. This is not to say that pre-modern Jewish religious thinking that also conceived of exile as a mental category was ironic because the religious thinking is grounded in cosmology and teleology, which is quite another thing.

241. White 1973: XI.
242. Raz-Krakotzkin 1996.
243. Dinur 1969.

tion of historical studies and perspectives in both public and academic discourses. The principle of return functions as a key element of the larger discourses and plots of Zionist history and it unifies Jewish history as chronology and linearity centred around the territory of *Eretz Israel*/Palestine. The uniformity of Jewish history around the longing for a return to Zion makes Zionist history unable to appreciate the plurality and inconsistencies of Jewish history.[244]

That Zionist history fails to appreciate aspects of Jewish history that do not correspond well to a principle of homecoming is not only a lack of recognition of the plurality of Jewish history. It is also a matter of marginalizing alternative utopian, religious and ideological options to the historical imagination of Zionism and thus part of the power struggle of making Zionism's conception of exile versus homecoming the realistic version. As pointed out by Hanan Hever, the effort to achieve hegemony, and thereby possess the power to define what is real and what is speculation, is a striving for a universalization of a certain discourse.[245] The universal is the self-evident, the commonsensical and the natural, which are conceptual attributes to the dominant ideology and discourse in a society. The principle of return in Jewish history is by Raz-Krakotzkin seen as a universalization of a particularly nationalist principle of conceptualizing belonging, history and identity to account for the relation between a people and a territory in all times and places.

Raz-Krakotzkin shows that Dinur and other disciples of the principle of return are mistaken in their view on Medieval Jewry's relation to *Eretz Israel* as a physical territory in terms of empirical proof. But what interests us here is rather that Raz-Krakotzkin has a very different perception of the meaning, use and structure of historical thinking than the Zionist historians. At the center of Raz-Krakotzkin's philosophy of history is the concept of exile understood as a mental category.[246] In this thinking history is part of "labouring for the present" and therefore not only a matter of establishing the past but more a matter of writing a history of and for the present that feeds certain discourses of identity

---

244. Raz-Krakotzkin 1996: 333-334.
245. Hever 2002: 28.
246. Raz-Krakotzkin 1994a, 1994b.

and Jewish existence.[247] These discourses are ones that question the universalism of Zionism within Jewish history and are highly critical of the political and cultural role played by the Palestinians in Zionist and Israeli culture and historical imagination as the immediate "Other". Raz-Krakotzkin's main perspective for studying and re-evaluating exile in Jewish history is the Israeli-Palestinian conflict and thereby he aims to contribute to a working for the present that opens possibilities for establishing equal relations between the parties. A central assumption is that the concept of exile carries a potential as the opposition that Zionism sought to eradicate. Jewish identity grounded in the mental category of exile can mobilize solidarity with the Palestinian refugees while Zionist historical consciousness is completely incompatible with solidarity with the Palestinians and their basic collective rights.[248]

Logically, such exile is not physical in as much as it is not a suggestion to the Israelis about leaving Israel to the Palestinians. It is a suggestion to recognize the repression of others by monolithic and universalizing ideologies of history that claim an essential and biological relationship to a territory.[249] Such ideologies like Zionism are invariably connected to power. Zionism equals power, in both Israeli and Palestinian understandings, while exile has connotations of powerlessness. As pointed out by both David Biale and Yoav Peled, exile is not powerless either and free of

---

247. "Labouring for the present" is a slogan deriving from the intense cultural debates among Zionists at the beginning of the 20th century. It means to work for improving the present and implies an understanding of progress as evolutionary. In the context of early Zionism it was the position of the more pragmatic trends within the movement that prioritized the improvement of Jewish conditions also when the improvements did not exactly fit in the ideology of territorial nationalism. Those trends perceived the completion of Zionism's goal as a long evolutionary process. Adi Ophir uses the slogan as the title of his 2001-book and thereby rearticulates its meaning in the Zionist cultural debates in a very different historical context where such cultural debates are called post-Zionist. See Ophir 2001, Hever 2002: 11-45.
248. Raz-Krakotzkin 1994a.
249. In fact, it is a complete reversal of the philosophy of nature of Johann Gottfried Herder (1744-1803) whose romantic thinking is a cornerstone of the philosophy of nationalism. Herder basically conceived culture, identity and language as stemming from the relationship between the habitat and its dwellers in ancient times. A nucleus of this original nature of a people is preserved up through the generations as a bond between them and this nature and its territory, and accordingly preserved as their very nature.

the politics of interests even as a mental category and these are aspects that pose a dilemma for the historical philosophy of Raz-Krakotzkin but also for other "Diasporists", as we shall see.[250]

Raz-Krakotzkin's re-invigoration of the Diaspora is comparable to the notion of Diaspora or exile in Ezrahi's history of exile in Jewish literature. Ezrahi re-evaluated Diaspora as a utopian, fictional opposition to normalizing culture and as a cultural invigoration of the community already living within sovereignty not as a rejection of sovereignty all together.[251] The inspirations that permeate the thinking of Raz-Krakotzkin are the philosophy of history of Walter Benjamin and the critical thinking of post-colonial studies as particularly laid out in Edward Said's book *Orientalism*.[252] Benjamin's idea that historical writing must "brush history against the grain" provides Raz-Krakotzkin with a distinction between two typical histories, namely the history of the powerful and the history of the subjected. The history of the subjected is both the history of the powerful and a critical principle.[253] Said's theory of orientalism is employed a long the same lines to juxtapose the categories of the Orientalist-Oriental and the colonizer-colonized. The powers of definition and description in concordance with real-political power create these categories as value systems that feed perceptions of history, progress and identity politics. Proper history should brush the self-evidence of this development against the grain in order to both explore history and provide criticism.[254] The interpretive and conceptual categories of the Orientalist-Oriental and the colonizer-colonized are expanded beyond what they nominally signify to be construed as "floating signifiers" of the structural relationship between the powerful and the subjected, the universal and the particular, within realms of culture, values and language. It seems that the theory of critical history derived from Benjamin and Said appropriates a principle of criticism of power discourses both in their concrete and cultural manifestations from the point of view of the subjected. The permanent dilemma of such positions is that the subjected

---

250. Biale 1986, Peled 1994.
251. In opposition to the classic post-WWII Diasporists Edmond Jabés and George Steiner. To Jabés and Steiner, the Jewish homeland is the Book. See Jabés 1991, Steiner 1985.
252. Said 1978.
253. Raz-Krakotzkin 1994a, 2004: passim.
254. Raz-Krakotzkin 2004.

can never become a concrete entity, a collective with equally totalizing counter-ideologies, because then the initial problem remains unsolved. On a conceptual level, the subjected operates the same vocabularies as the powerful if they enter the discourses of orientalism and colonialism.[255] If the subjected comes to represent the legitimate and natural existence and self-representation in opposition to the violence of real-political power and its cultural ideologies then the critical perspective is overruled by ideology and identity politics. Raz-Krakotzkin does not entirely escape this dilemma in his philosophy though it is clear that his ideal-type of the *Mizrahi* is a metaphor for the exilic experience, which is not fully embedded in any hegemonic narrative, in the case of the *Mizrahi* neither Zionism nor Arab nationalism.[256] Raz-Krakotzkin writes:

> "The concept of exile constitutes a kind of alternative tool on reality, not on the basis of its negation – but in it and in its language. Exile is not a marker for a general outlook fit for the repair of reality, but a marker for the sensitivity that enables the renewed turning to the theological aspiration. Especially relevant is the use of the concept for the purpose of the historical consciousness regarding Zionist culture".[257]

The concept of exile is capable of expanding the horizons on Zionist culture and the pluralist possibilities of the present because:

> "Here in the most salient way the meaning of the concept of exile becomes clear as historical consciousness in the Benjaminian understanding: Exile enables the guarding of the relative autonomy of the different histories, without disregarding the linkage to the present, without disregarding the strength of the definitions of this present".[258]

Exile is in the philosophy of history of Raz-Krakotzkin a Benjaminian concept, which can be equalled with a historical consciousness that safeguards the multitude of histories inhabiting a social field. This safe-

---

255. An analytical and ethical problem of the same kind as identified by Robert Young 1990.
256. Ibid.
257. Raz-Krakotzkin 1994b: 130.
258. ibid. 130.

guarding is needed for the sake of pluralism in history and is ultimately a counter-measure against totalitarian tendencies in the present, e.g. in Zionism, and for the recognition of the autonomy and legitimacy of Palestinian histories. As previously mentioned, the philosophy of history of Raz-Krakotzkin is oriented at history as a present time activity or social process that configures collectives in temporal trajectories. These temporal trajectories function as imaginaries of larger collective identities. They are in Zionism operationalized as ideology, as they are in all other nationalisms as well. To brush history against the grain is then to perceive such developments from the perspective of exile or more correctly from the perspective of "the negation of the negation of exile".

Exile is a metaphor for the in-between, the uprooted, who dwells in between parties struggling for hegemony, for the power to define the real and write history. The exilic's potential is thus to see things from the side of their consequences not their intentions and to be enough of a relativist to see the destructive logic behind powers of universalization. The Israeli *Mizrahi* persona is the example/symbol of this potential in the recent article by Raz-Krakotzkin: in-between Jews and Arabs eradicated by Arab nationalism from the history of the Arab states and subjugated by Zionism as primitive Orientals.[259]

In summary, the philosophy of history of Raz-Krakotzkin attempts to re-place the concept of exile outside its conventional place as one of the poles in the binary of exile-homecoming. Exile is perceived as a mental and an oppositional cultural category, not as physical existence outside a natural habitat. Sovereignty is recognized as a political, organisational principle within which mental and cultural exile is appropriated as cultural and historical criticism of power structures and violent conflicts. Raz-Krakotzkin theorizes a sort of secular spiritualism in opposition to the Zionist-nationalist territorialization of redemption. The range of cultural and critical, legitimate, options within Zionist discourse to articulate hope, redemption and to lead counter-lives is understood as very limited, and these options ought to be expanded in order to create the pluralist society that is a basis for recognition of the Palestinian histories. The concept of exile implicates an aspect of contingency towards political sovereignty and territorial identities, which then have no essential relation to individual or

---

259. Raz-Krakotzkin 2004.

collective ontology but are practical, real-political measures. The aspect of contingency concerning the understanding of existing political structures is in direct opposition to the Zionist historical teleology, which has the political and territorial autonomy of the Jewish people as the secular equivalent to redemption and furthermore this autonomy is part of the very definition of the natural existence of the Jewish people. Exile points to the contingencies of the power to define the commonsensical and natural on the basis of territorial nationalism.

Raz-Krakotzkin also uses the concept of exile as a suggestion for a principle of history inspired by Walter Benjamin's thoughts on history. This history is written against the powerful ideologies that define the universal and in praise of the multitudes of histories that inhabit a social field. As we saw, Raz-Krakotzkin parallels Benjamin's concept of history with his own concept of exile when it comes to its perspectives regarding the writing of the history of Zionism. Thus, Raz-Krakotzkin describes his exile as relevant on two levels; on the one level as a secular spiritual principle and on the other as a principle for the writing of history. The philosophy of Raz-Krakotzkin is not Diasporist in a concrete meaning but it constitutes a suggestive post-modern hermeneutics in which contingency and criticism is coupled with history. The "negation of the negation of exile" is meant to pluralize Jewish history for the purpose of the present. Philosophically, Raz-Krakotzkin is situated within a post-modern hermeneutics occupied with both historical understanding, and the powers that influence such an understanding, within a context where the effects of nationalism and the modern Israeli state are countered with a post-nationalist concept of exile.[260]

Post-Colonial Diasporism as Identity Politics

Diasporism is not a dominant ideology of Jews living outside Israel. Rather, it is an ideology of the few who wish to ground this existence in "exile"

---

260. As such it is both an explorative and suggestive philosophy of history. Theoretically, the difference between more conventional understandings of history and purposes of history and Raz-Krakotzkin's is that conventional history conceals its suggestiveness with common sense while Raz-Krakotzkin is open about his histories' philosophical implications for conceptions of the social field.

beyond pragmatic concerns such as family, career, living standards and peace. Practise has shown convincingly that there is no contradiction between being Diasporic Jews, citizens of many states and ardent Zionists. Thus, in the lives of the millions of Diasporic Jews of the world, the theoretical incommensurability, if not direct opposition, of the concepts of exile and homecoming bears no practical significance. The Jews of the Diaspora do not immigrate to Israel or reject Zionism and Israel; they mostly live in the Diaspora and embrace Zionism and Israel.[261] The diasporist grounding that few have or seek beyond Zionism understood as a Jewish ideology of ethnic identity is to be found in religion or political ideology, or as we shall see in a mixture of the two.

The groups that demonstrate the most vocal diasporism in the Diaspora are some orthodox communities who are against Jewish state-building, because God is seen as the instigator of exile and, ultimately, as the author of history. Other smaller groups are Jewish Marxist, radicalist or Bundist organisations who are either opposed to capitalism, nationalism or have an alternative political agenda of cultural, ethnic, autonomy of the Jews within larger state frameworks.[262] In Israel some of these tendencies have also had an impact on the identity politics of the state. This goes for the radical left of Israeli politics with parties such as Matzpen and united Jewish-Arab lists, but also through minor anti-Zionist, orthodox groups in Jerusalem. Generally speaking, such attitudes to Zionism and Israel are directed by radical interpretations of Judaism or radical interpretations of Marxism.

In the 1990s, alternative variations of Diasporism have surfaced, as we have seen, which have attempted re-descriptions of the traditional conceptions of Diaspora, Diasporism and Home. The nation-state boundaries and political hegemony are not any longer the cardinal issues of contention and such concepts are increasingly placed in the background as

---

261. Berkowitz writes of his efforts to explain the history of this phenomenon: "I have attempted to illuminate a history of the institutionalization of a contradiction – of a permanent self-re-creating diaspora Zionism, among a Jewish polity which was unlikely ever to set foot in Zion except as tourists" (Berkowitz 1997: 194). As part of the reason for the circumvention of this contradiction, Berkowitz finds this: "Zionism became a compartmentalized variant of Jewish ethnic identification, and a basis for local and international Jewish solidarity and sociability – and obviously, politics" (Ibid. 196).
262. It should be noted that these groups are extremely marginal compared to Zionism as an ideology of Jewish ethnic solidarity.

necessary aspects/evils of real-politik, while identity politics, criticism and ethics are concepts at the top of the agenda. This development is connected to the broader re-descriptions of politics and international cultural, economic and political relations, which took place during the 1990s in Israel and elsewhere in the West. In such re-descriptions, the nation-state and its borders are no longer the creators or the limits of politics and identity-building. These processes are increasingly individualized and globalized with the effect that the nation-state and the classical modern left-right politics no longer acculturate citizens within views of actions for political change and narratives for identity.[263] The state is loosing power over the political and private acculturation of people to global culture, media and politics and simultaneously the nation-state ceases to be a value in itself and instead to be considered more a result of a historical, thus contingent, development. As pointed out by Appadurai, globalization gives rise to new "scapes" of history and identity that leave the modern nationalist parameters increasingly irrelevant or as part of the globalized "scapes".[264]

The diasporic and exilic thinking which was re-described in the 1990s in Israel and other places expresses concern and involvement in a globalized, post-modern, Jewish ethno-scape in which Israel and Israeli society naturally play a significant part being the main cultural centre of the varieties of Jewishness.[265] The interplay of Jewishness and Zionism in the global Jewish ethno-scape is a primary concern for the American scholars Daniel and Jonathan Boyarin. Daniel Boyarin is a professor of Talmudic studies at Berkeley and Jonathan Boyarin is an independent anthropologist but both brothers attempt re-descriptions of Jewish history and identity in a critical dialectic with Zionism.[266] The following

---

263. Particularly works such as Bauman 1993, 2000, 2001, Giddens 1994, 1999 and Harvey 1989. To name but a few.
264. Appadurai 2003: 31
265. Surely, this thinking is marginal because it attempts to re-describe histories and identities beyond the commonsensical but it nevertheless addresses key aspects of the problematic of globalization. The increased tendency of radical nationalism in Israel is in fact a reaction to the same local and global tendencies. Bauman 2000, Ram 1999.
266. Daniel and Jonathan Boyarin are included in this study of Israeli diasporism because the distinction between Israeli-Diasporic is permeated by this thinking itself. So though they are American, they are among the most significant

analysis will primarily focus on the work of Daniel Boyarin, who is the most explicitly oriented towards Jewish identity politics of the two, but the analysis will be supplemented with writings of Jonathan Boyarin and co-authored texts.

In 1994, the Boyarins published an article in *Theory and Criticism* dedicated to an analysis and evaluation of Diaspora in Jewish history.[267] The article is politically suggestive but introduces the perspectives of this particular diasporism in the Israeli context. The political agenda of the article is the renunciation of territorialism and ethno-political hegemony based on a reading of Jewish history in sharp contrast to the historical conventions of Zionism and at the same time a commitment to Jewish cultural difference. Hence, the article is in diametrical opposition to Zionism's historical imagination and the principle of return in this history.

The Jewish cultural particularity that the Boyarins wish to preserve without confining the Jews to a certain territory is complemented with an equal commitment to social justice. Thus, there are two lines in the identity politics of the Boyarins, namely a particularist commitment to Judaism and a universalist commitment to social justice, which are not considered mutually exclusive. The commitment to social justice is not anchored in perceptions of Judaism as a specific spiritual message and it is not pre-conditioned on a specific mode of Jewish existence such as Jewish territorial sovereignty.[268] It is anchored in a perception of ethics in a general human experience and politics. The particularist commitment

---

      contributors to the discussion of the place of exile in Jewish history and identity through criticism of Zionism. Thus, there is a familiarity to the other writers treated in this text not bound by national borders.

267. Boyarin 1994. The version in *Theory and Criticism* is translated and re-arranged from the journal *Critical Inquiry* (1993 (19) 4). Its original title is *Diaspora: Generation and the Ground of Jewish Diaspora*. The same article figures in a cultural studies anthology *Theorizing Diaspora* (2003) which I also use. Furthermore, articles and books such as Boyarin & Boyarin 1997 and 2002 re-articulate many of the same points.

268. In this connection, A.B. Yehoshua's famous statement that moral responsibility is only mobilized under conditions of political hegemony is noteworthy. This statement represents the critical Zionism of Yehoshua and other Israeli cultural icons of his stature such as Amos Oz. Still, it is an expression of a limited view on morality and power and it clearly feeds the notions of the return to history and the Diaspora as an immoral existence. Yehoshua is paraphrased from Boyarin 1994.

to Jewish difference is anchored in a wish for continued Jewish collective existence and a specific reading of Zionism as ultimately a radical normalization of Jewish difference.[269] Cultural difference without political power based on that cultural difference is in the discourse of the article the opposite of identity based on shared territory and hegemony over that territory. This is in fact a reversal of current, and liberal, perceptions of how identities most favourably develop within states. The prevailing liberal notion of positive identity building is the idea that people who inhabit a shared territory develop a common political and social identity centred around shared duties, responsibilities and benefits within the system.[270] The Boyarins suggest a return to collective identities based on family, culture/religion and memory, which to their minds have been tainted by European racism, but nevertheless is the most viable identity option in a globalized world.[271] Their alternative to liberal state theory is a Buberian idea of bi/multi-nationalism/ethnicism within a shared territory where the political governance is "neutral" regarding ethnic culture besides enabling such multiculturalism.[272]

The political suggestiveness of the article is not only based on private opinion but firmly grounded in post-colonial theory, feminism and other

---

269. I will go into this reading of Zionism in detail when treating Daniel Boyarin's book *Unheroic Conduct*.
270. Smith 1991.
271. Zionism proves their point. Political hegemony and shared identity based on territory, which was Zionism's historical goal, fail in two respects. It leads to the eradication of Jewish difference and it excludes others living on the same territory who are not part of the majority identity.
272. The Boyarins do not explicitly adhere to multiculturalism but is seems to be the implication of their wish for collective Jewish identity based on difference. Their proposed notion of difference is not part of a discourse for private identity projects but for Jewish cultural particularity, which creates something of a contradiction between the writers as critical liberals and liberalism. Multiculturalism poses many problems to liberal state theory in particularly due to multiculturalism's collectivist dimensions. Put crudely, society under multiculturalism will be divided between Jews, Christians, Muslims, Atheists instead of being composed of citizens. Of course, the universalism of making citizens, i.e. sameness out of difference, is a colonial enterprise but the same logic exists within the ethnic-religious communities. There is not more logic to the claim that the multicultural society is more open to difference than to the claim that the traditional liberal-civil society is open to difference.

of the main streams within the area of cultural studies.[273] Cultural studies is perceived as an arena for critical studies of identities, histories and the ethnic and religious divisions of societies founded in the dichotomies and dialectics of colonialism and imperialism. As such, cultural studies are the studies of colonial and post-colonial structures and experiences uplifted to a paradigm for cultural configurations in general not only for the study of the historically colonial situations. The Boyarins place the studies of Jews and Judaism in this context in order to acclaim Jewish difference in context of other differences such as Blackness, Feminism, Homosexuality and minorities in general. According to the writers, cultural studies open up for both critical reflection on and solidarity between particular cultural interests and universal concerns:[274]

> "Christianity plus power has also yielded horror. If particularism plus power tends towards fascism, then universalism plus power produces imperialism and cultural annihilation as well as, all too often, actual genocide of those who refuse to conform. Our thesis is that Judaism and Christianity, as two different hermeneutic systems for reading the Bible, generate two diametrically opposed and mirror-image forms of racism – and also two dialectical possibilities of anti-racism. The genius of Christianity is its concern for all the peoples of the world; the genius of Judaism is its ability to leave other people alone. And the evils of the two systems are the precise obverse of these genii. The genies all too easily become demons. Christian universalism, even at its most liberal and benevolent, has been a powerful force for coercive discourses of sameness, denying, as we have seen, the rights of Jews, women, and others to retain their difference."[275]

The Boyarins attempt to articulate a discourse that is capable of entering critically in the normative culture system of both Christianity and Judaism, and normative culture systems in general, in order to point to the violence of the generalizations made from such systems. By adding power to the perspective of culture, they reach the conclusion that

---

273. In particular the works of Homi Bhabha and G. Spivak's are relied upon in the articulations of Jewish difference and Jews as both colonial subjects and colonizers.
274. Boyarin & Boyarin 1997: XI.
275. Boyarin & Boyarin 2003: 97

the possibility of political extension of the culture of an ethnic system inevitably leads to violence towards others. Judaism's particularity can lead to fascism when coupled with political and territorial power, while Christianity's universalism and power can, and has, lead to imperialism.[276] The key problem is therefore power for the commitment to social justice, which is weighted equally with the commitment to Judaism. The effects of power based on both particularism and universalism is a threat to difference but power is also a threat to the morality of the ideology of difference, if power is obtained on such a basis. The aim thus becomes to liberate culture from power and power structures such as territory. This is obviously a utopianism based on a desire to both free Judaism from the real-politik of Zionism and reclaim the culture(s) of pre-WWII Jews as a both moral and particular existence.[277] Theoretically, of course, a governing system is not neutral and will be a place of contest between the particular collectives sharing power, or the governing system will promote a universalism to optimize governing and prevent eventual struggle between minorities. The lesser utopia promoted by the Boyarins is that Israel should share the land and the power with the Palestinians and free the state of religion and ethnic supremacy.[278]

The discourse of the Boyarins is not only theoretical and political but grounded in a specific historical reading of Judaism that entails re-descriptions of practically the entire time-space parameters of identifiable Jewishness, primarily derived from classic rabbinic sources. The key to the re-description is the notion of space and how it is interpreted with regard to the land of Israel. The article suggests that the giving of the land by God to Israel should be read as an "always already coming from somewhere else". The divine promise itself is a destabilization of myths of autochthony because it is a sign of a guilty conscience towards the people already living there. At the same time the Jewish narrative of the land imagines the land as an attribute of the people, which creates a tension, an "unsettlement":

---

276. They obviously see Zionism as a very dangerous path within Judaism, which is not only hinted at in the article: "Any notion, then, of redemption through Land must either be infinitely deferred (as the Neturei Karta understands so well) or become a moral monster". Boyarin & Boyarin 2003: 103.
277. This reclaiming of Diasporic Jewish culture is not romantic or retrospective but critical as we shall see.
278. Ibid. 103.

> "The Jewish narrative of the Land has the power of insisting on the connection without myths of autochthony, while other narratives, including the Zionist one, have repressed memories of coming from somewhere else."[279]

The binaries that come to exist as principles for locating and grounding an existence, which in the Jewish biblical case would be wilderness-Canaan, wandering-settlement, diaspora-sovereignty, should not be regarded as choices between a first part and a second. Instead, they should be regarded as a permanent tension, which points to dynamics of culture – a tension that points to the mistake being made when something is held as an autochthony or locked in a certain image. In the discourse of the Boyarins, imaginations of Jewish history that see the first part of the binaries as diseases are not continuations of Jewish culture but a betrayal of Jewish culture.[280] This conclusion reflects a certain ambivalence in the discourse between nominalism and metaphysics. On the one hand, the discourse clearly alludes to nominalist and relativist theories of culture, history and identity when describing logics of culture and in using the concept of binaries to expose the dialectics of culture yet on the other hand, the engagement on behalf of particularist Jewishness enables essentialist judgment as to what true Judaism is. The brothers present a discourse which can hardly be claimed traditionally Jewish, but still it purports to re-read Judaism and not to betray Jewish culture. In fact, their re-description of Jewish history and culture is as novel as Zionism's was 100 years ago.

The central point of the Boyarins' re-description of Jewish history is, as mentioned, place. Place is considered a genealogical and mental capacity developed out of tradition and family with the feeling of being indigenous to a place, not to be confused with autochthonous. Compared to the philosophy of history of Raz-Krakotzkin, the Boyarins hold place as the mental category, not Diaspora as Raz-Krakotzkin. Diaspora is considered an attribute of Judaism; something which is intrinsic to Jewish culture and the Jewish experience as a historical phenomenon. In this sense, the Zionist perception of Diaspora as an unnatural condition is turned upside-down making Diaspora the natural condition of Judaism and territorialism an unnatural condition. Ultimately, the

---

279. Ibid. 104.
280. Ibid. 105. The binaries are lent from Harry Berger as presented in Boyarin & Boyarin 2003: 105.

Boyarins consider Diaspora Judaism's major contribution to the world; even more important than monotheism because Diaspora's lesson is that people and land are not naturally or organically connected.[281] Judaism simply provides the historical proof that the Herderian naturalism, which imagines people as organic products of territory, is mistaken. Judaism is therefore in the Boyarin optics a significant difference with a positive political message to the world.

As a philosophy of history, the discourse of the Boyarins not only appropriates Diaspora as a critique of normative culture. Further, it seeks to replace the normative culture of territorial political identities with a diasporism in which identities are based on pre/post-nationalist organisations of tradition, family and ethnicity. Stabilizations of identity and origins are rejected in favour of a notion of "always already coming from somewhere else", which is a philosophical import from post-structuralist philosophy in general and Jacques Derrida's perspective on language and history in particular.[282] Traditions, family and ethnicity are considered, in the Boyarin outline, identities that do not need stabilization or naturalist origins while nationalism's myths of autochthony epitomize the opposite. Hence, history cannot be stabilized in origins but only in genealogies and in this respect, the Boyarins think that Judaism has a particular message to the world because the history of the Jews is evidently not a history of a collective grounded in territory and political power. At the same time, history is written with a contemporary perspective. The perspective is not about "the past for its own sake" or about "wie es eigentlich gewesen" but about recognizing history as part of a social field where history legitimizes certain discourses and deems other discourses utopian or ideological. For the Boyarins the writing of history is predominantly an engagement in the particularity of Jewish culture and universal social justice.

---

281. Ibid. 110.
282. The concept of the always-already is applied and developed in structuralist and post-structuralist linguistics and philosophy meaning that there to every utterance, being, creation ect. is a pre-condition, which includes this utterance, being, or creation in its discourse or structure, and to this pre-condition counts the same premise. Thus, an anti-foundationalist, relational logic is established in which it is impossible to isolate an original moment.

Zionism Psychoanalyzed

Daniel Boyarin has worked most extensively on the writing of histories of aspects of Judaism that had the potential of separating Judaism from Zionism. As previously mentioned, Boyarin considers Zionism a betrayal of Jewish culture because it dismisses all diasporic and, theoretically, genealogical aspects of Jewish culture in favour of myths of autochthony and territory. In this perspective, Zionism constituted a radical change of Jewish culture and it ultimately led to a change of the Jewish experience in general. Zionism is a nationalist ideology, which saw the illnesses, or problems, of diasporic identity by and large in the same way as other nationalists, and anti-Semites when specifically related to Judaism. The agenda was to cure the Jewish problem as both an outward and inward strategy. The oppression, discrimination and violence against Jews would stop if the Jews obtained respect as a nation and this would help both the Jews and Europe. Inwardly, the Jews needed a new *Bildung*, which was perceived as both a rescue operation and a necessary and legitimate work ultimately because the anti-Semites rightly saw that the Jews had "de-generated".[283] The new Jewish *Bildung* should be European in accord with the highest ideals of German, French and English civilisation, education and nationhood while preserving Jewishness in the same way that the great culture nations preserved their national identity.[284]

In his *Unheroic Conduct. The Rise of Heterosexuality and the Invention of the Jewish Man*, Daniel Boyarin presents a series of readings of human ideals in Judaism. Special concern is given to ideals of manliness, femininity, sexuality and gender in general in Yiddish culture, the Talmud and modernity as exemplified by Freud and Herzl. Through his focus on ideals of gender in Judaism, Boyarin provides an analysis of Jewish cultural difference and the stereotypes placed on Jews and Jewish culture by the dominant European Christianity. In this analysis, modernity and one of

---

283. The best overview of Zionist ideology is Shimoni 1995. It must be noted that there was a huge difference between Zionism in the international organisation and in Palestine. To the Zionism of Palestine, there was a markedly nativist tendency to the effect that *Eretz Israeli* Zionism very much was for itself (the new Jews and Hebrews) and not for the Jews in the Diaspora.
284. This was surely done in numerous ways but the invention of the modern writing of history, the development of the integrated nation-state and centralized education are the most important larger factors, which influenced Zionism.

its most significant Jewish consequences, Zionism, are described as a very important juncture in Jewish history where Jewish difference was under the most pressure and provided a highly problematic answer.

Freud's texts are key texts of modernity as well as the founding texts of psychoanalysis. Freud is also central to the analysis of his population segment of Jews' relations to modernity and anti-Semitism. Freud's psychoanalytic works, so to speak, open a window to the cultural and emotional dilemmas for Jews of his time reflected by himself and his analysis of others. Thus, Boyarin psychoanalyses Freud, and as we shall see Herzl, in order to clarify the cultural and emotional stakes of Viennese Jews in the early 20th century. Freud was, of course, occupied with Judaism and anti-Semitism and his reflections over the issues, as well as the "in-voluntary" insights given by Freud, provide Boyarin with a view of the emotional factors influencing the invention of Zionism as a Jewish ideology.[285] The psychoanalysis of Freud and Herzl is integrated into the cultural studies/colonial paradigm, which on another level places the European Jews in a subaltern colonial dilemma: the desire to become like the suppressors while knowing that this desire only reflects the power of the suppressors and therefore the desire is unrealizable. Imposed agendas and discourses are taken over by the subjected who seek to re-invent themselves, re-create the individual and the collective as unique and autonomous through what the dominant discourses hold as legitimate categories and stereotypes. This is basically counter-violence and mimicry, which Franz Fanon pointed out in his works on colonial identities and violence.[286]

In the *Interpretation of Dreams*, Freud refers to a dream he had about Rome, which he names *My Son the Myops* – a dream he had after seeing Herzl's play in Vienna 1897.[287] In the dream, Freud envisions himself sit-

---

285. Freud was also occasionally occupied with Zionism but Boyarin carries his analysis of Freud into an analysis of Zionism and Herzl. In fact, Freud went to the theatre to watch Theodor Herzl's play *Das Neue Ghetto* before he dreamt one of the dreams that figures prominently in Boyarin's (and Freud's) analysis. It was an inter-textual moment between Freud and Herzl. As Boyarin aptly phrases it, Herzl wanted Phallustine not Palestine. Boyarin 1997: 222.
286. For example Fanon 1967.
287. We do not really know whether Freud saw or read the play, or if he had the dream right before or right after encountering the play. As Boyarin explains, it does not matter for the analysis but it makes for a better anecdote if Freud dreamt the dream right after seeing the play. Boyarin 1997: 221.

ting by a fountain at the Porta Romana at Siena almost in tears after the children had been brought to safety. In his own analysis Freud associates the dream with Psalm 137, which refers to the exile from Jerusalem.[288] In Freud's own analysis, this association is provoked by concern for his own children whom he cannot give a country of their own and who therefore need education to be able to move across frontiers. Thus, Freud himself offers a Zionist interpretation inspired by Herzl's play in which Rome means Jerusalem and bringing the children to safety means saving them from slaughter in analogy with the Biblical story of Pharaoh's slaughter.[289] In the same vein, educating them means enabling them to return to Zion. In Boyarin's analysis, however, Rome is not Jerusalem but exactly Rome. In line with Freud's general confusion of Christian and Jewish holidays (Freudian slips), Freud has also in his dream converted Jerusalem with Rome. His object of desire is simply Rome and Empire as well as the affiliated types of masculinity and heterosexuality, which his Jewishness in the discourse of anti-Semitism makes impossible. Freud is sitting, weeping, at Siena remembering Rome wishing for his children to be Roman. Weight is given to this argument by the fact that Freud as a child imagined himself as Hannibal understood as a Semite and returns to this theme in his interpretations of dreams. Hate and affection intermingle in the desire for Rome.[290]

In Boyarin's post-colonial analysis, the Freudian conflation of Christian and Jewish myths and of Rome and Jerusalem is an indication of the complicated relationship developing between the colonizers and the

---

288. The "By the rivers of Babylon"-psalm.
289. Except that it is not really the Jewish Biblical story that inspires Freud but the Christian story of Herod's slaughter of the children, as Boyarin shows. I will not go into this theme in detail but Boyarin convincingly shows that Freud conflates Jewish and Christian mythology. Boyarin's significant point is that Freud is entangled in the imaginaries of the Moses anti-type, namely Jesus, and thus Christianity not Judaism, which gives the saving of the children theme a new meaning. Freud's desire is to erase Jewish difference but still have Jewish pride. This is the product of a significant ambivalence between Jewish self-disdain and pride. Boyarin 1997: 225.
290. As Boyarin also notes, possession and being possessed are aspects of eroticism. Freud was "homosexualized" through his Jewishness and its place in the cultural economy of the day. To Freud (and Herzl) Zionism is a means to oust this homoeroticism. Boyarin also comments that for Jews such as Freud and Herzl, the Dreyfus trials were analogue to the Oscar Wilde trials. They were both about manliness. Boyarin 1997: 229, 222.

colonized. The Jewish "queer" position in the cultural economy of upper-class Vienna influenced by nationalism, anti-Semitism and German *Bildung* produces an ambivalence in Jews such as Freud and Herzl, who desire Rome (Germany) with both attraction and hate and are taken over by the ideal types of the dominant discourse and struggle with their queer identity. Freud thinks he sits by the rivers of Babylon weeping for the loss of Zion but he is in fact sitting at Siena longing for Rome. The differences and implications of the interpretations are highly significant for a description of Zionism.

***

Daniel Boyarin's account of Jewish identity in modernity as exemplified by Freud circles around the question of how and why the Jews were interpreted as being homeless, weak, emotional, feminine and Other in European political, psychological and racial discourses – and indeed did so in the self-interpretations of Jewish intellectuals. What were the cultural and psychological logics and structures behind these developments? In Boyarin's discourse normality and normalization constitute pressures and violences on cultural differences. Dominating discourses that produce the definitions and categories through which reality is conceptualized and ordered create powerful identifications of otherness. The orders of discourse are creative and re-creative for both the upper and the lower end of the hierarchy and therefore Jewish intellectuals did also take over the notion of Jewish queerness. This is a similar cultural dialectic as the one found between colonizer and colonized though in this case the Jew was a mulatto. White but not quite – or off-white – as Boyarin phrases it.[291]

Thus, in the first place, Boyarin's agenda is to question the discourses of normality and normalization. He does not accept the a priori assumption that the Jews were in an unnatural situation and he does not accept the a priori assumption that Zionism represents Jewish self-defence of cultural particularity against anti-Semitism; assumptions shared by both apologists and critics of Zionism alike.[292] Secondly, Boyarin's agenda is

---

291. Boyarin 1997: 262.
292. The commonsensical understanding of Zionism is that Zionism is a defence against anti-Semitism and assimilation, which is indeed the dominating plot of histories and analysis of Zionism. Critics of Zionism, to my mind, also most

to show that Zionism as formulated by Herzl seems to come closer to an ultimate rejection of historical Judaism through an assimilation of Jews into German cultural norms and discourses.

In his adult life, Herzl continuingly reflected over his status as a Jew in a German culture. He admired German culture immensely and he considered himself as part of this great culture nation. In his student days, Herzl was a member of a nationalistic and anti-Semitic student organisation, which he didn't perceive with any ambivalence until the day he had to quit the organisation because of his Jewishness. Herzl simply considered his Jewishness as an involuntary badge not of honour but of an unpleasant difference. Basically, Herzl did not hold this derogatory identity marker against the German culture that he loved but he held it against Jewish culture and ways of life in Europe. Boyarin's readings of Herzl's plays, political tracts and diaries show that Herzl's sources of inspiration and his cultural language were thoroughly German.[293] Zionism was a passage that should assimilate the Jews into German culture, as Herzl wrote: "Through Zionism Jews will again be able to love this Germany to which, despite everything, our hearts have clung".[294]

Carrying the analysis of Freud's ambivalence towards the cultural position of Jews in German culture and the produced desires thereof through to Herzl, Boyarin argues that Zionism was born of the same desires formulated as a political programme. To Freud it was enough for Jewish men and women to become real men and women and thus to get rid of the queerness of Judaism but to Herzl there were practical measures to be undertaken before this could happen. Herzl was in line with the Christian reformists who started the Jewish enlightenment by arguing that it was not Jewish race that was the problem but Jewish culture and social status. The Jews could be civilized and integrated in the European cultural economy if re-educated. Boyarin sees the enlightenment heritage in Herzlian Zionism as pure colonialism. The Jews were,

---

often accept this understanding but criticize the cultural particularism, nationalism and colonialism of Zionism. Boyarin completely, and refreshingly, avoids this parameter by stressing that the cultural horizons, plots and tropes of Zionism are not particular but identical to European nationalism and in line with the cultural economy of German society. Of course, there are in history many Zionisms and the focus here is on the Herzlian type.

293. Boyarin 1997: 271-312.
294. Quoted from Boyarin 1997: 278.

in the eyes of the Christian reformists such as Dohm, seen the same way as the natives of the colonized territories outside Europe were seen by benevolent colonizers within the spirit of the civilizing mission to the world. Herzl was "a good Indian" who participated in the reform of Jews and thereby their subjugation to the colonizers. Herzl was a sort of native collaborator:[295]

> ""I have, and know no other, blood than German blood," wrote Walter Rathenau, "no other tribe, no other people than the German. Expel me from my German soil, I still remain German, nothing changes". Herzl, with somewhat greater insight, had realized that only by leaving German soil and founding a Jewish State would he ever be truly German, but his identification with the Germans and desire to fully be one were the same as Rathenau's."[296]

Why not just convert to Christianity, we could ask? Herzl did indeed speculate on that possibility already in 1893 when he imagined himself bringing the Jews before the Pope for a mass-conversion.[297] Herzl and other Jewish leaders would, according to the fantasy, deliver the younger generations to baptism while they would remain the last Jewish generation. In line with Boyarin's reading, the important thing to note here is the double-bind between the desire to be normal on the one hand, and the internalized ideal of manliness on the other that makes it impossible for Herzl to convert himself. Instead, a theme of honour is invoked and Herzl and the Jewish leaders choose to go down with the ship instead of rescuing themselves. Just like real men would do. Herzl cannot abandon his nominal Jewishness because that would ironically make him even more Jewish. Instead, he sets out to transform the *Bildung* of modern Jewishness to be a mirror-image of German culture and thereby he can integrate himself and the Jews in the love of German culture by practicing it under a different name.[298]

---

295. Boyarin 1997: 279-280.
296. Ibid. 279.
297. Herzl's diaries quoted in Boyarin 1997: 281.
298. Woody Allen once, famously, stated that whenever he listened to Wagner he felt like conquering Poland. Herzl actually listened to Wagner in real time and one can speculate that he also felt like conquering something. That Herzl listened to Wagner is mentioned in Elon 1986: 3 and Boyarin 1997: 276.

Boyarin exemplifies this transition through Herzl's and Nordau's obsession with duelling. Manliness and honour were cardinal points to these Zionist heroes and occasionally it seems as if the agenda of their politics was to make manly men out of the Jews so they could defend their honour in a proper way.[299] The new Jew or the muscle Jew is a man who, when insulted, challenges his opponent to defend his honour. Herzl's play *Das Neue Ghetto* elaborates on the theme of Jewish honour and manliness, which works as a dominant plot for the entire play. The lead character Jacob Samuel had, before the time of the play, been challenged on his honour but he refused to duel. The incident troubles him still because of his Jewishness. The events of the play circle around the question of how to install pride and honour into Jewish life and only one solution is provided, namely the duel/violence/death. The duel will bring the Jews out of the new ghetto and show the world that the Jews are made of the right stuff. Actually, Jacob Samuel dies in a duel at the end of the play. On his death bed, Jacob says to his father: "You can understand, Father. You're a man".[300] *Das Neue Ghetto* is Boyarin's key example of Herzl's wish to transform Jewishness into Germanness. Jacob becomes a Siegfried and the Jews can be re-created.

Herzlian Zionism was, furthermore, caught in a peculiar colonial/post-colonial moment in as much as it was born out of the dialectics of cultural colonization of European Jews and, at the same time, had actual colonization of foreign territory as a central aspect of the entire raison d'etre of Zionism. The Zionist colonization of Palestine is not colonization as it is found in its typical forms in British, French or Spanish colonization. The Zionists did not have a concrete motherland or the

---

299. Boyarin also relies on Berkowitz (1993) and Biale (1992). In their more conventional historical studies, Berkowitz and Biale argue that the ideal of manliness was very important to Zionism and this ideal was to a large degree accountable for the popularity of the movement. Part of this was also the Jewish gymnastics clubs springing up at the turn of the century, which very often took names after ancient Jewish warriors such as the Maccabees and Bar Kochba. These gymnastic clubs were the ideal of Nordau's desire for the "muscle Jew".

300. Surely, this is an expression of wishful thinking because the ideal of manliness reflected in these dying words is very *goy*. Desperately, Jacob hopes that his father now in the face of the death of his own son sees the value of dying with honour. Jacob is, symbolically speaking, a Christian/Greek hero under a Jewish name.

structural basis in political and economical terms to be comparable to colonialism. Zionism is only the same as colonialism; it is a simulacrum of colonialism. In Boyarin's understanding Herzl wanted a colony to complete the transition of Judaism to Germanism. The colony and the process of colonizing would then make men and a nation out of the Jews and integrate them in the "family of nations" that Herzl writes about in *The Jewish State*. The natives of Palestine were either irrelevant or would be induced with civilization in the same benevolent manner as the Christian reformists envisaged for the Jews themselves.[301] This is what Boyarin entitles the colonial mimicry.[302] Zionism is, even though it is conceived as a liberation movement by its adherents, incapable of solidarity with the Palestinian struggle for liberation because the "liberation" itself in shaped in the discourse of nationalism and colonialism. It is a discourse that articulates freedom as the freedom to exercise power and control a territory.

In sum, the Boyarins, and Daniel as we have seen in more detail, create re-descriptions and re-conceptualizations of Jewish history and ethnography as an alternative to Zionism. The quest is not to question Jewish community or nationality, on the contrary, it is part of a universal

---

301. The clearest example of the civilizing mission of Zionism is expressed in Herzl's novel *Alt-Neuland* (1902). The novel is almost pathetically open about the mental dispositions that guide Herzl's visions. The protagonist, David Littwak, shows his British visitor, Mr. Kingscourt, the fabulous Altneuland with eager desire to impress and supersede him (as an icon of British imperialism and colonialism). In very telling passages, the model native, Reshid Bey, explains the wonders brought to the region by the Jewish colonizers. The novel brings Benedict Anderson's reflections over the intellectual poverty of nationalism to mind: "The "political power" of nationalisms vs. their philosophical poverty and even incoherence. In other words, unlike most other -isms, nationalism has never produced its own grand thinkers: no Hobbeses, Tocquevilles, Marxes, or Webers. This "emptiness" easily gives rise, among cosmopolitan and polylingual intellectuals, to a certain condescension. Like Gertrude Stein in the face of Oakland, one can rather quickly conclude that there is "no there there" (Anderson 1991: 5). Tom Nairn fits the psychoanalytic perspective by stating that: "Nationalism is the pathology of modern developmental history, as inescapable as "neurosis" in the individual, with much the same essential ambiguity attaching to it, a similar built-in capacity for descent in to dementia, rooted in the dilemmas of helplessness thrust upon the world (the equivalent of infantilism for societies) and largely incurable". (Quoted from Anderson 1991: 5).
302. Boyarin 1997: 271.

struggle for social justice that attempts to articulate alternative patterns of social and political organisation. Centrality is given to the concept of Diaspora for two primary, and in the Boyarin optics related, reasons. One reason on the universal level is that Diaspora is seen as a model for rehabilitating the organisations of identity around "racial", cultural and traditional parameters combined with a multiculturalist ideology that envisages the sharing of power. The second reason is the Boyarins conviction that Judaism is the incarnation of such a Diaspora. Judaism delivers the historical proof for the possibility of a de-territorialized identity, which is at the same time very integrative and communitarian. The Talmudic and Rabbinic tradition and the ways this tradition has contributed to Jewish continuity is subversive not only to territorialism but also to the Christian and Greek ideals of gender and power. The psychology and culture politics of gender in traditional Judaism versus the same in Christianity is re-articulated within the context of power and identity politics. The white Christian male is a colonizer and the male Jew is a queer whose queerness, difference, should be appropriated as an alternative model for social organisation.[303] The Boyarins not only invigorate Diaspora as a critical alternative or a critical principle but hold it as a past-future utopia in realistic and concrete terms.[304] Considered as a historical sociology and a philosophy of history, the Boyarins, with Richard Rorty's word, "re-weave" the patterns of Jewish history and identity within an ironist apprehension of the radical contingency of history and identities. Judgement is based on ethics, solidarity and tradition not on primordialism and autochthony. These criteria are in themselves suggestive for a postmodern, globalized, Jewish ethnoscape.

---

303. Daniel Boyarin is not blind to the fact that Orthodox Judaism itself is highly repressive towards women and queers and therefore the critical project is also directed at his own turf, which he elaborates on in a chapter on Bertha Pappenheim (Boyarin 1997: 313-359).
304. In this connection it is important to note the dialectics between utopianism, the desire for control and the freedom from ambivalence, danger and difference, as pointed out by Harvey 2000: 133-196 and Gur-Ze'ev as we shall see. The typological difference between Zionism and Diasporism as Utopias is not made explicit in Boyarin's thinking but I think part of the answer to this question is found in Boyarin's idea of not erasing or choosing any side of the binary impulses of Jewish culture. It still remains a dilemma, though.

An Israeli-Palestinian Homeland past Territory – or the Philosophy of Negative Utopianism

Though not a diasporist in the manner of the Boyarins or a historian in the manner of Raz-Krakotzkin, Israeli philosopher Ilan Gur-Ze'ev articulates alternative interpretive sensibilities and presents significant re-descriptions of the Israel-Palestinian cultural economy that are related to the post-nationalist, de-territorialized, discourses of the former. Whereas criticism of Zionism, Zionist history and identity and territoriality is an explicit agenda of the Boyarins and Raz-Krakotzkin, Ilan Gur-Ze'ev's philosophy constitutes an overtly universalist work towards criticism of culture production, education and normative discourses. Israel is the context of much of Gur-Ze'ev's work but its philosophical territory is that of critical theory and the articulation of a *Bildung* for the era of postmodernity. With its focus on the human being, the forces that influence it and lay out its possibilities for autonomous existence and its interaction with a social domain, Gur-Ze'ev's philosophy is a pedagogical thinking, which final reference is the human being or human categories such as Spirit, Creativity or Love.[305] Gur-Ze'ev is even more difficult to compartmentalize than the previous thinkers treated in this text due to the scope, many facets of the work and the wide variety of references and connotations in it. Therefore, I will only engage in two aspects of the work, which are connected to the theme of diasporism and these aspects are the notions of an Israeli-Palestinian homeland and counter-education or displacement as a re-articulated diasporic notion. History is not overtly treated in Gur-Ze'ev' texts but the texts have, however, some implications for historical discourse, which we will look at in the following.

As mentioned, Gur-Ze'ev's philosophical territory is that of critical theory in the tradition of Max Horkheimer and Theodor Adorno. Horkheimer and Adorno's criticism of modernity, instrumental rationality and the loss of human spirit is continued by Gur-Ze'ev and this creates an

---

305. In this we see a hint at education and pedagogy's pivotal position in contemporary humanistic and social sciences. After critical theory, pragmatism and discourse theory much of humanistic and social sciences can be read as education and pedagogy. The recognition of human language and thereby human categories as the final reference and the following replacement of truth in knowledge with the effects of knowledge place to my mind education and pedagogy at the center of postmodern human and social study.

important difference between this philosophy and the anti-humanistic tendencies in thinkers such as Foucault and other writers associated with post-structuralism. Gur-Ze'ev maintains that there is a human spirit and he holds humanism as a positive universal ideal. In our context, this also distinguishes Gur-Ze'ev from the Boyarins, whose multiculturalism is in opposition to the universalist mission of humanism. In fact, Raz-Krakotzkin is closer in perspective to Gur-Ze'ev than the Boyarins in as much as the inspirations in Raz-Krakotzkin's thinking from Walter Benjamin and Edward Said are derivations of the school of critical theory.[306] Gur-Ze'ev, however, significantly expands the critical theory perspective of Horkheimer and Adorno to include many other insights from other philosophical and pedagogical sources and inspirations. Another aspect of the universal humanism of Gur-Ze'ev is his concern with the dialec-

---

306. Benjamin was surely placed in the mental territory of critical theory and Edward Said claims in his *Representations of the Intellectual* (1994) that one of his primary sources of inspiration is the thinking of particularly Adorno. Actually, "exile" is to Said part of the habitus of an intellectual. Not quite at home anywhere and always discontent with popular cultural tendencies. Obviously, there are parallels between Said's Palestinian exile and the criticism it feeds and the way the notion of exile feeds Said's favourite, non-nationalist, Jewish thinkers such as Horkheimer, Adorno, Benjamin and Chomsky. This is an affinity, which I believe is quite important to the increased interest in Said among Israeli and Jewish academics and intellectuals such as ones treated here. The Boyarins hold Said in high regard and have had interesting debates with him, Raz-Krakotzkin is directly inspired by Said's work and Gur-Ze'ev has in several articles written about Said though in a highly critical manner towards Said's self-professed "Jewishness", which Gur-Ze'ev sees as a sophisticated rejection of Jewish historical self-understanding (Said in *Ha'aretz* 18.08.2000, Gur-Ze'ev 2003: 46-48). The occupation with Said comes surely not only from his theoretical work but also from his identity as a Palestinian intellectual in exile. He obviously poses a dilemma as an ambivalent ideal as the type of intellectual who in the 20th century had a "Jewish" identity but in this case is also a relentless critic of Zionism from a Palestinian (nationalist) perspective. If we see Said as an ambivalent ideal to these Jewish thinkers, we add another ambivalence and that is the fact that these Jewish thinkers by and large agree with Said's criticism of Zionism but at the same time Said represents the Palestinian intellectual who can to some degree appreciate Jewish history and identity and not the least acknowledge the significance of the Holocaust while remaining a Palestinian nationalist. Thus, on several levels, Said plays an important role in the formulation of an Israeli-Jewish identity after Zionism and territorialism, both on the level of theory and critical interventions and on the level of approaching genuine Palestinian recognition of Jewish history, identity and the Holocaust.

tics of the Israeli-Palestinian experience. The Palestinian struggle for liberation from Israeli occupation is not per definition a just struggle. It is also confronted with severe criticism of its violence and negations of Israeli-Jewish identity and suffering.[307] It seems to be a deliberate agenda for Gur-Ze'ev to position his philosophy in critical attachment to anti- and post-Zionist academic agendas within the Israeli academy. To get a constructive angle to Gur-Ze'ev's philosophy, it is crucial to understand that Zionism, its history books, identity politics and institutions are understood as a normalizing educational project, which aims at shaping the individual and collective capacities and beliefs of Jewish men and women.[308] Such a project is per definition violent because it seeks to defeat external and internal opposition to it and normalize the difference of the members of the projected collective into sameness.[309] The agenda of critical theory and Gur-Ze'ev's derived counter-education is therefore to provide criticism, re-description and enable moments of freedom and individuality in which the possibility of the experience of an alternative totality is present.[310] This otherness is not perceived as an alternative history, which is truer or more ethical than the commonsensical; it is more of a transcendence from history.

***

---

307. An interesting discussion of this theme can be found in the article *Beyond the Destruction of the Other's Collective Memory* in which Gur-Ze'ev and Ilan Pappé debate the issue of justice and violence in the Israeli-Palestinian conflict (In the collection *Destroying the Other's Collective Memory*, 2003).
308. Gur-Ze'ev 2003: 1-24.
309. Thus, when the term violence is used it signifies concerted and structured affects on the individual to educate or re-educate her/him into a normalized existence. Violence is therefore both constructive and destructive and a condition of social existence but always an attack on freedom, individuality, love and creativity and other conceptual representations of spirit in Gur-Ze'ev's texts.
310. Ibid. 4. Gur-Ze'ev insists on the possibility of the universal and the total despite the recognition of radical contingency. In opposition to Derrida, Rorty and Laclau and Mouffe (and other anti-foundationalists), Gur-Ze'ev believes that there still is something beyond contingency, discourse and politics. That something is most frequently in the texts phrased in religious/metaphysical language as Spirit, Infinity, Transcendence and Messianism. That something is grounded in the essence of Being as an ethical relationship before cognition and culture in the line of Levinas' ethics.

"The quest for homeland, even the reflection on homeland, is never at home. The moment "homeland" enters the linguistic space and receives its "voice" it comes to the brink of loss, of distance, or of exile from what homeland refers to. Entering the language of homeland, quest for homeland, or overcoming being exiled from homeland as it is, or as it should become, entails entering the Platonic cave within which a collective or a realm of self-evidence and the *Same* is created. It is constituted by powers, that are effective enough to secure the invisibility of their manipulations for the collective, which it creates, activates, represents, and victimizes. It is exactly the depths of the evidence of selfhood, orientation, yardsticks, and aims of the individual that feel at home in their "homeland" which represents their effective victimization and loss of themselves. In this sense the language of homeland or Heimat as its history reveals, might also open new possibilities of overcoming the hegemonic system.[311]

According to Gur-Ze'ev, homeland is never a concrete place of home. It is an emotional, reflexive, individual space that resembles an inner longing for infinity (timelessness), identity and totality. In a sense it is a Messianic dream. We can never be at one with our homeland. If homeland is collectivized and articulated ideologically it is part of the violences, educations and manipulations that produce the commonsensical and the self-evident. If an individual feels at home in her homeland, she is truly victimized and estranged! In this human need and capacity to individually sense and reflect on Home lies both the potential of totalitarianism and transcendence. The Heimat-feeling that can make promises of transcendence from the realm of self-evidence, of violence, in Gur-Ze'ev's texts is the individual, never quite at home, homeland, which reaches for infinity and totality.

Gur-Ze'ev effectively removes the concept of homeland from its conventional sociological descriptions and provides it with a description that addresses the more fundamental psycho-cultural dimensions of the concept. Conventionally, we would understand homeland as our place of birth, socialization and the place where we have duties, rights and protection under the law. In such a description homeland is objectivized and collectivized and it enters a dialectic in which it also serves as a concept that represents the powers of socialization and these powers'

---

311. Ibid. 25.

control over our imagination. Nationalist ideologies have understood the importance of the concept of homeland as the place of complete identity, unity and peacefulness. This longing is given a concrete object, namely a land or a territory of the past, present or future in a collective vision. This homeland is a safe haven for an individual who is also part of an articulated "us". In this regard, Zionism in its initial stages can be seen as serving a dual purpose as both an attempt of many individuals of transcending their entrapment in Europe and as a production of self-evidence through which homeland is articulated as an ideology.[312] The same is the case for Palestinian nationalism. It both provides an individual passage into the possibility of freedom but it is also an ideology which on a collective basis takes possession of the otherworldliness of the homeland. In a sense, the notion of homeland articulated in Gur-Ze'ev's texts has close resemblance to commonplace nostalgic and romantic imaginations of childhood harmony. The safeness of parental love and concern, the timelessness of play, the innocence and openness of encounters with the strange, the unfamiliar and the totally other, which are attributes often connected to imaginations of the perfect childhood. The un-prejudiced, un-acculturated face-to-face meeting with the world in its totality is quite similar to the Levinasian ethics of pre-discursive communication.[313] Gur-Ze'ev surely recognizes the debts to the romantic poets when is comes to

---

312. In this regard we can notice the present strength of the "safe haven-ideology" as it has manifested itself during the second intifadah and in the debates about the so-called new anti-Semitism 2000-2004.
313. We must not forget, though, that this is a romance not children psychology but that is also a little beside the point in relation to Gur-Ze'ev's perspective. It is not a matter of whether the romance of perfect harmony and face-to-face relations to the world is true in a factual sense. It is rather a matter of the creativity of the imagination to envision real, free and unrestrained dialogue with the world as a whole. More critical to the romance is its contextualization and integration in theories of the psyche/personality and theories of discourse. Such work "disenchants" or "de-mystifies" this childhood romance or Homeland and denies it its claims to originality in the sense of its being beyond contextualization and discourse, which is something that Gur-Ze'ev insists on (Gur-Ze'ev 2003: 1-24). Homeland-as-transcendence cannot escape historicity and rules of interpretation when it is perceived as more than a capacity of the human; that is as a representation of something else in the psyche or as a cognitive characteristic. Regarding Levinas' ethics, I have drawn on Bernhard Taureck's *Levinas zur Einführung* (1991).

his notion of Homeland as the individual imagination of the unmediated relation to the world.[314]

In this perspective, the history of Zionism and of modern, Zionist Jewish identity as an ideology is conceptualized as a development and a dialectic that cannot be understood properly without the integration of the development of modern Palestinian identity. This is a radical contextualization of history as something which crystallizes into narratives and identities through categories, rules and relations. The categories, rules and relations in a social field define central aspects of the self, the collective and the other. These are aspects, which plot history as a discourse that presents different realities as they are perceived, operated and consumed in a society. The other, who visibly or invisibly, inhabits the histories usually has a totally connected and mutually dependant mirror-history. In this respect, Palestinian nationalist history and Zionist history are intertwined as two systems of production of knowledge, which depend on each other for situating the self, the collective and other in their proper places. At the same time, the Israeli-Palestinian situation is unique in as much as the exile versus homecoming binary is so explicit and dominant in the respective collective identities and histories. This adds further to the similarity between Israeli and Palestinian identities but it also leads to total mutual rejection of the other's memory, suffering and truths.[315]

Gur-Ze'ev points to the Palestinian rejection of any sort of legitimacy of Jewish claims to the land of Palestine. Jews are mere colonizers whose identity as Israelis is completely criminal and illegitimate, which is something that Gur-Ze'ev equals to the robbing of any spirit of the Israelis and to a process of de-humanization.[316] Zionist ideology and education construe the same image of the Palestinians primarily through the instrumentalization of Holocaust memory as an icon of Jewish history in a transcendental historical understanding in which Amalek is always present and most recently represented by the Palestinians. It is of prime concern to Gur-Ze'ev to point to the dialectics of Israeli-Palestinian relations to avoid categorical understandings of the other:

---

314. Gur-Ze'ev 2003: 26.
315. Gur-Ze'ev 2003: 41.
316. Ibid. 41

> "The philosophical and the political relations between the Holocaust and the *Nakbah* and who owns Israel/Palestine and whose homeland it is have become a unified element for Israeli and Palestinian internal and external violence, which at the same time is also a fruitful *constitutive* element of reproducing each of the warring side's ethnocentric collectivism".[317]

In contrast to both the Boyarins and Raz-Krakotzkin, Gur-Ze'ev does not judge the victimhood, suffering or nationalism of either Zionism or Palestinian nationalism as being better or worse or attempts to create a hierarchy of whose suffering or ethnocentric collectivism is the more relevant or just. Both exist and feed on each other through the same cultural and psychological mechanisms, which essentially are educational violences taught by ideology and institutions. Both collectives emphasize suffering and exile in their cultural economy as the key to their identity and the key to their consequent rejection of the other's suffering.[318] The Holocaust and the Nakbah are placed in opposition to each other in these ethnocentric histories as identities and ethical narratives that are exclusive and fundamental. They do not open for any universal recognition of the suffering of others but serve rather as the yardstick for moral rights when it comes to claiming ownership of Palestine. At the same time, the narrative of the Nakbah is also construed as a rejection of the Holocaust and Jewish historical relations to the Land of Israel within the plot of mere colonization. Holocaust education in Israel is equally not the same as Nakbah education but it is its rejection or moral-historical superior in the hierarchy of suffering.[319] This leads Gur-Ze'ev

---

317. Ibid. 41.
318. Something which is almost self-evident to anyone who has only a superficial knowledge of Zionist and Palestinian literature. Exile is constitutive for the collective self-understanding. Exile forms the strong desire for homeland in an organic understanding of the relationship between collective and the lost land, which can be seen in both Palestinian and Zionist, even Canaanite, poetry and this leads to the categorical rejection of the other's rights of the same land. There is no room for contingency in such an understanding.
319. Gur-Ze'ev's perspective is controversial in the context of Holocaust education. It is a perspective that in literature resembles the story *Siren* by Etgar Keret in which Holocaust education is also an instrument and a system in opposition to real compassion. Holocaust education has led to a number of discussions in Israel in recent years and the same has the introduction of Palestinian nationalist literature in the Israeli curriculum. These discussions show the depths

to suggest that in the cultural economy of Israelis and Palestinians it is in fact the Holocaust/Nakbah that is the Homeland of the collectives.[320] This homeland is perceived from the perspective of an organic relationship to the land from which follows that Jews/Palestinians are the true flowers of the Land and the others are either colonizers (rapists, usurpators) or impostors (incompetent natives, Arabs, Bedouins).[321] In this perspective, the territory cannot be apprehended purely as a territory in itself. It is always an interpretation to which there is attached an imaginary geography of which things, peoples and histories are part.[322]

---

of the influence of Holocaust memory in Israeli culture and the effects of this memory's instrumentalization in the service of nationalist politics. Holocaust education leaves no room for a work towards the understanding of culture production based on suffering and exile in a relational perspective. This is indeed a highly complicated question, which at least has two important dimensions. One is the question of how to preserve factual historical knowledge of the Holocaust/Nakbah and the second is the question of how to educate people to recognize and resist stereotyping and categorizations of others on a collective basis. I would argue that these two dimensions are not the same. To possess a factual knowledge of the Holocaust/Nakbah does not lead to recognition of the suffering of others *par se* (see for example the movie *Apt Pupil* by Bryan Singer 1998). In fact, the second dimension of educating to recognize the other is also a work to counter the effects of commonsensical moral lessons derived from the self-evidence produced by knowledge of the Holocaust/Nakbah. In discussions over the issue of Holocaust/Nakbah education it is very often unclear what the purpose of such education is; is it part of claims made to certain rights or a certain collective status or is it part of a work to counter violence, discrimination and fascism? In my perspective, the bottom-line is not constituted by knowledge but by the imagination, criticism and solidarity.

320. As already suggested in the title of the article *Holocaust/Nakbah as an Israeli/Palestinian Homeland* to which I refer.
321. The impostor-theme is quite strong in Israel after the integration in public discourse of the fact that the land was not empty before Zionist immigration which is reflected in many aspects of Israeli culture from rightwing politics to literature. In this perspective, Palestinian nationalism is not seen as self-creative but as a result of opposition to Zionism. The Palestinians are Arabs and serve larger purposes of Arab nationalism/fascism and anti-Semitism. They are an invention of the Arabs to lead guerrilla warfare against the Jews returning to their Homeland. Of course, the issue here is not whether or not Palestinian nationalism in fact was one of the results of Zionism colonization, which it among other things was, but whether this nationalism is a genuine collective identity/imagination or an evil scheme. Kimmerling and Migdal 1993, Khalidi 1997.
322. See Harvey 2000 for reflections over how places and spaces (geographies) represent utopias and changing imaginary geographies (my phrasing).

It is the interpretation that needs to be addressed and indeed countered if Israel is to move beyond the violences of Zionist education and take steps towards Israeli-Palestinian peacemaking, to use Gur-Ze'ev's terms, and because of the dialectic relation with Palestinian education the same is needed with regard to the Palestinian relations to the land. In spite of philosophical differences, what unites the writers treated here is the awareness of the need to address the interpretations of histories and identities on the Israeli-Palestinian scene. Exile or Diaspora as the starting point for a new outlook offers an alternative perspective to the groundedness of territorialism and nationalism.

Gur-Ze'ev distinguishes himself, however, from the other writers treated here in as much as he finds it appropriate to direct equal criticism towards the Palestinians, their history and identity. As we have seen, the Boyarins and Raz-Krakotzkin either fully accept the colonization paradigm with regard to Zionism or get trapped in an ambivalence towards the justifiability of the history of the weak. They do not discuss the inter-relatedness of the Israeli-Palestinian histories and identities as mutually dependent narratives. Exile is ultimately the option of the Jews/Israelis as an anti-territorial community or a critical position while the Palestinians are victims to the Jewish transformation to a territorial community. In fact, Gur-Ze'ev believes that the Palestinian rejection of Zionism is much stronger, unified and grounded than the Zionist rejection of the Palestinians both presently and historically. The Western, advanced, technological and capitalist state of Israel has structurally undermined the Zionist rules of interpretation and enabled a pragmatic, individualist middleclass, which, by and large, accepts the Palestinian narrative and wishes to share the rights to the land.[323] The violence directed at this segment of

---

323. Gur-Ze'ev 2003: 44-45. With this description of Israeli society's recent developments Gur-Ze'ev is in line with sociologists such as Shafir and Peled 2002 and Ram 1999. I find, however, that there is an inconsistency in the level of critique. When the Israeli undermining of the traditional Zionist narrative of the land is bound to social changes then the Palestinian (maybe increased?) rejection of Jewish/Israeli legitimate presence in the land is also tied to social structures and configurations. Palestinian society has not had the opportunity of developing into a Western, capitalist economy amongst other things (definitely not only) due to Zionist/Israeli oppression. Did we in the 1990es witness a gradual break-up of the inter-dependency of the Israeli-Palestinian narratives due to the unequal affects of globalization in economy and post-modernization in culture?

the Israeli population is in Gur-Ze'ev's perspective both strategically and emotionally at the heart of the Palestinian struggle against Israel. The violence is not directed at the army, the police or the government of Israel as politics by violent means, but against the spirit, accomplishment and love of the land of the Israeli middleclass citizen. The bombing of a bus full of the children of middleclass, educated, liberal Israelis in Haifa, Tel Aviv or Jerusalem is a strike against *them* as people; as illegitimate human beings; against the best/most detestable they represent. Their love of Israel, life and freedom is a rape of Palestine in a Palestinian nationalist understanding.[324] The sad irony of it is, of course, that it is this segment of the Israeli population who represents the individualization that enables recognition of the Palestinian suffering and historical narrative.

Gur-Ze'ev finds that Homeland is an essential part of the cultural and psychological landscapes of individuals as a romantic longing for totality and transcendence. This longing is always translated into a concrete object in politics and education, which leads to its collectivization. What, then, can be done to counter this translation from a humanist perspective? The answer is: only countermeasures, not a replacement with other concepts and ideologies.[325] The place from where Gur-Ze'ev sees possibilities of countermeasures that can challenge Israeli and Palestinian violence and competition to take over the others self-representation is not really a

---

324. When an Israeli soldier shoots to kill a Palestinian child (I find it beyond discussion that this happens intentionally) and is supported and excused by the system, it is basically an expression of the same de-humanization.

325. Gur-Ze'ev has developed a concept of counter-education, which is his contribution to an answer to the problematics of educational, institutional and ideological violences that disable individual moments of transcendence towards the world and the other. Counter-education shares the commitment of critical philosophy to permanently challenge the existing order of things. It is committed to never accepting the facts and reality and to focus on what produces these facts and realities. It is not supposed to replace normalizing education (then it would be normalizing itself) but it insists that education is more than acculturation. In this respect, counter-education's focus is the recovery of the "other I" that is not the same as the others and the acceptance of the other's absolute difference. Success is only momentary and measured by the (occasional) individual capacity to criticize and see the real as an ideology. Its utopia is negative in the meaning of undetermined by any normalizing education or ideology. It is a utopia consisting of the momentary transcendence provided by criticism. Gur-Ze'ev adds to the concept of counter-education in many articles so surely my representation here is a reduction. See for example Gur-Ze'ev 1998, 2001, 2003.

place; it is the opposite of conceiving of territory in metaphysical terms; it is homelessness.

***

In the spring of 2003 Ilan Gur-Ze'ev formulated a call for action towards a beginning of the end of the Israeli-Palestinian conflict. This call reflects both his concepts of counter-education and such a view's consequences for public discourse and action. It is one of the very few attempts to radically advocate for real change of the evil dialectic between Israel and the Palestinians in a public tone formulated by either Israelis or Palestinians. Surely, it is doomed to controversy in as much as it addresses both the issue of just existence and exile/Diaspora/homelessness.[326] Gur-Ze'ev's call quite closely resembles the Boyarins' political agenda of a transformation from the prevailing idea that identity and nationhood grow out of a territory and its political organisation to a pre/post-modern notion of identity and nationhood constituted of race and culture. If not articulated the same way with significant differences between the Boyarins' historical and ethnographical re-descriptions of Jewish history and (male) identity and Gur-Ze'ev's philosophically grounded, universalist critique, the two perspectives still advocate a Jewish return to the Diaspora as homeland. In his call, Gur-Ze'ev writes:

> "The ongoing genocide in Southern Sudan, the daily Russian assaults against the Chechen people, the uprooting of the Tibetan people and culture by the Chinese, the oppression of Christians and the condition of women, homosexuals and other minorities in Saudi Arabia, or the oppression against the Russian majority in Estonia are only a few of examples of today's lack of courage and widespread dishonesty in the treatment of Israel. At the same time it is true, and one should face it, hard as it is to acknowledge, that Israel has become a space where there is less and less room for genuine creative spirit and for social justice. Israel has become the ultimate Diaspora of the Jewish spirit. Here, more than anywhere else, there is no room for "the Jewish heart", or for Jewish intellectual independence and avant-garde creativity. It is a sad actuality, but I cannot avoid, must not avoid, facing it even if it is so hard for me to acknowledge: there is no room for a just State of

---

326. Gur-Ze'ev 2003b.

Israel. St. Augustine knew this was so for all the manifestations of "the earthly city". In the case of Israel it has become so clear that unreserved siding against injustice inevitably endangers the very existence of Israel, not solely its current policies".[327]

The commitment shared equally by the Boyarins and Ilan Gur-Ze'ev to justice as a commitment, which is not superseded by their commitment to Jewish history and identity but a central part of this latter commitment, leads to, and in fact demands, that Zionism and Israel are deemed unjust. To Gur-Ze'ev as an Israeli, it is the development of Zionist and Israeli society from its early beginnings until today that shows that the paths of A.D. Gordon, Ahad Ha'am and Martin Buber have been rejected for a Sparta of Judaism. To Daniel Boyarin, Zionism is colonial mimicry and he rhetorically declares himself an anti-Zionist in the tradition of Judah Magnes and the Brith Shalom group.[328] In comparison, Gur-Ze'ev understands Zionism in a more nuanced manner and will not abandon his personal share of this history.[329] To all three writers presented in this essay, globalization and postmodernization provide the structural and cultural developments that in effect can lead to a diaporization or contains the conditions of possibility for Diaspora. In the globalized cultural logic Jewish abandonment of territory as homeland and a reaffirmation of Diaspora as the historical homeland of the Jews, Jews and Judaism can re-enter their telos as an avant-garde; a new description of a Chosen People.

The course of modern Jewish history and Zionism, as it has been projected by the clear majority of historical works on the subject and by the categories and concepts by which it is dealt with in public discourses, as

---

327. Gur-Ze'ev 2003b: 3.
328. Boyarin 1997: 278. Judah Magnes and the Brith Shalom did obviously not consider themselves anti-Zionist but Daniel Boyarin's point is that an attitude like theirs to the Palestinians and Zionism is considered anti-Zionist today.
329. "This means that this counter-education should also prepare Diasporic life for those people, like myself, who insist on living in Israel at all costs, even as it becomes before my eyes a Zionist Sparta of the wicked. This means that the interconnectedness between *Gola* and *Geula* (Diaspora and redemption) should offer a very specific, concrete, and detailed counter-education in current Israel, for preparing not only the exodus from Zionism and the State of Israel but, what is more important, the possibility of Diasporic life in Israel itself". Gur-Ze'ev 2003b: 12.

a return to history and a negation of the Diaspora is severely criticized and exposed by these writers as a normalizing ideology. Direct historical re-description seems to be of lesser importance to Gur-Ze'ev than to Boyarin and Raz-Krakotzkin who also produce histories of the past that can address the present within a critical, diasporist perspective. The equally crucial re-descriptions by Gur-Ze'ev are interwoven in his counter-educational project and commitment to critical theory though these commitments make concrete, positive utopian alternatives impossible. To Gur-Ze'ev radical criticism is the negative utopian alternative.

Final Comments

When we with the Boyarins, Raz-Krakotzkin and Gur-Ze'ev reconsider the Zionist return to history and the negation of the Diaspora, we not only see a radical and marginal critique of the Zionist ideological project. We also see the contours of a reorganization and re-description of the concepts and inter-relatedness of history, identity and territory within a Jewish context that answer to the universal developments of globalization. The bulk of the theoretical and historical literature on the topics of nations and nationalism emphasizes the relative modernity of the conceptions of a collective as autonomous and organically related to specific territory in a way that describes this territory as the property of the collective. In this way, the academic literature on the topic stands in sharp contrast to popular and ideological national, collective identities, which primarily emphasize the deep historical grounding of a community on a territory. The nation, its identity and territorial relation, is in its own ontology deeply historical, while any historicization of it shows that it is a relatively recent phenomenon. Reflexive political attempts to overcome this schism and envision the contingent, liberal, national community inevitably struggle with the dilemma between the integration of collective identity with Homeland/territory and its force as a community builder, on the one hand, and the weakness of the reflexive, contingent community on the other. The central issues in this regard are philosophical, social and psychological. Conceptions of truth, knowledge, history and justice are very important and, at the same time, it is clear that social configurations influence exactly the dominant understanding of such concepts. Psychology's importance comes from the fact that, as Gur-Ze'ev points out, we have a deep need for the peacefulness, unmediated communication and acceptance of Home-Homeland. In each their own way, the Boyarins, Raz-Krakotzkin and Gur-Ze'ev attempt discourses of how to conceive of Jewish-Israeliness and its history within the recognition of the contingency and discursivity of truth and history, changing social configurations and the need for Homeland.

Zionism radically changed the prevalent Jewish discourses of history and identity in a dialectic with contemporary developments of modern Europe. Modernity, nationalism, anti-Semitism and colonialism are among the most important influences that shaped Zionism both in a negative and positive sense. Zionism was at the same time a Jewish reaction to the pressures, or with Gur-Ze'ev terminology violences, of modernity, nationalism, anti-Semitism and colonialism and a Jewish adoption of these ideologies and developments. Jews were both colonised and colonizers, natives and white, liberators and conquistadors in a history of Jewish modernity, which doomed the traditional diasporic Jewish way of life in Europe as unnatural, parasitic and non-historical. The issue of history is, in this regard, very important for an understanding of how the imagination of proper Jewishness changed during the formation of Zionism, and was again open for change during the 1990s. History is a discourse of identity in a temporal perspective, which aims at showing why things are the way they are in a realistic style with the teleology determined by an already known present or an envisioned utopia. Zionist history manifested the historical, realistic, relation between the Jews as a collective and the Land of Israel and articulated this relationship as being constitutive for the very character of Jewishness. The utopia of Zionism was normality as a Western nation with its ideological affirmations of history, culture, manliness and enlightenment which included the reverse rejection and destruction of the characteristics of traditional Jewishness. To the Zionists this meant freedom, or at least an escape of the negative stigmatizations of Jews, to Daniel Boyarin as a Jew this was mimicry to its most radical extent and an ultimate success of Germanism.

The Zionist return to history is and was also intimately connected to the coming into being of Palestinian national identity and history. The conflict between the two collectives has undoubtedly strengthened the metaphysical discourse of history of Zionism as part of the all-out war. This issue is central in particular to both the re-descriptions of the Jewish relationship to the land of Raz-Krakotzkin in history and the counter-educational project of Gur-Ze'ev.[330] Both seek to open up the historical possibilities, create awareness of the contingencies and criticize the normalizing versions of history that feed and is fed by the conflict. The most particular, and to my mind interesting, commonality between these writers is their identification of the possibility of an alternative in the historical concept of the Diaspora. In the modern Jewish cultural economy in the light of Zionism Diaspora is inevitably in opposition to Zionism, which entailed the project of its eradication. To Boyarin, Diaspora is indeed the opponent of Zionism and it is in the history of traditional Judaism as a diasporic community that the Boyarins find the counter-history to Zionism that could legitimate a post-modern Jewish Diaspora as a truly historical Jewish community, which at the same time incarnates difference as a cultural and social possibility. Diaspora is to Raz-Krakotzkin a critical, cultural, alternative perspective through which to see the commonsensical and the powerful; it is to brush history against the grain in Walter Benjamin's words. In Gur-Ze'ev's perspective, Diaspora is a symbol of a homelessness, which enables the freedom that comes from being in a different place than home. In this perspective Diaspora/Homelessness can mean the re-entering of Jewish spirit, creativity and heart, which have been colonized by Zionism and the Israeli-Palestinian conflict. Despite the differences, Diaspora is identified as both something lost and something to possibly gain through the loss of the modern conceptions of homeland/nation/territory. The recognition of the waning power of the nation-state and the increased force of globalization is paradigmatic to the philosophies of these writers as well as for the condition of possibility for these philosophies legitimacy in cultural debates.

The search for truth and absolute knowledge understood as traditional epistemology of history and philosophy is replaced by what Richard Rorty calls "a re-weaving of patterns of beliefs" in open, critical and analytical gestures which engage polemically in both academic enquiry and subjective, political projects at the same time. In the texts of the Boyarins, Raz-Krakotzkin and Gur-Ze'ev it is impossible to reject the academic achievement but is also impossible to find even attempted objectivity and to separate the academic from the political projects. These are features

---

330. As well as Raz-Krakotzkin's projection of the Mizrahi as a persona representing the in-between Arab- and Israeliness and of course also the Boyarins' view on the Palestinians as colonized subjects.

that to my mind characterize the type of academic texts that correspond to the cultural logic of late capitalism.[331] Thus, these texts expand the vision on the topics that they treat but simultaneously engage in constructing discourses by which we can apprehend these insights favourably in relation to the current order of things in Israel and Palestine. As identities and histories, collective as well as private, are based on what we know to be true both factually and imaginatively, academic texts are equally important as a source to knowledge of the hegemonies and divisions of a society to public and political discourses. The academic texts of writers such as the Boyarins, Raz-Krakotzkin and Gur-Ze'ev show us the contours of academic, critical, discourses that seek to articulate knowledge and uses there of with a commitment to Jewish ethnicity post nationalism. In these discourses, Diaspora is the key concept of a Jewish ethnoscape for the age of globalization and postmodernity.

---

331. To paraphrase the title of Fredric Jameson's book *Postmodernism, or, the Cultural Logic of Late Capitalism* (1991). Late capitalism is not only globalization but also economy and culture within the nation-states. This cultural logic is postmodernism within Jameson's Marxist perspective. Within this outlook it is of course impossible to separate the political from the academic. I would argue, though, that generally attempted objectivity is still the commonsense of humanistic studies and viewed through this perspective, the texts of these writers pose problems due to their explicit agendas. As we have seen, I do not either separate the knowledge production from the political projects in my treatment of the texts.

History on TV: The *Tekumah* series

"The Israeli-Palestinian context manifests a clash between two normalizing educational systems, which produced and re-produce two collectives committed to negating the otherness of the Other as a vital part of each one's self-constitution. This self-constitution of the collective is actually the act of the negation of the self-constitution of the individual human. It is the act of robbing by the system of human potentials for overcoming collectivism and false love and relation to Spirit, creativity, and responses to a *call* of something higher than life as the aim of life. It demolishes the potentials for dialogical self-constitution. It is actually the self-constitution of the system. It uses the consciousness of self, identity, collective memory, and quests for a freed homeland in each collective for self-reproduction. It is committed to denying the concept of the homeland of the Other and to "liberating" the geographical space as well as the symbolic arena as part of its normalizing education, which also has its explicit and occasional military violences."[332]

Introduction

Public history is a history that is produced by or for the state either as part of educational programmes, institutions such as museums and commemorations and increasingly through mass media. Surely, public history is not only narratives nominally identified as historical but also the very communicative community created by mass media where a vision of a common reality of media users is laid out in discourses that also define what is new, controversial and debatable, on the one hand, and what is historical and commonsensical on the other. Mass media is a radically contextualized producer of history in as much as its prime concern is the direct acceptance of its discourse of history by the consumers. In a sense, mass media seek to represent the reality of its consumers so direct

---

332. Gur-Ze'ev 2003: 29

and fast that it is a reality which is only recognized by the consumers as real on TV. In this respect mass media is a shaper of the optics through which the totality of the real is perceived. Occasionally, as I will discuss in relation to the Israeli TV series *Tekumah*, public history in the mass media is overtaken by other, stronger, experiences of reality. TV can also be produced in a utopian moment that is itself history when the programme is eventually broadcasted. Then public history has the potential of escaping its role as producer of self-evidence for a moment until re-normalized by public interests. The *Tekumah* series was indeed such a public history which can be viewed and analyzed from several perspectives. Aired in 1998 as the highpoint of mass media commemoration of Israel's 50th anniversary with the aim of unifying and celebrating the nation, it instead came to be viewed as intellectualistic, post-Zionist propaganda. I will in the following discuss a number of contexts through which we can read the history presented in *Tekumah* as the history of 1990s Israeli liberalism.[333]

The *Tekumah* series has been discussed a number of times in relation to the so-called post-Zionism debates and the debate over the new historians. The series has often been represented as evidence for post-Zionist influence on the media and academia though this has been denied by the producers of the series.[334] I will try to transcend these politically local and contextual debates about the series and view it from both the angle of critical theory as the ruling system's reproduction of itself and from a contextualized perspective of creating a history of the present in the Israeli public. At the conception of the series right after the signing of the declaration of principles in 1993, this present was a utopian moment where huge openings of possibilities appeared between Israelis and Palestinians and this moment heavily influenced the entire historical perspective of the series. Thus, there seems to be two interwoven lines open for interpretation in the series namely the degree of reproduction of the hitherto hegemonic historical discourses of Zionism and the specific historical moment which indeed did present the possibility of creating a history that was at the same time a break with Zionist history and completely legitimate as public history.

---

333. The liberalism and optimism of peacemaking, globalization and economic growth as also discussed in the anthology *Peacemaking and Liberalization* by Shafir and Peled (2000).
334. Pappé 1998, Green 1998.

***

Ilan Gur-Ze'ev tells us that the Israeli and the Palestinian collective are determined to aim for the destruction of the other collective. Israelis and Palestinians are as collectives created by normalizing educational systems which actually have a twofold purpose that are the destruction of the other's collective identity/memory and the negation of the individual human being. The other's collective memory is conceived as being the negation of the legitimacy of the claims of one's own history and identity which in the most explicit manner is the case for the Israeli and Palestinian collectives.[335] The aim of destroying the collective memory of the other is a community building strategy that is basically a general negation of otherness which separates the real and genuine from the false and ideologically constructed. It creates the common knowledge of the authenticity of the "we" and de-centres the otherness of the other to a permanent outside the realm of common sense. To the logic of collectivism the negation of the individual is central. To genuinely identify the individual with the collective and for the individual to conceive of her own identity as identical with the collective representation of it, individual difference or otherness must be erased. Sameness and collectivism rule when histories, ideologies and literatures can legitimately or uncontested create discourses which claim to represent or claim to be an icon of the real history or experience of a proper name. Thus, the concern for this normalizing education project is not the individual's self-creation in a dialogue with others and the system but the reproduc-

---

335. The fear of the righteousness of the claims of the other to the real natural and historical relationship to the land is itself a producer of violence. Traces of the other's history in the land are systematically being erased or re-described in a way that does not challenge the nationalist claim to the land. Part of this effort is the description of the Jews as being solely a religious community which Zionism transferred into a colonialist movement and another aspect is the radical hebraization of Palestine after the 1948 war. The Palestinian geography was both physically and culturally erased or re-described and the Palestinians themselves driven out of the land or placed under military administration until 1966 when Zionist hegemony was thoroughly established. Still, a ghost of the former cultural identity of the land haunted Israeli culture from particularly the 1960s onwards most clearly reflected by A.B. Yehoshua's short story *Facing the Forests* (Yehoshua 1968) and the debates over Yizhar's *Hirbet Hiza* and *The Prisoner* (1949) in several rounds. See Benvenisti 2000 and Shapira 2000.

tion of the system as a guardian of a collective history and identity. In this way, Israeli history, Israeli institutions and Israeli media are reproducers and guardians of the history and identity of a proper name, not the individuals inhabiting the geography of Israel and Palestine. Israel as a system becomes through the official narratives of the state the guardian of the memory of Jewish suffering, the guardian of the memory of the Holocaust and the guardian of the tale of liberation in 1948. These are the narratological cornerstones of Israeli history and identity.[336] The above basically draws on the insights of the school of critical theory and its concern for the individual in opposition to instrumental rationality, collective reasoning and mechanical reproduction. In this perspective, the mechanical reproduction of culture, history and identity via the modern state and the capitalist system are violences against the individual human being and the possibility of transcendence, art, spirit, creativity and other humanistic attributes to human nature.[337] In general, critical theory is highly critical towards mass communication media such as TV even though the theorists very early had a clear understanding of the importance of TV and films for the culture of late capitalism. The position towards mass media such as TV of Horkheimer and Adorno in the *Dialectic of Enlightenment* and Marcuse in *One-Dimensional Man* might seem

---

336. This guardianship prevail it must be noted, in negation of the way of life and traditions of the Diaspora. The memory is safeguarded not to remember the Diaspora but to negate it with the moral lesson that Zionism and Israel is the only way to preserve the Jewish name. Of course, the same logic dominates all other national educational systems.
337. Experts on critical theory can surely identify substantial differences between Horkheimer, Adorno, Benjamin and Marcuse and several phases in their thought. To the purposes of this present essay, it suffices to note the general occupation with man's freedom and the critique of enlightenment, positivism and science. Actually, Marcuse saw the welfare state and the warfare state as an interplay of systems operating in the advanced societies. The welfare state takes man's freedom by taking possession of his time and the warfare state makes him think about the enemy instead of his own society. Mass media communication creates a togetherness and abolishes the distinction between private and public; the state, the corporations and the workers are gradually united and society moves towards a state of administration which is a totalitarian society just without terror. If we replace the Cold War with the Israeli-Palestinian conflict, Israel could be such a welfare-warfare state. Marcuse 1964: 19. Already in 1944, Adorno and Horkheimer envisioned that TV would amount to a total experience that will make it irrelevant to even hide that its products are all the same. Adorno and Horkheimer 1944: 179-180.

outdated today in the light of the rapid developments of such media and the theories thereof. Nevertheless, their understanding of mass media as a producer of the Same and togetherness seems right to the point or at least one of the points of mass media. Mass media's bottom line is still money making as it was when Horkheimer and Adorno published *Dialectic of Enlightenment* in 1944; things on top of this are just an ideology to justify the uniformity of mass media products. In Horkheimer and Adorno's phrasing, it is a circle of manipulation and retroactive need, which reinforces the strength of the system.[338] From a critical point of view, the question becomes whether this perspective can cover the role of mass media in an era of globalization when mass media communication can be said to be at the same time a producer of global togetherness and uniformity and a key element of the erosion of the cultural particularity of the nation state. Mass media indeed reinforces a system through production of the same but it also undermines other systems such as a national media culture. In this way, the development of Israeli media is not different from that of other advanced societies. Israeli media of the 1990s was highly globalized in its cultural aesthetics and in its variety of products and the TV-series *Tekumah* attempted to be, at once, globalized in its expression and discourse and to frame a particular national experience. The *Tekumah* series creates, as we will see, a particular positive optimism as national history anchored on the one side of the striving forces of the historical moment of the first half of the 1990s. Yet, it reproduced a historical plot of the reproduction of the Israeli system that only aspired to newness due to the fragility of the moment.

There are diverse theories of the role played by mass media in the production, distribution and reception of history and the ways this role influence or has changed patterns of collective memory in a society.[339] TV-series, both drama and documentary, are widely held to be the most important source of historical knowledge for the average citizen of advanced societies. The perspective on this development is most often critical from a positivist historical position where the concern is the precision of the information provided by TV and the shallowness of the inevitable focus on biography and iconic events.[340] TV focuses primarily

---

338. Horkheimer and Adorno 1944: 179.
339. See Landy 2001 and Edgerton & Rollins 2001.
340. Edgerton 2001: 1-16.

on narrative and biography, which serve perfectly TV's personalization of presented public events. Histories without a clear narrative line, clearcut heroes or villains are not TV material or are re-described to meet the requirements of good TV entertainment. At the same time, immediacy is of paramount importance to TV-history. Histories on TV have to be immediately recognizible to the average consumer. The consequence of this TV parameter is that the relevance of the history presented on TV for contemporary public discourses is very direct and commonsensical. Great national TV histories such as the *Tekumah* (Israel 1998), *Roots* (USA 1977), *Holocaust* (USA 1978), *Heimat* (Germany 1984), though three of the mentioned are dramas, represent important themes in contemporary cultural and political discourses in a highly personalized manner and have a high re-creative potential on both knowledge and public awareness of the actuality of certain historical events.[341] Surely, there are differences between history as documentary and history as drama but documentaries such as the *Tekumah* employ the individual narratives in an equally important manner. History is personalized as experiences of Israeli men and women, soldiers, farmers, mothers and fathers who are interviewed in a way for the viewers to feel the emotions of the time and most importantly the commonality between the interviewees and "us". The footage that accompanies the interviews places the interviewees in the dramas of the past as people caught in the storm of history as both agents and victims at the same time. The documentary base of series such as the *Tekumah* is plotted and narrated as drama in itself.

The concern for the quality of the history presented on TV and the critique of TV as an instrument of state, market and capital to normalize individuals into collectives such as consumers, Israelis, Danes or Americans are not the same. The concern for the quality of the history

---

341. The same can be said about historical films. The important debate after Steven Spielberg's *Schindler's List* over how to represent the Holocaust shows us some of the dilemmas of history on TV or film. Claude Lanzmann, who directed the film *Shoah*, was very critical towards Spielberg's dramatized and personalized Holocaust commemoration. Lanzmann argued that the Holocaust could not be replayed as a narrative of survival when it is both unrepresentable and a narrative of death. Lanzmann's and others' concern was that the history of the Holocaust as both plot and moral lesson after *Schindler's List* had been altered in a way that challenged the core of Holocaust memory. See Miriam Bratu Hansen's analysis of both the debate and *Schindler's List*. Hansen 2001.

product on TV with regard to the facts of the past is largely irrelevant to our purposes here. The media of collective memory is TV and a focus on what actually happened in the past in a critique of this development basically misses the point.[342] Instead, a focus on what kind of history is presented on TV is relevant. The relevant questions in this present essay are questions that address history on TV from the perspective of critical theory and investigate possible discursive openings in the Israeli context that could alter the position of TV history as mere official history. Such a contextualization of the *Tekumah* will point to tendencies of change in the historical discourse of Israeli public conversation in the 1990s.

Commemorative History

History, memory and their prime media TV are sites of discursive struggles even under the perspective of critical theory. History, collective memory and TV are official histories in the sense that they are in general controlled and distributed top-down through culture, institutions and mechanisms for controlling their allegiance to the conventions of historical discourse in a society. From a critical perspective they are in principle non-oppositional. Still, within hegemony there are generally accepted margins for social, political and historical dissent and in this respect alternative histories of minorities can operate the field of memory and become a challenge to hegemony. Michel Foucault stated that: "Since memory is actually a very important factor in struggle, if one controls people's memory, one controls their dynamism. And one also controls their experience, their knowledge of previous struggles."[343] In Foucault's perspective, memory control becomes gradually more and more effective with the development of TV and films and it hinders a presumed previous flow of collective memory; flows that are "reprogrammed" by these mass communication apparatuses.[344] Like Horkheimer, Adorno and Marcuse, Foucault seems to believe that control has increased in

---

342. Netta Ha-Ilan's interesting study shows how the Israeli news shows on TV are the most important producer and distributor of collective memory. In these shows, daily events are framed in historical plots that are very important to creating a togetherness and collective memory between the viewers. Ha-Ilan 2001.
343. Foucault cited from Anderson 2001: 22.
344. Ibid. 22.

modern (and postmodern) societies and that the, in Foucault's term, reprogramming of memory represented by modern mass communication media is a hindrance to creativity and freedom.[345] Despite these reservations and criticisms of the possibility of counter-history in a world of global mass communication, marked and open social and political conflicts within a society such as the Israeli can create a context in which TV history and other commemorative histories can both represent state interests and function partially, not as counter-history, but as alternative, critical history.[346]

The Israeli state, institutions and culture produce and reproduce commemorative history in school books, museums, political discourse, the arts and the media.[347] The icons and myths of commemorative history are not eternally fixed but are re-described or re-placed over time in response to socio-cultural development and changed public reception.[348] These changes are not changes that question the legitimacy of

---

345. Others like Michael Curtin argue that TV does not reprogram memories as a control mechanism but it organizes and re-organizes difference within the global economic order. In his perspective, TV does not homogenize identities but it organizes them on the global arena in a hierarchy of values and attitudes that are designated to certain places. Curtin 2001:338. I do not find the two perspectives incompatible. When TV functions as a producer and distributor of a global hierarchy of values and attitudes and fixes these values to places through the creation of icons representing the values of certain places as in nature documentaries, adventure programmes, ethnographies and political reports, power and control is the precondition for the ability to create a hierarchy. The power to organize and re-organize to a large extent equals control. Yet, Curtin's argument is important for reminding us that TV distributes a synthetic organization of cultural difference and that TV does not make Asians into Americans but actually contributes to a fixation of such identities.
346. Counter-history in the Foucaultian sense can not be part of the hegemonic system. Foucault following Nietzsche argued for a counter-history in three steps: 1. Against realism – official history or monumental history. 2. Against identity – history that conceals the heterogeneous systems that make the self. 3. Against truth – history that conceals that knowledge rests upon injustice. Foucault 1977: 163. The *Tekumah* is in no way that critical but it attempts to include or domesticate a Palestinian narrative which in itself is not a counter-history to Israeli history but a mirror-history. Counter-history is per definition equally critical towards both Israeli and Palestinian history.
347. Zerubavel 1995, Ha-Ilan 2001.
348. Zerubavel 1995 shows how central Zionist myths have a history of uses and receptions since their invention. She tracks the working of myths such as Masada and Josef Trumpeldor from the 1920s until our time.

the commemorative history itself but are part of its reproduction. The most important aspects of Israel's commemorative history are focused on Holocaust memory and the establishment of the state in 1948. These two historical events are intertwined as a metahistorical function of each other. Palestinian history is conceived as a denial of both the Holocaust and the historical justice of the rebirth of the Israeli nation which is why the Israeli-Palestinian conflict is the generator of the sanctity of particularly these aspects of Israeli commemorative history.[349] The critical engagement in both Holocaust memory and 1948 by academics and intellectuals since the late 1980s has not changed commemorative practice or the broad public acceptance of this practice which in line with Gur-Ze'ev's argument is due to the perpetuation of the conflict.[350] Israeli commemorative history thus upholds events that are highly important to the collective self-identity of Jewish Israelis but this history is at the same time an active partner in concealing the injustices this knowledge is based on and the conflicts it is engaged in. It represents not the individual Israeli but the ideology of the collective.[351] In this perspective, the promises of peace made in the early 1990s opened for the possibility of a different commemorative history of which the *Tekumah* was the first large and prestigious product.

The Tekumah-series

In his 1998 review of *Tekumah,* Ilan Pappé wrote that the series was almost post-Zionist in its presentation of Israeli history. Pappé's review appeared in *Journal of Palestine Studies* after he earlier in three consecutive articles in the same journal had explored the key word of Israeli cultural debates of the 1990s, namely post-Zionism:

> "But while the history is still told as a Zionist story, there are indications that there is a counterstory as well. The fact that the other side's story does not receive as much coverage as the Zionist one creates an imbalance that might dictate to the viewer whose story is more truthful. Still, the programme on several occasions provides

---

349. Gur-Ze'ev 2003: 25-50.
350. Among the critical works are Segev 1986, 1993, Zertal 1998, Morris 1987, Pappé 1992, Shlaim 1988.
351. Of which Etgar Keret's short story *Siren* is an example. Keret 2002.

verification by Israeli participants of Palestinian claims. Indeed, at times even the narrator himself presents the Palestinian view as just, and in so doing leaves an ambiguous and probably confused impression with the viewers"[352]

Pappé's prism is that of the specific coining of the term post-Zionism that he himself has been one of the most important shapers of. Pappé judges the series solely from a commonsensical perspective of the level of truth and justice attributed to the Palestinian historical narrative. The episode that Pappé refers to in the citation is about the 1948 war in which several Israeli participants, now old men, give testimony to the fact that they witnessed and even participated in creating the Palestinian exodus. These sequences are indeed among the most important in the series but the testimony of the elderly men is not in principle the same as deeming the Palestinian historical narrative just and the Zionist unjust. Pappé's review shows some of the ideological and identity-political stakes of a series such as *Tekumah*. It seems as if Pappé wants that the series should devote as much time to the Palestinians as to the Israelis in what is an Israeli history. This is surely part of an internal Israeli anti-Zionist struggle which basically aims at replacing Israeli history with Palestinian. This approach does not solve the problem of totalizing histories or has any counter-historical perspective because Palestinian history is not counter-history it is mirror-history, as previously mentioned. Other critics of the series such as government ministers Ariel Sharon and Limor Livnat also focus on the presence of a Palestinian historical perspective and they also think that its presence casts shadows over Zionist achievements but from the opposite point of view. They think that the Palestinian narrative does not belong at all in an Israeli history.[353] Both examples point to the Palestinian historical narrative as opposition to and even negation of

---

352. Pappé 1998: 99. Pappé's articles on post-Zionism were the first to attempt a coherent analysis of the buzz-word of the 1990s. I find Pappé's attempt rather unsuccessful. Pappé does not differentiate clearly between political, ideological and social developments and attributes to post-Zionism as mixture of philosophical insights and political ideologies which primarily serve to legitimize post-Zionism as the position of a re-organized radical Left to which Pappé himself belongs. Pappé fails in bringing the term post-Zionism to mean something beyond a certain political opinion on Zionism and the Israeli-Palestinian conflict. Pappé 1997a, 1997b, 1997c.
353. Green 1998.

Zionism but from opposite poles that show us the spectrum of the Israeli struggle over memory. The optics of both Pappé and Sharon-Livnat are oppositional to the ideological legacy of *Tekumah* which can be characterized as Oslo-optimism.[354] These critics do not engage in the question of commemorative history's normalizing project in a principled manner but advocate its replacement with another normalizing project. Thus, their perspectives are not against history, identity and truth or the culture industry only these concepts' particular representations in *Tekumah*. In the following, I will attempt to analyze whether *Tekumah* itself contains counter-historical perspectives.

***

The *Tekumah* series consists of 22 episodes of one hour duration each. Each episode treats a period or a theme of Israeli history which is conventionally regarded as important to the history of the nation. The first three episodes deal with the Jewish settlement in Palestine, the period after World War II and the 1948 war and these episodes serve as an introduction to and the central plot of the entire series. In the three inaugural episodes, the meta-narrative of Zionist history is presented through historical events that are of great importance to collective memory in Israel; Zionism, the Holocaust and the 1948 war. Other significant episodes of *Tekumah* deal with the integration of Arab Jews in Israel, the Palestinian minority within Israel, the Palestinian struggle against Israel and the mutual recognition of Israelis and Palestinians in 1993.[355] I have singled out a number of sequences from some of these episodes to consider as both aesthetic, historical and moral statements within the context of mass media communication and the production of culture.

Tekumah was conceived as a unifying narrative to commemorate Israel's 50th anniversary in 1998. It was produced by the IBA (Israel Broadcasting Authority) which since the beginning of public TV broadcasting in the 1960s has been the official institution for the production, distribution

---

354. I will return to this theme after presenting aspects of *Tekumah*.
355. The question of significance is of course subjective. In my version, the episodes that deal with the contested history between Israelis and Palestinians and between Israelis are significant for the critical perspective of counter-history and for an evaluation of level of conformity with hegemony that the series presents.

and organization of Israeli TV.[356] Therefore, it can be considered official and commemorative history. The 22 episodes of *Tekumah* ran on Israeli TV in the spring of 1998. The individual episodes were introduced by Israeli singer and cultural icon Yehoram Gaon and narrated by Yigal Naor. The choices of Gaon and Naor as presenters of the series represent the integrative agenda behind the series. Gaon is a *Mizrahi* Jew who has made it to the centre of Israeli culture and Naor is a former *Palmach* commander who incarnates the Israeli Man with his military elite background and pure *Ashkenazi* accent. Anyway, during the production of the series Gaon quitted his job as presenter due to the public debate it aroused and in particular due to the episode about the Palestinian struggle against Israel.[357] Executive producer and chief editor of *Tekumah* was Gideon Drori who took the initiative of the series and conceptualized it. The series itself was directed by 19 different Israeli directors. According to Drori, facing criticism, the series was not intended to be post-Zionist or outright pro-Palestinian, as some critics claimed, but indeed Zionist only of a dynamic 1990s type.[358] To my mind, Drori's statements in the face of criticism capture the dynamism of this particular historical moment. The *Tekumah*, produced by the IBA, was surely intended to be commemorative and ceremonial[359] which its entire picture-sound impression testifies to, but it furthermore intended to be progressive in line with the cultural

---

356. IBA has since 1965 been the authorized institution for Israeli TV broadcasting. It is directed by a board appointed by the political parties according to their parliamentary representation. Only in 1993 monopoly was broken and private news and history programmes could be broadcasted as Israeli TV. The public and representative control of the IBA reflects a concern for public service, education and collective memory but also a political struggle for the control of the same. See Ha-Ilan: 208.
357. It is not entirely clear whether Gaon quitted or was made to quit. It is clear though that the reason was the public debate the series aroused. The issue was debated broadly in Israeli media at the time. See e.g. Green 1998.
358. ibid.
359. The preferred term of Netta Ha-Ilan. Ceremonial history is a history that affects people emotionally and creates bonds between them. It is part of a society's social knowledge that assists the creation of the experience of "us". It is an emotionally based knowledge, not necessarily cognitive or ideological. I find that Ha-Ilan's concept of ceremonial history is not entirely the same as commemorative history. Ha-Ilan's focus is on knowledge while my use of the term commemorative emphasizes differences between histories in a typological manner. Thus, the terms are not meant to be interchangeable. Ha-Ilan 2001: 227.

debates of the early 1990s and reflects the potential of the Declaration of Principles and the economic boom of the time. These developments were met with a large sceptical opposition in Israel who were sceptical not only to the peace negotiations with the Palestinians but also towards globalization in particular its cultural dimension.[360] At the same time, the entire regional as well as global contexts that should ensure the success of the Oslo-negotiations were highly volatile which made the total investment in liberal discourse of the series quite premature. Therefore, the *Tekumah* came to reflect memory struggles in Israeli society between sides battling for hegemony.[361] Gaon, Naor and Drori are as characters aspects of this struggle and worked to universalize the historical memory presented in *Tekumah* as the history of all Israel. This is probably what Ilan Pappé saw as an ambiguity in the series which might translate into confusion for the viewers.

The visual side of *Tekumah* is characterized by classic Zionist themes. Each episode has as its introduction a sweeping aerial perspective that moves between images of past and present underscored by a dramatic and emotional sound image. The pictures show the flourishing fields of Israel and its labouring inhabitants. The image presented of the land is clearly dynamic with a focus on progress and the achieved prosperity intertwined with classic romantic themes of the beauty and innocence of the Homeland. To be sure, the visual and audio introduction to the episodes is a remnant of the modernistic, Zionist and progressive epic with its emphasis on the working of the land, conquering it from the wilderness and integrating it into civilized nature.[362] We should not underestimate the affect of headlines and introductions in the reception of a historical narrative or news story for that matter. The headline and the subsequent framing of the narrative are both a plot and a trope for the historical discourse and as such it has already established a meta-historical context and the type of discourse. In the first episode, we are introduced to the so-called "Generation in the Land" which refers to the nativized Jews in Palestine who build the Jewish pre-state community. The episode

---

360. Ram 1999, Shafir and Peled 2002.
361. Here, it is important to recall Foucault's argument that the one that controls memory controls both action and experience.
362. *Tekumah* can be purchased in its entirety as video. I refer to the series of videos published by IBA in 1998.

deals with the period from 1936 to 1946. Accordingly, the focus is on the Arab-Palestinian uprising from 1936 to 1939, the influx of refugees from Europe but also on the culture of the pioneer-generation. The pioneers are Zionist icons who established settlements, drained swamps, worked the land and defended themselves if necessary. In *Tekumah*'s first episode they are presented with some nostalgia and several times with the adjective "very ideological". This reference is in the episode made to the pioneering youth movements and some former pioneers are interviewed about the movements and life in general in the times of the *Yishuv*.[363] Several times in the first episode the issue of the Palestinian presence in the land is touched upon. An elderly woman says: "We didn't know that it was somebody else's land". In the interview with this woman and other veterans of the days of pre-state settlement retrospective comments on the right to the land and justice in the Jewish settlement enterprise are numerous which reflects the contemporary concern on this issue and the legitimacy of such debates in the 1990s. The Palestinian uprising and resistance against Jewish immigration are not portrayed as terrorist activity but as a sort of misunderstanding of Zionist intent and lack of recognition of the catastrophe facing European Jewry from the 1930s onwards. The conflict between Jews and Palestinians before the 1948 war is articulated within the liberal Zionist discourse which measures the situation as a tragedy where the major evil (anti-Semitism) leads to a lesser evil (Palestinian uprooting and eventually expulsion).[364] The tragic portrait of the situation is in concordance with the rather sinister and low-key description of the historical events that are cornerstones of Zionist memory. These event are clearly viewed with a historical distance that transforms the representation of the events from a rejoicing and celebratory mode to a more bitter-sweet, nostalgic memory with a clear awareness of the pain and suffering involved for the people who lived that historical moment. This historical distance is not purely chronological. It is the result of changing social configurations, cultural and historical re-descriptions that surely grant legitimacy to the ideologies and actions of the period but at the same time construct a reflexive distance. Among these changes, the peace process of the early 1990s and the debate about

---

363. Yishuv means settlement in Hebrew and is the most common term for the Jewish pre-state community particularly in Zionist and pro-Zionist literature.
364. *Tekumah* episode 1.

the new historians were the most important. In the liberal Zionist discourse of *Tekumah*, the history of the Generation in the Land is not a call for action or a model of imitation. The relation between the historical events and the present is not linear and determinative. It is an emotional and cultural relation like a heritage that does not prevent the present and ultimately the future from being all together different.[365]

The episode about the generation in the land is followed by an episode entitled *A State in the Making*. The focus in this episode is on the first years after WWII up to the UN resolution that decided to partition Palestine between Jews and Palestinians in November 1947. As a piece of TV production it is almost completely similar to the first episode. The line of narration is continued and many of the same people are interviewed to account for the history of this period. Among the new interviewees are Meir Davidson, a veteran of the Givati brigade, and Yacoba Cohen who served in an intelligence unit. Davidson and Cohen add considerable ambivalence to the narrative as they emphasize the horrors and injustices that are flipsides of the heroism which the Jewish-Israeli actions usually are plotted within. Cohen was an undercover agent posing as a Palestinian in Haifa's Palestinian neighbourhoods. He is very moved by this memory and the fact that he personally knew the people who were uprooted. He eventually met personal friends of his as refugees in Lebanon and recalls this event as horrible. The interview with Cohen is very emotionally charged and appears central to the episode due to the affect of his display of feelings for the enemy and representation of the events as tragic. The personalized history of *Tekumah* works effectively as a bonding between these veterans and the new historical moment of the 1990s in which their sorrows, pains and regrets can be integrated with their strong sense of national pride. The perspective that emanates from the interviews with Davidson and Cohen perfectly fits producer Drori's idea of a modern, dynamic Zionism capable of looking the past into the eye, recognize the tragedies of history and still be proud of the achievements of this history.

In *A State in the Making* we find another interesting sequence. Golda Meir was one of the leaders of the Zionist organisation. She spearheaded

---

365. This un-linear representation of the past and its bitter-sweet nostalgia are signs of the atmosphere of liberal optimism of series. The present of the production of the series is clearly understood as "better" than the described past.

negotiations with King Abdallah of Jordan regarding the status of Palestine after the withdrawal of British forces and eventually became Prime Minister of Israel from 1969-74.[366] Meir was furthermore known for her hardliner position on the conflict with the Palestinians. In the episode a section from Meir's report to the Jewish Agency is read aloud. Meir describes how she felt when she came to Haifa under the Palestinian flight from the city.[367] She pays particular attention to the empty houses which were left in a hurry with coffee still standing on the tables and rooms full of furniture and things as if their inhabitant were just out shortly. Meir comments that it must have looked like this in many cities in Europe just a few years ago. This chilling comment casts light on the magnitude of the Palestinian disaster in an imagery very central to Israeli collective history and it further revises the common impression of Meir as intransigent and unsympathetic to the Palestinians. From the perspective of Israeli commemorative history the sequence with Meir's visit to Haifa is highly revisionist as she was one of icons of the denial of the Palestinians' rights to Palestine and placed in middle of the spectrum of Israeli politics as a historical leader and heiress of Ben-Gurion's Zionism.

The third episode of *Tekumah* is entitled *The Silver Platter* after a poem by Nathan Alterman. It refers to the birth of the state in May 1948 and the 1948 war which began in earnest after the declaration of independence on the 14th of May. Alterman's poem celebrates the birth of the new Jewish nation with lines like these: "Heartsick, but still living, a people stand by/ to greet the uniqueness/ of the miracle// Readied, they wait beneath the moon,/ wrapped in awesome joy, before the light./ Then, soon,/ a boy and a girl step forward/ and slowly walk before the waiting nation.[368] Alterman's poem is about the rebirth of the Jewish nation out of 2000 years of suppression. It has the qualities of the epic drama that presents a vision of the totality of history from one beginning to the next. Out of the chaos and terror of history steps the collective subject,

---

366. In Shlaim 2001 Meir's work in the period is treated extensively.
367. Haifa was the first city from which the Palestinians fled from the beginning of December 1947 until April 1948. Morris 1987:41-45.
368. Alterman 1973: 154. Regarding the translation, I follow the selected and translated reading material for Remembrance Day and Independence Day in Israel published on the Israeli Foreign Ministry's web site: www.mfa.gov.il/MFA/History/Modern%20History/Israel%20at%2050/Selected%20Readings%20for%20Remembrance%20Day 30.09.2004. Translator unknown.

afraid but willing to take action. History is collectivized to the ultimate extent in a few lines, which incarnate a cosmology of Zionism where the emotions of the Jewish "we" are articulated. On the surface, the title *The Silver Platter* could seem ambiguous considering the hardships endured by the Zionists and the refugees from Europe under the 1948 war when the outcome was unclear to the participants. But, if we consider the particular place for youth and youth movements in the Zionist ideology of renewal and the following lines of Alterman, we find a tribute to the young Israeli soldier:

> In work garb and heavy shod
> They climb
> In stillness
> Wearing yet the dress of battle, the grime
> Of aching day and fire-filled night
>
> Unwashed, weary unto death, not knowing
> Rest
> But wearing youth like dew drops in their hair
> Silently the two approach
> And stand
> Are they of the quick or of the dead?
>
> Through wondering tears, the people stare
> "who are you, the silent two?
> And they reply: "we are the silver platter"
> Upon which the Jewish state was served to
> You.[369]

The Silver Platter thus refers to the young people who created the Jewish state on the battlefields on the 1948 war and served it to the Jews. As the title of one of the key episodes of *Tekumah*, it serves to capture the tragedy, the glory and the dept to the veterans who made the historical vision of the Zionists real. The reference to Alterman's poem makes this episode a particularly powerful trope for the historical discourse of the series.

The Silver Platter also makes use of Givati veteran Meir Davidson as a character who personifies the Zionist youth who made the vision of Jewish independence real. This episode in particular goes into detail

---

369. Alterman 1973: 154-155.

with the horror of the fighting and it does not spare the viewers of the injustices committed by the Zionist side. The ideology of Zionist heroism has conventionally presented the violence committed by Zionism and Israel as defence and as conducted by an ethic of so-called purity of arms. Zionist and Israeli weapons were simply not applied as a way of creating horror and bloodshed but as a reluctant and as pure as possible way to defend the higher goals of Jewish freedom. Meir Davidson's testimony in *Tekumah* thoroughly revises this ideology as an unconscious mirror of Benny Morris' book *The Birth of the Palestinian Refugee Problem, 1947-1949*. Davidson comments both on the expulsion of the inhabitants of Lydda-Ramle region in centre of the country and on what actually happened in the course of fighting. He recalls that: "The villages burned like bonfires" and replies to a question about the so-called purity of arms that: "Who speaks about purity of arms? There is no such thing as pure arms." Davidson states this as a commonsensical refutation of a more or less ridiculous ideological claim and therefore he strikes at the heart of the romance of the 1948 war. Along the same vein, the narrator and Davidson speak about the expulsions of the inhabitants of the region Lydda-Ramle and both clearly give the impression that the orders to expel these Palestinians came directly from the top and were executed by Yitzhak Rabin.[370] These sequences of *The Silver Platter* are almost a perfect reflection of the description of the same events in Morris' *The Birth of the Palestinian Refugee Problem* and as such enter directly in the polemic over the new historians but as a univocal statement from a participant.[371]

In *The Silver Platter,* there is also a reference to one of Ben-Gurion's grander designs for a Middle East re-worked by the 1948 war. A passage from Ben-Gurion's diary is referred to in which he contemplates on the

---

370. In Hebrew the word for expulsion is "girush" which is used directly by the narrator without any circumventions.
371. In fact, Benny Morris was consultant on this particular episode and he can only be satisfied with the result as it is almost a remake of his book just as a TV documentary. The Lydda-Ramle expulsions were the largest direct expulsions of Palestinians during the 1948 war. 40.000-50.000 thousand people were expelled by direct order from Ben-Gurion who with the military leadership considered the expulsion a strategic move. The towns had surrendered but the Zionist leadership wished to flood the roads towards Jordan with refugees to prevent an attack from the Arab Legion and to burden the economy of the Legion as much as possible. Lydda and Ramle were re-populated with Jewish refugees from Europe. Morris 1987: 207-212.

possible scenario if the war was to fall out in the most hopeful way in a Zionist understanding. This particular passage shows that the Zionists did not indorse UN resolution 181 on the partition of Palestine to more than a practical extent. The passage reads as follows:

> "We should establish a Christian state in Lebanon whose southern border would be the Litani. We shall conclude an alliance with it. When we have broken the force of the Arab Legion we shall annihilate Transjordan, and then Syria would fall. And if the Egyptians dare continue fighting, we shall bombard Port Said, Alexandria and Cairo."[372]

Ben-Gurion's wishful thinking of the above clearly reflects that the Zionists had ambitions for the Palestinian region and did not consider visions such as Ben-Gurion's out of place. The making of a new order for the Palestinian region was, it seems, among the Zionist perspectives for engaging in the war of 1948. This was a perspective that was obviously not only concerned with the defence of the Jewish settlements but it was concerned with creating facts on the ground that would radically alter the partition resolution approved in the UN through expansion of the Israeli territory, destruction of the prospected Palestinian state and political changes in the surrounding Arab states.[373] The insertion of this passage from Ben-Gurion's diary in *The Silver Platter* shows that the producer of the series considered it a part of his dynamic Zionism that the Zionists of the 1948 war not only defended the establishment of the Jewish state but also actively worked for the expansion of its territory and for its Judaization. Such a perspective would be quite unthinkable in relation to the logic of the purity of arms and David against Goliath representations that are at the centre of Israeli collective memory. This does not mean, though, that veterans such as Davidson appear to be non-Zionist or especially critical because they do indeed underline the difficulties facing the Zionist forces and the heroism and entrepreneurship the situation demanded of them. The veterans interviewed in *Tekumah*

---

372. These lines are also quoted in Pappe 1992: 141.
373. The vision of Ben-Gurion has been a permanent perspective in Israeli politics with disastrous effects such as the Lebanon war 1982-2000 where the objectives of Begin and Sharon were very similar to Ben-Gurion's grand design of 1948.

simply appear to be realistic in their assessment of what happens during wars such as the 1948 war where aspects of ethnic, civil and conventional war intermingled. Meir Davidson, Yacuba Cohen and the others are in the historical narrative of *Tekumah* the silver platter on which the Jewish state was served to the people. The Zionist youth achieved this in an ugly, bloody and tragic war during which many unjust deeds were committed but out of chaos the Jewish state arose. The core of the Zionist historical narrative remains intact but its tarnish of purity and innocence is stained. The producer of *Tekumah*, Drori, and others involved in the production of the series refer to this openness as a sign of maturity.[374] We should however consider the fact that the possibility of looking at the past as something other, but related culturally and emotionally to the present, stems from discursive and structural conditions of the present in which the series is written. Maturity becomes a euphemism for stating that the present is better, things have been learned and other stages have been reached. *Tekumah's* historical presentation of the 1948 war reflects the producers' historical discourse and its conditions.

As the last of my presentations of sequences from the *Tekumah* I will shortly discuss the episode entitled *Ingathering of the Exiles* which is number four out of the 22. The four episodes singled out here deal with the historical situation around the establishment of the state and that is why they are central for an analysis of the history presented in the series in general. They simply lay out the discourse that was intended to articulate the norm for the Israeli understanding of the birth of their state. *Ingathering of the Exiles* is of course also a Zionist ideological slogan that derives from the vision surrounding the idea of a Jewish state from the 1880s onwards but it was articulated directly in the Israeli Declaration of Independence as one of the most important goals of Israel and a work that immediately needed to be put in action.[375] In the episode, a sequence shows Ben-Gurion declaring that the ingathering of the exiles is one of Israel's most important tasks and he furthermore comments on the historical importance of gathering in Israel Jews. To Ben-Gurion,

---

374. Green 1998.
375. In different variations the slogan of "ingathering of the exiles" appears in Zionist writings from its earliest beginnings. It surely reflects not only a Zionist ideological dictum but also a much older messianic hope within Jewish religious tradition.

the Jewish collective "aliyah"[376] was a necessary step to save the Jews from persecution and discrimination. He included the Jews of the Arab countries as having the same need though is was primarily the displaced persons in Cyprus, Germany and elsewhere that needed rescuing in the immediate after-war period. To integrate the Arab Jews in a Zionist ideology based on European Jewish experiences and the European Jewish Holocaust was of high importance to the Zionist leaders. The primary reason for the importance of the Arab Jews was ideological, namely that Zionism claimed to be speaking on behalf of all Jews. Nationalist ideologies such as Zionism are based on historical and organic arguments that ascribe a natural and historico-cultural sense of togetherness to all Jews. When the nation is conceived as an extended family all Jewish populations become a target for integration into the family. A secondary reason for the importance of the Arab Jews was demographical. Control, development and expansion of the territory would be insured with a massive influx of immigrants.[377] The 1948 war obviously made the massive immigration of Arab Jews to Israel possible due to the engagement in it of virtually all the Arab countries.

The Arab Jews were largely un-acculturated to Zionism and the dominant European Jewish culture, which set the ideological and cultural agenda of Israel. At the same time, Zionism was thoroughly integrated in European colonialist and orientalist discourses that at once romanticized the Arab Jews and considered them inferior and basically uncivilized. Arab Jews were placed in satellite cities, transit camps and systematically stripped of as much of their Arab identity as possible in the process of re-educating them to Zionism. *Ingathering of the Exiles* emphasizes the really striking differences between e.g. Yemenite Jews and the completely modern, European ways of life in Israel. The episode shows much original

---

376. "Aliyah" means ascent in Hebrew and is in a Zionist connection used for the immigration to Israel.
377. Conditions for the Arab Jews did indeed deteriorate during the 1930s and 1940s over most of the Middle East but this was primarily caused by the political upheavals in the wake of colonialism, nationalism and the gradually increased awareness of Zionism as a threat to the rule over Palestine. The Zionists also conducted campaigns in the Arab countries to push Jews to immigrate to Israel. The gradually more difficult conditions for the Arab Jews was not caused by a transformation of historical anti-Semitism coupled with fascism as was the case in Europe from the 1880s onwards. See e.g. Stillman 1991.

footage from the transit camps and several veteran immigrants from the big waves of immigration are interviewed. These interviews often stress the social divisions of Israel and the cultural difference of Arab Jews even after 50 years of living in Israel.[378] In his review article of the *Tekumah*, Ilan Pappé also notes the chilling meeting between a former *Ashkenazi* volunteer to the transit camps and one Arab Jewish woman who met each other then. The Arab Jewish woman asks the former volunteer if she helped them because she was a Zionist or for human reasons.[379] This question illustrates the process of integration from the side of the ones to be integrated; the objects of a social, ideological experiment and a normalizing project. In general, this episode follows the line of presentation carried out by the other episodes in mention but it touches upon the sensitive issue of internal others. People who are Jews but still Arab pose a dilemma to the European nationalist and colonialist heritage of Zionism because among the central tenets of Zionism was exactly the normalization of Jews into a European nation with the same cultural and territorial dimensions. The Arab Jews also became an object of colonisation, which has resulted in major social, cultural and political divisions in Israel between *Ashkenazis* and *Mizrahis* since the 1950s. Despite its *Ashkenazi* and hegemonic perspective, this episode exhibits many of the basic divisions of Israeli society through original footage and interviews. The conflicts and cleavages of the integration project at the centre of the political goals of the young Israeli state are not presented as critical, subversive revelations against Zionism but as common sense.

Contextualizing Tekumah

The 1990s was a decade in Israeli history when this very history was re-described in many aspects. The first Gulf war, the election of the Rabin–

---

378. The journal *Theory and Criticism* has a number of times addressed the issue of racism and the suppression of Arab Jewish culture. Research in the history and culture of the so-called *Mizrahi* (Eastern) Jew has increased from the 1990s and researchers such as Hannan Hever, Amnon Raz-Krakotzkin, Yehuda Shenhav, Gabriel Piterberg and Ella Shohat have published significant books and articles about the subject. The episode of *Tekumah* about the integration of the Arab Jews does not involve the level of criticism applied by these authors but it nevertheless illustrates some of the points made by them. See e.g. Hever 2002, Shenhav 2002.
379. Pappé 1998: 104.

Peres government and the Declaration of Principles between Israelis and Palestinians meant real-political changes of the power structures of the Middle East and real-political changes between Israelis and Palestinians. In a nutshell, the first Gulf war enabled the isolation of the Palestinians from the political struggles of the wider Arab world and increased American active involvement in the region which empowered its ally Israel to take steps towards a settlement of the Israeli-Palestinian conflict. By and large, the Palestinians gave up their struggle for the lost homeland and accepted the rules of interaction set by Israel and USA. This proved to be a tremendous opportunity for Israel to settle the conflict and uphold most of the territorial, political and economical advances made through the hitherto permanent state of war. At the same time, major socio-economic changes took place in Israeli society. State involvement in the economy, the unions, health care and cultural institutions was reduced and re-organized in a development with many resemblances to the changes in the North European welfare states in the same period. These changes were basically seen by the governments as necessary to meet the demands of increased globalization. The effects of these changes are varied but among the central aspects are the privatisation of identity politics, individualization and an increased focus on a politics of values. The politics of economy and social structure are no longer the most contested areas between a left and a right. From the 1990s onwards, political divisions in advanced societies became re-organized along identity political lines in relation to which struggles over memory and imagination are central.[380] The technicalities and complexity of globalization, international capitalism and state-organisation-corporation interaction cannot be controlled, understood or explained by politicians in a singular perspective which makes the idea of real, controlled socio-structural change unviable.[381] Roughly put, the left-right perspective dominated by ideas of concrete and profound changes of the structures of society has been supplanted by a national-postnational perspective, in which single issues are articulated as to represent a central value of a national or post-national/cosmopolitan political position, as the major political line of division in Western

---

380. The above follows the descriptions formulated by Ram 2003 and Bauman 2000.
381. When it comes to concrete social change such as of capitalism and globalization the TINA (There Is No Alternative) principle rules.

societies.³⁸² In the Israeli context, these developments are basically of the same character but the dominance of the Israeli-Palestinian conflict in the shaping of Israeli politics and culture makes the conflict the central arena of which the changed political struggle took place.

Through the 1990s, Israel received several hundred thousand Russian immigrants of Jewish decent. This huge wave of immigration changed the demographics of Israeli society, led to new social and identity political conflicts and changes of the entire political spectrum. Former strategies of immigrant integration were given up on and the integration of the Russians relied on the forces of the market and minimal state involvement. State involvement was reduced to Hebrew language acquisition, housing and a minimal financial integration aid.³⁸³ The waning of the former Zionist educational project that the people of the immigration waves of the 1950s and 1960s experienced at full force, is one of the most obvious signs of the gradual dissolution of the modern Zionist project. The Russians in Israel challenge the received notions of Jewish nationality in as much as many of them never have lived with a strong Jewish self-identity, have not achieved one in Israel and do not even consider themselves Zionists. Many among the Russians simply wished for their immigration to Israel that it would lead to improved life conditions, not necessarily a new self-identity.³⁸⁴ The population influx of the 1990s contributed to the social, structural and discursive changes that made the 1990s a decade of memory and imagination struggles with the potential of decisive re-descriptions of Israeli history, experience and Israeli-Palestinian relations.

The foremost political icon of the developments in Israel of the 1990s was the so-called peace process between Israelis and Palestinians since 1993. In reality, this process was very soon taken of track and deprived of all its potential except in the international media which until this day still represent Israeli-Palestinian relations within the discourse established between 1993-95. Violence is in this discourse considered a setback as though there existed a peace process and the goal of the international community is to get the parties "back on track". This track was only open for passage in a short utopian moment between 1993-95

---

382. Ram 1999.
383. Shafir & Peled 2002: 308-334.
384. Shafir & Peled 2002: 308-334.

if even then. More significant for our perspectives, though, than the real-political development between Israelis and Palestinians which so far has only amounted to increased settlement activity, violence, terror and increased impoverishment of particularly the Palestinians but also the Israelis was the opening up of the struggles of memory and imagination most often referred to as post-Zionism. As previously mentioned, Ilan Pappé is among the key shapers of the discourse of post-Zionism.[385] In his series of articles in *Journal of Palestine Studies* Pappé explored the notion of post-Zionism and came to the conclusion that post-Zionism influenced academia, the arts and the media but not the general public. It was by and large an intellectual trend informing or at least influencing sections of Israeli mind-workers who increasingly accepted at least parts of the Palestinian historical narrative and leftwing critique of Zionism.[386] Pappé makes acceptance of the Palestinian historical narrative some kind of proof for the influence of post-Zionism which if re-formulated is convincing: The memory and imagination struggles have the Israeli-Palestinian conflict as well as the nature of Zionism as key topics and as icons of the value systems and historical discourses that the participants in the debates adhere to. The *Tekumah*-series simply became a site of contest because the iconic events and narratives that were integrated into a TV show can be considered both commonsensical and counter-historical at the same time. Thus, Palestinian History is not a yardstick for the development of Israeli understandings of history but the types of history appropriated are. Palestinian History is not even symbolically counter-historical to Israeli and Zionist history but exists in a relationship of dialectical re-enforcement with Zionism. The post-Zionist position as coined by Pappé in the Israeli struggle over memory and imagination

---

385. Other important shapers of the discourse of post-Zionism are sociologist Uri Ram and historian Tom Segev. Many others are considered post-Zionists by commentators but I consider that to be a convenient placing of particularly younger intellectuals and academics in a catching category. Ilan Pappé and Uri Ram describe the post-Zionist condition differently but generally agree on its basic outline. Pappé considers post-Zionism an ideology influenced by philosophical notions of post-modernity and Uri Ram considers post-Zionism to be a social condition and the rather un-ideological and pragmatic Israeli middle class to be the post-Zionists. Pappé 1997a, 1997b, 1997c, Ram 2003.

386. Pappé 1997c.

thus uses Palestinian History as an icon of a historical discourse and value system as much as Zionist opponents do.

Tekumah was according to producer Gideon Drori conceived and planned in a very different political climate that when it was aired in 1998. Planning began already in 1994 when peace euphoria was at its highest peak. The last episode of *Tekumah* entitled *The Gun and the Olive Branch* is almost an End of History in as much as the narrative of Israeli history in the light of conflict with the Palestinians was about to come to an end. As such *Tekumah* is a historical journey, an epic, from the joyous yet tragic, bitter-sweet, establishment of Israel to the reconciliation with the "lesser victims" of the same inaugural events. This is in effect the story that evolves from a *Tekumah*, rebirth, to an imagination of normalization. It develops from one beginning to another analogous to Nathan Alterman's poem of the 1948 war. The perspective of *Tekumah* is through all the episodes the perspective of peace making and liberalization, reconciliation and normalization. The liberalizations of Israeli society, immigration of hundred thousands of ambivalent Jews from Russia, the Declaration of Principles and the post-Zionism debates all contributed to the sense that the early 1990s was the end of an era and the beginning of a new. In such context where Zionism itself has become part of history, when a booming economy and increased globalization individualize society and create a strong, pragmatic and bourgeois middle class with an immediate view to improved life conditions for themselves and their children, then the hardships and ideologies of even the near past are discursively placed in a different time. This understanding of time is obviously not chronological but discursive.[387] *Tekumah*'s historical discourse is located in a particular sense of newness and change fostered by the hope and positive utopianism of the early 1990s.

The Declaration of Principles can itself be considered as both the proper trope and imagination of the *Tekumah*. If we conceive of the Declaration of Principles as a historical document and at the same time a historical vision in line with our general understanding of history as both proper and philosophical as un-separable characteristics. The very short introduction to the Declaration simply contains the vision of

---

387. This conception of time is furthermore ironic in opposition to a linear understanding of the past in which one time necessarily comes after another and passes things on in an evolutionary manner.

a new time with mutual recognition and future cooperation between the parties.[388] It defines the period of confrontation as being over and states that both parties have legitimate political rights which could have been a revolutionary statement in the light of decades of mutual denial of the other's rights to existence. *Tekumah* is the dramatic, historical narrative version of the consequences of the Declaration for the Israeli perspective of history though it still upholds Zionist collective memory as a ceremonial past. The reason that the series became controversial is due to its conception in a liberal, positive utopian moment which, as the real-political circumstances changed, became ideological on behalf of the legacy of the Rabin-Peres government. The integration of Palestinian history thus became only an icon of the historical discourse and value system of this particular side in the Israeli struggle over memory and not truly counter-historical.

Final Comments

In an article in *Jerusalem Quarterly File*, Israeli film director Dorit Naaman comments on *Tekumah* from a perspective of the history of documentaries and the debate over the new historians.[389] Naaman contends that *Tekumah* adopts a fashionable polyphonic style but that it remains only a style. Regarding the content of the series, nothing differs significantly from what can be considered official Israeli history.[390] With her analysis, Naaman touches on the same topic as Fredric Jameson when he in *The Seeds of Time* questions whether the aesthetic pluralism often equalled with postmodernism really is genuine pluralism or just a new "cover" for the same ideological and ethical universalism that has always existed.[391]

---

388. The Declaration of Principles can be read at: www.mideastweb.org/
389. Naaman 2003.
390. Ibid. 38-39.
391. Jameson 1994: 1-71. This is a central aspect of Jameson's critique of the postmodern perspective. From his Marxist perspective, Jameson claims that culture is a product of socio-economic configurations and not vice versa. This means that post-modern theories reflect socio-economic conditions and that these are just as determinative as they have always been. This critique is quite fundamental because post-modern theories' emphasis of imagination and discourse indeed foster the reverse or at least a dialectic perspective on the relation between

Naaman calls *Tekumah* for postmodern fashion not post-colonial history.[392] The criticism that Naaman levels against *Tekumah* seems reasonable when we consider that the series indeed is official history and was conceived as such. The question is if the pluralistic approach and the integration of aspects of the Palestinian tragedy of 1948 do a work towards another kind of history or if it is like Naaman says: the same old story. Is it basically the re-production of the same as Zionist collective history or can we find in it tendencies that point to changes in the public discourses of Israeli historical heritage?

Within the post-Zionist history perspective of Ilan Pappé, *Tekumah* can be considered a change of or a partial break with Israeli commemorative history. In this perspective change is measured by the level of acceptance of the Palestinian historical narrative and *Tekumah* does accept and explain several key narratives of this history. The Palestinian exodus is considered a tragedy that was not only self-inflicted and partially caused by the policy of expulsions carried out by the Israeli army. Israeli veteran soldiers are made to recall the horrors that befell the Palestinians and they look back on these events with sadness though things could not have fallen out otherwise according to their narratives. The liberal Israeli reasoning of the major disaster that led to a smaller disaster prevails in the key episodes of the series. Veteran Davidson who testifies to both the burning of villages and the expulsions of innocent Palestinians revises Israeli myths of pure intent and honourable conduct, such as the purity of arms, in a commonsensical manner. Even David Ben-Gurion and Yitzhak Rabin are drawn into the ambivalences of state making and the violent flip side of heroism as the leaders directly responsible for the expulsion of the populations of Lydda and Ramle in central Israel/Palestine. In many respects, the three first episodes of *Tekumah* resemble Benny Morris' book *The Birth of the Palestinian Refugee Problem, 1947-1949* (1987) and to an extent include his recent explanations that there are no contradictions between considering the Zionist project good, just and giving it full support and uncovering the more unpleasant sides of its implementation.[393] The series and Morris

---

"base" and ideology. I find, though, that post-Marxist discourse theories such as that of Laclau and Mouffe counter this critique. Laclau and Mouffe 1985.
392. Naaman 2003: 43.
393. In *Ha'aretz* and *The Guardian*, Morris has voiced his personal political opinions on the conflict and Zionism. It caused considerable debate because his books

follow the historical vision of the Rabin-Peres government (1992-1996) in which the history of Israel is not only sequences of just acts and strict self-defence but nonetheless the Palestinians are the enemy with whom peace is on the threshold.[394] Considering the works of the new Israeli historians and the debates they caused, this historical perspective is critical and revisionist against previous Israeli commemorative history which Morris himself already in 1988 in the Jewish-American journal *Tikkun* rejected completely as being part of the ideological making of Israel.[395] Central aspects of the new history by Morris, Pappé and Shlaim are incorporated in a new official history but the nature of a series such as *Tekumah* necessarily domesticates the subversive, revisionist character of the new history and we are thus faced with a completely different contextualization.

Considered as a state produced TV programme to commemorate Israel's 50th anniversary *Tekumah* is part of a culture industry that re-produces the discourse and a sense of togetherness that the state desires. *Tekumah* creates a common, historical, narrative frame that functions as a plot by which the present can be understood as progressively different and better than this past but it at the same time provides a common heritage, a sense of togetherness, for the viewers/consumers.[396] This shows us that *Tekumah* is both liberal in its perception of the present as the most prospective of times and official as a production of collective memory. The integration of aspects of the Palestinian historical narrative that do not significantly challenge the core of Zionist memory can thus be understood as being in the interest of hegemonic public discourse. TV is the most important source of historical knowledge and awareness and accordingly *Tekumah* can be considered highly important to the Israeli struggles over memory

---

are cornerstones of the revisionist historical literature. See the interview with Morris in *Ha'aretz* January 9. 2004, and his article in *The Guardian* February 21. 2002.

394. The idea of standing on the threshold to peace informs Morris in his articles and interviews in *Ha'aretz* and *The Guardian* and therefore he voices the same complaint as the Barak government and the Israeli peace camp about being "disappointed" about the Palestinians for not accepting the peace proposals at Camp David 2000.

395. Morris 1988.

396. Ha-Ilan's study of Israeli news media shows the same mechanism for news stories. Ha-Ilan 2001.

in the 1990s. It was a series that all sides of this struggle desired to design or control as we have seen it with both leftist and rightist critics. Due to its place of production at the centre of the culture industry and its self-conception as commemorative history *Tekumah* in no respects involve counter-historical perspectives. In concordance with Yael Zerubavel's arguments about the changing meaning of Israeli myths over time, *Tekumah* reflects the re-production of an official Israeli historical narrative.[397] The historical narrative is not static but it is re-produced to avoid the dislocation of its discourse and thus its hegemonic position. *Tekumah* is no less an expression of the self-constitution of the system and a denial of the otherness of the other than previous versions of Israeli collective memory. The integration of aspects of the Palestinian narrative reflects a domestication and pacification of their mirror-history which is only possible from a position of increased dominance.

On the surface of things it seemed quite different in 1998, though, as the series was aired. It caused a vigorous public discussion, as mentioned, and it was literally disavowed by the IBA itself due to criticism. Investigations were launched and an introductory programme to the series was introduced which by and large reduced *Tekumah* to a debate programme instead of the intended commemorative history. The reason for this unexpected development was that the Israeli memory struggle was all but resolved after the assassination of Yitzhak Rabin in 1995, the election of Benjamin Netanyahu in 1996 and the rapid deterioration of the peace process. The utopian moment of the Declaration of Principles, liberalization and peace making was over but it was exactly in the spirit of this moment that *Tekumah* was conceived. *Tekumah* reflects the discourse of history of the liberal Israel of the early 1990s but in 1998 the memory struggles had reopened and the series thus only became the reflection of an ideology instead of a reflection of hegemonic commonsensical discourse. Histories are written, or in this case recorded, in and for a present moment and as such *Tekumah* is the history of and for the peace process of the early 1990s.

---

397. Zerubavel 1995.

Post-Nationalist Discourse, Globalization and a New Jewish Ethnoscape – Postscripts

In the course of this inquiry, numerous issues regarding historical and cultural debates in Israel in the 1990s have been touched upon. In the following, we will pay particular attention to the issues that have appeared to be central in all the previous essays, namely the issues of post-nationalist discourse and its cultural implications, globalization and, in a word from Arjun Appadurai, a new Jewish ethnoscape.

Historical discourse in its broadest sense, that is as a discourse that articulates a relation between the past, the present and the future, is a highly important aspect of both collective and private identities. Historical discourse articulates the position of the individual in time and space and identifies the historical, political and cultural spheres of identification between individuals and collective, social domains. In a conventional sense, it gives answers to existential questions of the origins of the proper names that inhabit our social domains as indications of our belongings. Historicity is inherent in the nature of language and thus in the means we possess to articulate the world and our social relations. At the same time, historical discourses are parts of a social domain constituted by antagonisms. As any meaningful historical imagination is linguistic and discursive in nature, it struggles against alternative discourses and a general overflow of possible interpretations. Ultimately, the relations that we place historical events in cannot be decided on by other means than convention, common sense and personal convictions.[398] Conven-

---

398. In this respect, methodologies of historical research fall under the category of conventions.

tions and common sense are central ideological and cultural attributes of the hegemonic discourses in a given social domain.[399]

Thus, history provides us with the knowledge of our belonging and social identities, but this knowledge and these identities are highly contextual and change over time. They are not fixed by messages from the past about how things really were, but they are relatively stable in shorter periods due to their relations to other discourses of the social domain. Accordingly, historical discourses are intimately related to discourses of identity, culture and ideology. This relation can not be severed by even the most conscious attempts to be "objective". Thus, when we inquire into the historical discourses of a given period we inquire into the time-space dimension of the social domain and the ideologies that are vehicles of understanding this dimension. In these present essays, academic history, literature, philosophy and TV in Israel in the 1990s have been discussed within this perspective.

In Israel in the 1990s, we experienced a proliferation of debates about Jewish-Israeli history, Zionism and Israeli identity. The most central aspects of the more public dimensions of these debates were the character of Zionism, the Israeli-Palestinian conflict and the 1948 war. In academic and intellectual circles, more detailed aspects of Jewish-Israeli history such as Zionist historiography, the role of the Palestinians and the *Mizrahi* Jews in Israeli culture and the character of Israeli literature were debated and still are. Explained with the theoretical vocabulary of these present essays, Israel experienced an organic crisis. The 1990s proved to be a period of weakening of the relational system that defines the Israeli social domain. The so-called post-Zionism debates, as the above mentioned debates became known as, were caused by a proliferation of elements that were not already integrated in Zionist discourse or that could not be either integrated or rejected by it. These elements were of all kinds: works of history, peace process, globalization, liberalization and new literatures. The challenge to Zionism did not emerge from a single point but it was the result of an overdetermination of circumstances and it resulted in a general crisis of social identities in Israel in the 1990s. Thus, it was not a single incident or a set of related incidents that brought a profound crisis on Zionism in the 1990s. The crisis was a result of the influence

---

399. I follow the use of the concept of hegemony as developed by Laclau and Mouffe 1985.

of a multitude of new articulations to which Zionism did not constitute an adequate relation.

Some of these articulations were through the 1990s transformed into alternative discourses of Israeli history and identity that identified the emergence of a new historical situation after Zionism. This new historical situation was primarily characterized by the declining power of the nation-state and its integrative culture. The nation-state and its, in a word from Shafir and Peled, incorporation regime, finally lost its exclusive grip of Israeli society in the 1990s and it could not face the challenges of liberalization and globalization of the economy, the peace process and the integration of about a million Russians by way of educating to the traditional Zionist civic virtues. In this respect, sociological discourses such as the ones of Shafir, Peled and Uri Ram are parts of these alternative discourses, while they at the same time attempt to provide the re-descriptions that effectively capture the new historical situation.

In general terms, the process that led to the weakening of the power of the nation-state to incorporate its citizens under a common vision, and the weakening of the power to shape them as proponents of the same virtues, has been described by many sociologists. In these essays, we have primarily relied on the descriptions of Zygmunt Bauman and Uri Ram. This process leads to a proliferation of antagonisms between the ideology of the nation, which has lost its claim to hegemony and thus common sense, and the progressive and rationalist ideology of globalization. This new major demarcation line has replaced the traditional right-left axis of politics in the advanced societies. Uri Ram uses the metaphor of the "Great Transition" which conventionally has been applied to the transition to modernity in 19th century Europe as an equally appropriate metaphor for the current transition to post-modernity. In the 19th century, the old regime was replaced with the nation-state after a period of proliferating conflicts and currently the nation-state is being replaced with globalization as the most rational vehicle for development. This transition to post-modernity is the economic and cultural process that serves as the large scale development that led to the crisis of Israeli social identities in the 1990s.

The demands of economic liberalization and lessening of direct state involvement in the economy that have accompanied the process of globalization transformed the Israeli system from the end of the 1980s and brought about a privatization of key institutions of solidarity such as the *Histadrut*. The conflict with the Palestinians and the violence that follows Israel's colonial policies in the occupied territories became with the first Intifadah the primary hindrance to liberalization and economic growth. Thus, the liberal policies of the Rabin-Peres government of 1992-95, though both government leaders were Labor Zionist veterans, paved the way for the Declaration of Principles, which is the historical document that epitomizes the liberal-economic optimism of the period. The Declaration of Principles opened up for the possibility of a different Israeli history that had moved beyond the state of conflict with the Palestinians and accordingly the Declaration of Principles sparked off a process of historization of Zionism in the public realm. The TV series *Tekumah* of 1998 epitomizes this historization of Zionism and incarnates the atmosphere of the 1990s of Israeli society being on the threshold to a new and better era. The recognition of Zionism as a historical phenomenon instead of the incarnation of the real found in popular cultural products such as the *Tekumah* was very important to the proliferation of historical debates in Israeli society and accordingly to the possibilities of formulating alternative histories.

The term "post-Zionism" has been frequently used during the 1990s to describe the vigorous intellectual tendency to criticize Zionism that was experienced. It is noteworthy that during the 1990s, Zionism completely lost its ideological, cultural and philosophical vigour. No leading intellectuals, academics or politicians were able to articulate a Zionist discourse that was not only a defence of national values in the face of the wave of criticism published in the 1990s. Thus, criticism of the "post-Zionists" was and is widespread and some of it justified and interesting, but none of it is suggestive regarding the invention of new concepts for the present. This proves one of the points made by Uri Ram in his sociology of knowledge of Israeli society in the 1990s. Namely, that the intellectuals supporting the Israeli nation-state and its ideology Zionism are supporting the *Gemeinschaft* of Israeliness, while most of the critical discourses are developing the *Gesellschaft* of globalization in an Israeli context.[400] At the outer ends of the spectrum, extremist Zionist and anti-Zionist positions are found; positions which profit from the waning of the Labor Zionist incorporation regime.

---

400. Ram 1998, 1999.

Uri Ram's sociology identifies the middle class of Israeli society as the social background of post-Zionism. This segment of the Israeli population was the one to benefit the most from the liberalizations of the early 1990s in terms of economy and generally improved life conditions. It was the liberalism, optimism and momentum of the Israeli middle class that provided the conditions of possibility and legitimacy of the post-nationalist discourses presented in these present essays. This liberalism and optimism was by no means radical or counter-historical, and it is generally represented by the TV series *Tekumah*. The history of Zionism and Israel presented in *Tekumah* is the history of liberalism in the 1990s. We find in *Tekumah* the Israeli history suitable for a liberal period and a period of pacification of the Israeli-Palestinian conflict. *Tekumah* could have had the subtitle "Peace and Profit" as much as its attempt to integrate Palestinian history represents not a critical reckoning but an attempt at creating a new hegemonic formation in the image of the economic and political power at the time. Thus, as much as *Tekumah* is the history of liberalism and the history of Israel that creates the conditions of possibility for individualism, it is also part of the *fatamorgana* of peace making that dominated the same strata of Israeli society during the 1990s. The work of journalist Amira Hass of *Ha'aretz* provides us with the necessary insights from the Gaza Strip to deem the peace process a *fatamorgana*.[401]

When *Tekumah* was broadcast in 1998 at the 50th anniversary of Israel it was already history. The real-political developments between Israel and the Palestinians, the initiation of terror by extremist organisations and the deterioration of living conditions among Palestinians led, including the election of Benjamin Netanyahu in 1996, to a general Israeli disappointment over the peace process and to the fear that the Palestinians were not contend with the prospects of the process. The controversy caused by the series points to the nature of history as a discourse that seeks to stabilize identities of the social domain. *Tekumah* did not broadcast incorrect information, it was approved by a board of historians, and it was conceived as a highly incorporative event, yet it was received as being controversial. *Tekumah*, under the conditions of

---

401. Hass 1999 and her hundreds of articles in *Ha'aretz*. Journalist Gideon Levy does much of the same work of familiarizing Israelis with the inhabitants of their colonial possessions.

1998, stood out as an example of a historical vision of the aftermath of the Declaration of Principles. This vision died with the assassination of Rabin and the deterioration of Israeli-Palestinian relations following it. The liberal vision did not achieve hegemony and the memory struggle ensued.

The New Historians and post-Nationalist Discourse

It was the so-called new Israeli historians who became the first icons of the changes of historical discourse in Israel in the 1990s. Benny Morris, Ilan Pappé and Avi Shlaim shaped a new history of Israel and the Israeli-Palestinian conflict through studies of the 1948 war, the Palestinian flight and expulsion from Palestine and Zionist-Arab relations. This new history more or less confirmed the versions of Israeli history that been the accepted wisdom on the far left of the Israeli political spectrum and among Palestinian scholars of history. Benny Morris coined the phrase "the new historians" and paved the way for debates about Israeli writings of history by declaring that Israeli historians until the new historians had been "chronicler-participants" of a national liberation movement and thus unable to view their own achievements impartially.

The new history unambiguously perceived Israel as the strong, well-organized and modern part of the conflict, while the Palestinians were the opposite. The conventional Zionist wisdom that Israel had no choice but war and that the Zionists were fighting the fight of David against the Arab Goliath was proved erroneous. Instead, the new history portrayed a history in which several options were possible and with the Zionists as having the upper hand from the outset. The Palestinians were the victims of war and the Zionist ambition of a pure Jewish state. Even the Arab states proved to be much less intransigent than conventionally described in Zionist history.

At any rate, this presentation of history by the new historians could also have been included in a historical discourse acceptable to the ideology of Zionism. Zionist historians such as Anita Shapira and Shabtai Teveth do not explicitly reject the findings of the new historians apart from details, but they oppose the type of history proposed by Morris, Shlaim and Pappé. As discussed earlier in this inquiry, the new historians do indeed propose a new type of history though they adhere to the same theories and methodologies as most other historians. What had changed in the new history was the time-space parameters of Jewish-Israeli history. Historical discourses create places as parts of wider imaginations of history and the new historians detached Jewish-Israeli history from its Jewish-European context and the history of Jewish suffering. The new historians instead created a Palestinian space for Jewish-Israeli history. Zionism's internal discourses of self-legitimization and Zionist understandings of the so-called Jewish return to history (and the ancient homeland) were not considered as explanatory strategies for the evaluation of Zionist politics in Palestine. The major consequence of the exclusively Palestinian time-space parameters of Jewish-Israeli history of the new historians was a complete turn in perspective. From a Palestinian, territorial, perspective, the Zionists are European colonizers who in alliance with the dominant colonial power of the day, Great Britain, brought a process on Palestine, which inevitably ended in violent conflict. Without a Zionist meta-historical frame, the new history was several degrees more controversial than if it had just presented the horrors of the 1948 war as regrettable evils in the course of a higher good.

On a more detailed level, the new history applies different narrative strategies than traditional Zionist history. As we have seen earlier, the new historians arrange their histories as highly contextual studies and use tropes not conventionally used in Zionist history. Metonymical and ironic discourses that seek to solve in advance specified questions or replace existing histories implicitly reject the Comedies and Tragedies of Zionist, nationalist, history.[402] It must be noted that the new history is just as realist and representationalist as Zionist history and thus in no way represent any post-modernization of Israeli history. The new history is a replacement of one realist history with another but the form of this other history cannot be articulated within conventional Zionist discourse. Benny Morris' attempts after the failed Camp David negotiations in 2000 to do so in press interviews are ultimately unsuccessful. These attempts are not anchored in a positive Zionist vision, but in a pragmatic,

---

402. Anita Shapira notes the same aspect of the histories of the new historians but finds the satiric history useless. Shapira definitely respects history's literary and imaginative dimensions, in opposition to the new historians who have never questioned the factuality and objectivity of their own discourses, and she praises the edificial potentials of Comedy and Tragedy. Shapira 1995.

real-political assessment of what Morris personally deems good and bad and are as such quite primitive reflections on the history he himself has influenced greatly. The new history is the realist history that serves as the dominant historical imagination of the positions in the Israeli memory struggle of the 1990s most often identified with post-Zionism. If we follow Hayden White's theory of the relation between certain histories and corresponding ideologies, the new historians provide Israel with a liberal history that corresponds well with the overall critical tendency towards the nation and its ideology of the 1990s. The historical perspective of the new historians is theoretically conventional and much less advanced than the other discourses of the 1990s treated in these essays, but anyhow the new history should be considered the realist background of the globalist tendency of the 1990s. Phrased differently, we could say when the post-nationalists of the Israeli middle class need to resort to a version of how Israeli history really is they would by and large resort to the new history.

Post-nationalist discourse is a discourse that, such as the new Israeli historians, does not share historical imagination with the ideology of nationalism and accordingly does not hold the nation-state as more than a product of certain socio-economic and cultural relations dominating a certain era. Thus, post-nationalist discourses on Israeli history and identity appear inherently critical of the Zionist perspective because they treat Zionism itself as a historical phenomenon. In this way historization of Zionism in the 1990s served to de-universalize Zionist civic values and resurrecting them as just an ideology amongst others. Post-nationalist discourses cannot be positively defined, only negatively. The similarity between the post-nationalist discourses discussed in these present essays is that they are not Zionist. The discourse of the new historians is by no means anti-representationalist (Richard Rorty) or counter-historical (Foucault) and it is as such very different in nature from the literary and philosophical discourses also discussed in this inquiry, but nonetheless the new historians were among the most significant elements of the organic crisis of Zionism in the 1990s.

Irony and Liberalism in the 1990s

In his *Contingency, Irony, and Solidarity*, Richard Rorty claims that irony has nothing to offer public conversation but at the same time, he makes a very compelling case for private irony – in the interests of the common good.[403] In Rorty's vision of the liberal society, the intellectuals are ironists but people in general are just nominalist and historicist. In such a society, nominalism, historicism and contingency have become common sense. Because this society is liberal, there is no need to answer the questions of "Why do we care about the pain and suffering of others?" and "Why are we liberals?".[404] The public dimension of liberal ironism thus becomes the striving for reduction of pain and suffering and securing the possibilities of being alienated from this same society. This utopia is negative. Its discourse cannot be defined in positive terms as based on universal morality, or as based on the particularity of historical purpose. Its point of departure is a historically contingent "we" committed to the expansion of this "we" by way of encounters with the strange and different – the feat of ironism. Solidarity is not in this perspective based on shared vocabularies, Jewish, Moslem, Christian, but on the question "Are you suffering?". I claim through my inquiry into works of literature by Etgar Keret and Orly Castel-Bloom that a perspective on history, identity and society of this magnitude is visible in their texts, and is indirectly discussed through the consistent use of the trope of irony in their discourses. Therefore, the discourse of ironist liberalism was present in Israel in the 1990s as a legitimate public discourse: something, which I hold to be a function of the reduction of pain and suffering, or at least the experience of pain and suffering, and as suggestive to cultural alternatives to Zionism.

Irony has only a liberal potential. It is not essentially liberal. Earlier in these essays, I claimed that Foucault was a radical ironist and that his metaphor of the genealogist resembles the character of "Dolly" in Orly Castel-Bloom's novel *Dolly City*. Dolly is an ironist character because she

---

403. Rorty 1989: 73-95.
404. It is important to note that Rorty's project is a defense of ironism against the claim made by liberal metaphysicians such as Jürgen Habermas that ironism is a danger to social hope and generally ideas of a better society. Rorty seeks to make a case for ironism as an equally hopeful background for a liberal society and social hope as metaphysicism. Rorty agrees with Habermas that ironism cannot be a political philosophy but he disagrees that philosophy has to have a political potential to be really relevant. We can navigate between the private and the public, between the philosophical and the political, according to Rorty. Accordingly, Rorty should not be understood as attempting to create a positive political philosophy based on ironism, he just makes the point that a liberal society and the principle of hope is possible also for ironists.

questions the prevailing assumptions of history, identity and society. She is incurably alienated from her tribe and indirectly she questions whether this tribe is right for her. She is not sure that she has been given the proper language and wonders if she is the right kind of human being. In Dolly's case, this is not only a general manifestation of ironism but also an inquiry into the objectifications of womanhood and Mother-Son relations. The more radical her investigation goes, the clearer her rootlessness and entrapment becomes. Dolly fundamentally disturbs any edification of Israeli society as based on a Zionist ideology, but, furthermore, she does not empower alternatives such as feminism or political radicalism. Dolly's project of escaping domination fails and does not even in its failure disclose Truth. We cannot call Castel-Bloom's discourse in *Dolly City* an expression of liberalism because for that purpose its violence is all too significant. Violence is not the worst thing we do in the universe of Dolly, it is also a means for liberalization. Hence, Castel-Bloom's Dolly can only read as a private project. We can read it and feel solidarity with Dolly's striving for freedom and diagnosis, but we have to keep its radical ironism subordinated to the wish for the reduction of pain and suffering. Still, our reading of it might challenge our final vocabulary and diminish the realm of the self-evident in our social domain.

Particularly interesting about Castel-Bloom's discourse is that she with the novel *Human Parts* shifts perspective from a private project of liberation to a representation of an entire social domain from an apparent non-oppositional perspective. From the perspective offered in these essays, this turn does not implicate a renunciation of ironism by Castel-Bloom. Rather, it signifies her understanding of an imminent dissolution of the ethnocentric "we" that is, no matter what, our sole point of departure for our private projects. The shallowness and kitsch of the "reality show" of Israeliness exhibited in *Human Parts* leaves no room for private projects. The individual alienation is projected unto the entire social domain and "America" seems to be the only possible escape. The conditions that engendered the possibility of Dolly's challenge of vocabularies were, paradoxically, challenged themselves by violence. Castel-Bloom's radical ironism does not contain the potential of expanding solidarity beyond the Israeli "we" in a crisis situation such as the one experienced in Israel since the outbreak of the second Intifadah and the increase in terror bombings against Israeli civilians. Castel-Bloom's discourse is itself tangled up in violence and its premise for solidarity is not suffering and pain. Sublimation, self-creation and re-production are not subordinated to pain and suffering. The conclusion I want to draw is that Orly Castel-Bloom's discourse, though highly literary and philosophically relevant to the questioning of Zionist discourse and common sense, does not contribute to a lessening of pain and suffering in Israel and definitely not regarding the Israeli-Palestinian conflict. The discourse of Dolly and *Human Parts* contributes to a struggle against collectivization and objectification in a search for individuality, and its perspective on history as an embodiment of experiences, the physical marks of discourse, makes it radically subversive to the historical imagination of Zionism.

Previously, I called Etgar Keret an example of Rorty's liberal ironist. Keret's discourse is not on the surface as subversive as Castel-Bloom's but it is just as embedded in an ironist worldview. Keret's characters as we meet them in e.g. the story of *The Bus Driver who wanted to be God* and the story *Siren* are everyday people trapped in their respective peculiarities and absurdities. They are not characters for the edification of society, but people presented without the ideologies of idealistic virtue or rationalizations of reasons for their capacities. They just are, so to speak. Keret plays with normal-absurd dichotomies and dominant and commonsensical virtues, and his stories circle around the happenstances that becomes defining moments of the protagonists' lives. As we saw previously, Keret's stories rebel in a humorous and ironic tone against collective ideas of principles and good. They always set the system as an impersonal mechanism that is blind to the individuality of human beings, but this positioning does advocate a revolutionary or idealistic change. In Keret's discourse, history is the reproduction of a system that seeks to educate to certain virtues, which makes it inherently trivial and ultimately sets it against the individual. In the same way, public culture is regarded as a commercial product containing the characteristics of commercialism. It is very easy to consume but it never amounts to an experience. Instead, the experiences, happenstances, contingencies of life are the moments that create us and this awareness is the foundation of irony. Keret's stories are not as Castel-Bloom's permeated with a sense of estrangement and alienation. On the contrary, they are most often warm stories that produce a sense of togetherness despite the typical Keret character's difference from the system. This togetherness is not produced by shared vocabularies or an idealistic definition of a human essence that hides behind discourse and language. Rather, it is created through the ironist tone and liberal ideology that permeate Keret's little worlds, which at the same time makes it impossible to wholeheartedly embrace commonsensical views and possible to extend solidarity to the weak, the strange and the ones subjected to cruelty. As we saw in the story *Siren*, the history education supposed to install compassion actually saves a person, Eli, by an ironic twist. Protected by the siren on Holocaust Day, Eli escapes a beating. Morality in Etgar Keret's stories is not universal but situational. It is revised in the meeting with new people and new experiences but it is never an educational system on behalf of a state and an ideology. Thus, the public dimension of Keret's discourse is a project of extension of solidarity committed to the expansion/overcoming of the ethnocentric "we". Such a perspective on history and culture cannot partake in a Zionist educational project and its preferred social order is the liberal society of the Rortyan type where the contingency of beliefs is common sense and the intellectuals are ironists committed to solidarity with the weak in opposition to being committed to a particularistic historical cause or a metaphysical idea. The discourse of Etgar Keret is committed to a Jewishness that happens to constitute an ethnocentric point of departure but it even more committed to a sense of solidarity that extends beyond culturally induced ideology. It seems that the type of literature of Keret has some resemblances to the traditional Yiddish storytelling tradition, but that is a perspective that remains to be explored. Within the present perspective, Keret's discourse is not overtly suggestive to a Jewish ethnoscape after Zionism but it is an example of ironist liberalism in an Israeli context.

Taken together, the discourses of Castel-Bloom and Keret signal that Zionism does not any longer function as the commonsensical reality and the particularistic historical cause of a younger generation of Israeli writers. This generation vehemently distrusts the discourse of nationalism and ideas of supra-historical goals and purposes, and this to an extent that the exploration of the limits of nationalist, collectivist discourse figures prominently amongst the purposes of this literature. As we saw, Yerach Gover considers the purpose of the canon of Modern Hebrew writing to be the setting of legitimate borders for Jewish-Israeli history and experience.[405] Castel-Bloom and Keret question and expand these borders by way of philosophical surgery and ironist solidarity, respectively.

---

405. Gover 1994.

Diaspora

In the main stream of the writing of modern Jewish history, Diaspora has been considered an unnatural condition suffered by the Jews. The Jewish nation was displaced by the Romans almost two thousand years ago and it has wandered the earth suffering the wills of other nations until 1948. In 1948, the Jews returned to history. The history returned to was the history of nations, power, manliness, heterosexuality, colonialism and modern development and also an educational project to induce Jewish identity with the opposite stereotypes of Jewish existence prior to 1948. The entire perspective on history that permeates the ideas of Jewish powerlessness and displacement is itself a historically contingent understanding intimately related to the development of modern nationalism and the main sciences following this development, namely modern history and sociology. Within the varied positions of modern Jewish identity, Diaspora was institutionalized as an unfortunate historical circumstance that befell the Jews. This understanding has not been challenged by the millions of Jews not living in Israel, apart from small groups, which is something that points to the domination of Zionism as the background for the commonsensical togetherness of Jews. As Michael Berkowitz has shown, Zionism in the West has become a community feeling and the main philanthropic effort from Jews to Jews.[406]

Philosophical positions as the ones treated in these essays are in the light of the above highly controversial to commonsensical understandings of Jewish history and identity. Amnon Raz-Krakotzkin, Daniel and Jonathan Boyarin, and Ilan Gur-Ze'ev address the historical imagination of Zionism and its normalizing education because they, amongst other things, consider Zionism a violent, colonialist project. Zionism has not only contributed to violence in Palestine against the Palestinians but also against alternative Jewish lives and traditional Jewish perspectives such as that of Diaspora. This does not mean that these writers should be considered anti-Zionist in a traditional understanding of the Zionist/anti-Zionist dichotomy. Particularly Ilan Gur-Ze'ev explicitly appreciates the self-creative liberation project of Zionism but rejects its collectivist, ethnocentric dimension. I would suggest that we in the case

---

406. Berkowitz 1997.

of such writings as the ones presented here reject the Zionist/anti-Zionist dichotomy and replace it with a universal nationalist/post-nationalist dichotomy. First of all, this distinction makes no particular claim against Zionism but against nationalism in general and secondly, it indicates by generalization the imaginative dimension of concepts such as nationalist/Zionist and post-nationalist/anti-Zionist. A post-nationalist position does not seek to empower an alternative nationalist imagination such as the Palestinian or an alternative Israeli nationalism such as the Hebrew/Canaanite. The post-nationalist positions of Raz-Krakotzkin, the Boyarins and Gur-Ze'ev consider nationalism to be part of a particular rationality, logic and cultural ideology, which belongs to a particular imagination of history, belonging and identity. The process of globalization is the vehicle for a gradual dissolution of the nationalist paradigm and in the wake of this process, new conflicts and new possibilities occur. In a sense, the most historically obvious concept for a re-description of Jewish history and experience in an era after nationalism is Diaspora.

It is impossible to join the perspectives of all the writers presented in these essays in a positive description. They do not share an educational project, signify their critique of nationalism, or use the concept of Diaspora in the same way. We should not consider the writings of Raz-Krakotzkin, the Boyarins and Gur-Ze'ev a diaporist ideology but instead consider it a critical engagement in the dominant ideology of their cultural relations, and, at the same time, suggestive discourses to a Jewish ethnoscape in the age of globalization. As a consequence of their rejection of collectivism and ethnocentrism, Daniel and Jonathan Boyarin and Ilan Gur-Ze'ev explicitly state that their commitment is equally to justice and Jewish identity. This dual commitment in itself renders Zionism unjust in the form the dominant tendencies within it has currently and historically. Central to their respective writings is the belief that Diaspora both historically and as a philosophical concept has something important to contribute to the new possibilities surfacing in the age of globalization. For these possibilities to present themselves as critiques or alternatives to the current order of things, re-descriptions of Jewish history and identity are necessary.

In the essay *Disjuncture and Difference in the Global Cultural Economy*, Arjun Appadurai argues that the discourses of the global cultural economy cannot be reduced to simple center-periphery models or be exclusively located within compartments such as the nation-state.⁴⁰⁷ Technology, migrations, Diasporas and capital are all forces that have changed the imagined national community, and new global imagined worlds are in the age of globalization taking over as vital parts of the cultural imaginations of people. Appadurai suggests the term ethnoscape to capture the cultural, ethnic and religious togetherness of a group of people in an age when the nation-state is loosing its control over such identity formation. Benedict Anderson showed with his *Imagined Communities* that the nation is an imagined community, and Appadurai forwards this perspective unto a global cultural economy thus stressing the significance of the imagination as a social practice also in the age of globalization.⁴⁰⁸ Borrowing this terminology, I suggest that we in the writings of such philosophers as Raz-Krakotzkin, the Boyarins and Gur-Ze'ev find discourses that in many respects supersede the national paradigm of Zionism and Israel. These discourses point to a new diasporic sense of Jewishness for the age of globalization. The organic crisis of Israeli society in the 1990s has not come to an end with the second Intifadah from 2000, only the era of liberal optimism has. The Israeli memory struggle still stands between the supporters of traditional Zionist colonialism in defence of the national community and liberals. The liberals have been pressured as a political expression in the light of increased conflict and economic crisis, but the conditions for their existence as an alternative are the same; the process of globalization will not be revoked. The new Israeli historians, new types of literature, liberal TV shows and diasporic philosophy are elements of the organic crisis of Zionism that flourished in the 1990s. Jewish and Israel history and identity became the key issues of what I have termed the Israeli memory struggle. This struggle shows us the significance of historical discourses in the social domain as discourses that not only inform about historical facts. Historical discourses create places, shape the horizons of identities and partake in the struggle of deciding what is real and common sense, and what is the opposite.

---

407. Appadurai 2003.
408. Anderson 1991.

Bibliography

Ahad Ha'am (no publication date): "Flesh and Spirit", *Collected Writings of Ahad Ha'am*, The Jewish Publishing House, (Hebrew).
Alterman, Nathan 1973: "The Silver Platter", *Collected Writings of Nathan Alterman*, Hakibbutz Hameuhad, (Hebrew).
Anderson, Benedict 1991: *Imagined Communities. Reflections on the Origin and Spread of Nationalism*, Verso.
Anderson, Steve 2001: "History TV and Popular Memory", *Television Histories. Shaping Collective Memory in the Media Age*, (eds.) Edgerton and Rollins, The University of Kentucky Press.
Appadurai, Arjun 2003: "Disjuncture and Difference in the Global Cultural Economy", *Theorizing Diaspora. A Reader*, (eds.) Jana Evans Braziel and Anita Mannur, Blackwell Publishing.
Attridge, Bennington and Young 1987 (eds.): *Post-Structuralism and the Question of History*, Cambridge University Press.
Barber, Benjamin 1995: *Jihad vs. McWorld: How Globalism and Tribalism are Shaping the World*, Times Books.
Bauman, Zygmunt 1989: *Modernity and the Holocaust*, Polity Press.
Bauman, Zygmunt 1993: *Postmodern Ethics*, Blackwell.
Bauman, Zygmunt 2000: *Liquid Modernity*, Polity Press.
Bauman, Zygmunt 2001: *The Individualized Society*, Polity Press.
Benvenisti, Meron 2000: *The Sacred Landscape. The Buried History of the Holy Land since 1948*, University of California Press.
Berkowitz, Michael 1997: *Western Jewry and the Zionist Project 1914-1933*, Cambridge University Press.
Bhabha, Homi 1990 (ed.): *Nation and Narration*, Routledge.
Biale, David 1986: *Power and Powerlessness in Jewish History*, Schocken Books.
Boyarin, Daniel and Jonathan 1994: "The People of Israel Has no Motherland", *Theory and Criticism*, 5, (Hebrew).

Boyarin, Daniel and Jonathan 1997 (eds.): *Jews and Other Differences. The New Jewish Cultural Studies*, University of Minnesota Press.

Boyarin, Daniel 1997: *Unheroic Conduct. The Rise of Heterosexuality and the Invention of the Jewish Man*, University of California Press.

Boyarin, Daniel and Jonathan 2002: *The Powers of Diaspora. Two Essays on the Relevance of Jewish Culture*, University of Minnesota Press.

Boyarin, Daniel and Jonathan 2003: "Diaspora: Generation and the Ground of Jewish Diaspora", *Theorizing Diaspora. A Reader*, (eds.) Jana Evans Braziel and Anita Mannur, Blackwell.

Braudel, Fernand 1980: "History and the Social Sciences: The *longue durée*", *On History*, Chicago University Press.

Castel-Bloom, Orly 1992: *Dolly City*, Zmora-Bitan, (Hebrew).

Castel-Bloom, Orly 1997: *Dolly City*, Loki Books.

Castel-Bloom, Orly 2002: *Human Parts*, Kinneret Publishing, (Hebrew).

Castel-Bloom, Orly 2003: *Human Parts*, David R. Godine.

Curtin, Michael 2001: "Organizing Difference on Global TV: Television History and Cultural Geography", *Television Histories. Shaping Collective Memory in the Media Age*, (eds.) Edgerton and Rollins, The University of Kentucky Press.

Derrida, Jacques 1973: *Speech and Phenomena and Other Essays on Husserl's Theory of Signs*, North-western University Press.

Derrida, Jacques 1994: *Specters of Marx: the State of the Dept, the Work of Mourning and the New International*, Routledge.

Deleuze, Gilles and Guattari, Felix 1989: *A Thousand Plateaus. Capitalism and Schizophrenia*, University of Minnesota Press.

Diamond, James 1986: *Homeland or Holyland? The Canaanite Critique of Israel*, Indiana University Press.

Dinur, Ben-Zion 1969: *Israel and the Diaspora*, Philadelphia.

Dominguez, Virginia 1989: *People as Subject, People as Object. Selfhood and Peoplehood in Contemporary Israel*, The University of Wisconsin Press.

Edgerton, G. and Rollins, P. 2001 (eds.): *Television Histories. Shaping Collective Memory in the Media Age*, The University Press of Kentucky.

Elon, Amos 1986: *Herzl*, Schocken Books.

Evron, Boaz 1995: *Jewish State or Israeli Nation*, Indiana University Press.

Ezrahi, Sidra Dekoven 2000: *Booking Passage. Exile and Homecoming in the Modern Jewish Imagination*, University of California Press.

Fackenheim, Emil L. 1978: *The Jewish Return into History. Reflection in the Age of Auschwitz and a New Jerusalem*, Schocken Books.

Fairclough, Norman 1995: *Critical Discourse Analysis. The Critical Study of Language*, Longman.

Fanon, Frantz 1967: *Black Skin, White Masks*, Grove Press.

Feldt, Jakob 2001: "Post-Zionist Discourse", *Scandinavian Journal of Middle Eastern Studies (TfMS)*, (Danish).
Feldt, Jakob 2003: "The New Historical Situation. Israeli Imaginations of History and a New Israel", *A New Middle East?*, (eds.) Lars Erslev Andersen and Peter Seeberg, University of Southern Denmark Press, (Danish).
Foucault, Michel 1979: "What is an Author", *Textual Strategies. Perspectives in Post-Structuralist Criticism*, (ed.) Josué V. Harari, Cornell University Press.
Foucault, Michel 1977: "Nietzsche, Genealogy, History", *Language, Countermemory, Practice*, Cornell University Press.
Furet, Francois 1991: "From Narrative History to Problem-Oriented History", *The History and Narrative Reader*, (ed.) Geoffrey Roberts, Routledge.
Gadamer, Hans-Georg 1989: *Truth and Method*, Stagbooks.
Gellner, Ernest 1997: *Nationalism*, Phoenix.
Giddens, Anthony 1994: *The Consequences of Modernity*, Polity Press.
Giddens, Anthony 1999: *Runaway World. How Globalization is Reshaping our Lives*, Profile.
Gover, Yerach 1994: *Zionism. The Limits of Moral Discourse in Israeli Hebrew Fiction*, University of Minnesota Press.
Green, David B. 1998: "The Rebirth of a Nation", *The Jerusalem Report* (Anniversary issue).
Grinberg and Shafir 2000: "Economic Liberalization and the Breakup of the Histadrut's Domain", *The New Israel. Peacemaking and Liberalization*, (eds.) Gershon Shafir and Yoav Peled, Westview.
Gur-Ze'ev, Ilan 1998: "Towards a Non-repressive Critical Pedagogy", *Educational Theory*, 48, 4.
Gur-Ze'ev, I., Masschelein, J., Blake, N. 2001: "Reflectivity, Reflection and Counter-Education", *Studies in Philosophy and Education*, 20, 2.
Gur-Ze'ev, Ilan 2003: *Destroying the Other's Collective Memory*, Peter Lang.
Gur-Ze'ev, Ilan 2003b: "*Can't you see that the time has come in Israel for a counter-education that will prepare for a self-initiated Jewish displacement?*", unpublished paper.
Ha-Ilan, Netta 2001: "Images of History in Israeli Television News: The Territorial Dimension of Collective Memories, 1987-1990", *Television Histories. Shaping Collective Memory in the Media Age*, (eds.) Edgerton and Rollins, The University of Kentucky Press.
Halkin, Simon 1950: *Modern Hebrew Literature. From the Enlightenment to the Birth of the State of Israel: Trends and Values*, Schocken.
Hansen, Miriam Bratu 2001: "Schindler's List is not Shoah: The Second Commandment, Popular Modernism and Public Memory", *The Historical Film. History and Memory in Media*, (ed.) Marcia Landy, Rutgers University Press.

Harvey, David 1989: *The Condition of Postmodernity. An Inquiry into the Origins of Cultural Change*, Blackwell.
Harvey, David 2000: *Spaces of Hope*, University of California Press.
Hass, Amira 1999: *Drinking the Sea at Gaza. Days and Nights in a Land under Siege*, Metropolitan Books.
Hazony, Yoram 2000: *The Jewish State. The Struggle for Israel's Soul*, Basic Books.
Herzl, Theodor 1896: *The Jewish State*, (in an undated Danish translation from Hertz Forlag).
Hever, Hannan 2002: *Producing the Modern Hebrew Canon. Nation Building and Minority Discourse*, New York University Press.
Hobsbawm, Eric J. 1990: *Nations and Nationalism since 1780. Programme, Myth, Reality*, Canto.
Hoffman, Anne Golomb 2000: "Embodiments: An Introduction", *Prooftexts. A Journal of Jewish Literary History*, 20. 1 &2.
Horkheimer, Max and Adorno, Theodor 1995 (1944): *Dialectic of Enlightenment*, Gyldendal, (Danish).
Jabés, Edmond 1991: *From the Book to the book. An Edmond Jabés Reader*, Wesleyan University Press.
Jameson, Fredric 1991: *Postmodernism, or, the Cultural Logic of Late Capitalism*, Verso.
Jameson, Fredric 1994: *The Seeds of Time*, Columbia University Press.
Jenkins, Keith 2003: *Refiguring History. New Thoughts on an old Discipline*, Routledge.
Karsh, Efraim 1999: *Fabricating Israeli History. The "New Historians"*, Hakibbutz hameuhad, (Hebrew).
Katz, Jacob 1986: *Jewish Emancipation and Self-Emancipation*, The Jewish Publication Society.
Keret, Etgar 1996: "Siren", *Pipelines*, Etgar Keret, Am Oved Publishers, (Hebrew).
Keret, Etgar 1998: *Kneller's Happy Campers*, Keter Publishing, (Hebrew).
Keret, Etgar 2001: *The Bus Driver Who Wanted to be God & Other Stories*, St. Martin's Press.
Khalidi, Rashid 1997: *Palestinian Identity. The Construction of Modern National Consciousness*, Columbia University Press.
Kimmerling, Baruch and Migdal, Joel 1993: *Palestinians. The Making of a People*, Free Press.
Kimmerling, Baruch 1995: "Academic History Caught in a Crossfire. The Case of Jewish-Israeli Historiography", *History and Memory*, 7, 1.
Laclau, Ernesto and Mouffe, Chantal 1985: *Hegemony & Socialist Strategy. Towards a Radical Democratic Politics*, Verso.
Landy, Marcia 2001 (ed.): *The Historical Film. History and Memory in Media*, Rutgers University Press.

Marcuse, Herbert 1964: *One-Dimensional Man. Studies in the Ideology of Advanced Industrial Society*, Routledge.
Masalha, Nur 1991: "A Critique of Benny Morris", *Journal of Palestine Studies*, 21, 1.
Meyer, Michael A. 1967: *The Origins of the Modern Jew. Jewish Identity and European Culture in Germany, 1749-1824*, Wayne State University Press.
Morris, Benny 1987: *The Birth of the Palestinian Refugee Problem, 1947-1949*, Cambridge University Press.
Morris, Benny 1988: "The New Historiography. Israel Confronts its Past", *Tikkun Magazine*, 3, 6.
Morris, Benny 1990: *1948 and After: Israel and the Palestinians*, Oxford University Press.
Morris, Benny 2000: *Righteous Victims: A History of the Zionist-Arab Conflict 1881-1999*, John Murray.
Mouffe, Chantal 1997 (ed.): *Deconstruction and Pragmatism: Simon Critchley, Jacques Derrida, Ernesto Laclau and Richard Rorty*, Routledge.
Myers, David N. 1995: *Re-Inventing the Jewish Past. European Jewish Intellectuals and the Zionist Return to History*, Oxford University Press.
Naaman, Dorit 2003: "Old Wine in New Bottles. *Tekumah*, an Israeli Resurrection of Social Change?", *Jerusalem Quarterly File*, 19.
Ophir, Adi 2001: *Working for the Present. Essays on Contemporary Israeli Culture*, Hakibbutz hameuhad, (Hebrew).
Ottolenghi, Emanuele 2003: "Paradise Lost: A Review of Laurence Silberstein's "The Post-Zionism Debates. Knowledge and Power in Israeli Culture"", *Israel Studies*, 8, 2.
Pappé, Ilan 1992: *The Making of the Arab-Israeli Conflict 1947-1951*, I.B. Tauris.
Pappé, Ilan 1993: "There is no History, only Historians", *Yediot Aharonot Musaf LeShabat*, August 8, (Hebrew).
Pappé, Ilan 1997a: "Post-Zionist Critique on Israel and the Palestinians part I", *Journal of Palestine Studies*, 26, 2.
Pappé, Ilan 1997b: "Post-Zionist Critique on Israel and the Palestinians part II", *Journal of Palestine Studies*, 26, 3.
Pappé, Ilan 1997c: "Post-Zionist Critique on Israel and the Palestinians part III", *Journal of Palestine Studies*, 26, 4.
Pappé, Ilan 1998: "Israeli Television's Fiftieth Anniversary "Tekummah" series: A Post-Zionist View?", *Journal of Palestine Studies*, 27, 4.
Pappé, Ilan 2002 (ed.): *The Israel/Palestine Question*, Routledge.
Ram, Uri 1993 (ed.): *Israeli Society. Critical Perspectives*, Breirot Publications, (Hebrew).
Ram, Uri 1998: "Post-Nationalist Pasts: the Case of Israel", *Social Science History* 22, 4.

Ram, Uri 1999: "The State of the Nation: Contemporary Challenges to Zionism in Israel", *Constellations* 6, 3.
Ram, Uri 2003: "From Nation State to Nation-State: Nation, History and Identity Struggles in Jewish Israel", *The Challenge of Post-Zionism. Alternatives to Israeli Fundamentalist Politics*, (ed.) Efraim Nimni, Zed Books.
Ratosh, Yonathan 1944: *The Opening Discourse*, Havaad legibbush hanoar haivri, Tel Aviv, (Hebrew).
Raz-Krakotzkin, Amnon 1994a: "Exile within Sovereignty: Toward a Critique of the "Negation of Exile" in Israeli Culture part I", *Theory and Criticism*, 4, (Hebrew).
Raz-Krakotzkin, Amnon 1994b: "Exile Within Sovereignty: Toward a Critique of the "Negation of Exile" in Israeli Culture part II", *Theory and Criticism*, 5, (Hebrew).
Raz-Krakotzkin, Amnon 1996: *The Representation of Galut. Zionist Historiography and Medieval Jewry*, Ph.D. dissertation Tel Aviv University, (Hebrew).
Raz-Krakotzkin, Amnon 2004: "The Zionist Return to the West and the Mizrahi Jewish Perspective", *Orientalism and the Jews*, (ed.) Ivan Davidson Kalmar and Derek J. Penslar, Brandeis University Press (forthcoming).
Rogan, Eugene and Shlaim, Avi (eds.) 2001: *The War for Palestine. Rewriting the History of 1948*, Cambridge University Press.
Rorty, Richard 1989: *Contingency, Irony, and Solidarity*, Cambridge University Press.
Rorty, Richard 1999: *A Pragmatist View on Contemporary Analytic Philosophy*, published on Richard Rorty's homepage: www.stanford.edu/~rrorty/
Said, Edward 1978: *Orientalism. Western Conceptions of the Orient*, Routledge.
Said, Edward 1994: *Representations of the Intellectual. The 1993 Reith Lectures*, Random House.
Segev, Tom 1986: *1949, the First Israelis*, Owl Books.
Segev, Tom 1993: *The Seventh Million: The Israelis and the Holocaust*, Owl Books.
Segev, Tom 2002: *Elvis in Jerusalem. Post-Zionism and the Americanization of Israel*, Metropolitan Books.
Shafir, Gershon 1996: "Israeli Society: A Counterview", *Israel Studies*, 1, 2.
Shafir, Gershon and Peled, Yoav 2000 (eds.): *The New Israel. Peacemaking and Liberalization*, Westview.
Shafir, Gershon and Peled, Yoav 2002: *Being Israeli. The Dynamics of Multiple Citizenship*, Cambridge University Press.
Shaked, Gershon 1977- : *Hebrew Narrative Fiction 1880-1980*, (vol. 1-4) Keter Publishing, (Hebrew).
Shalev, Michael 2000: "Liberalization and the Transformation of the Political Economy", *The New Israel. Peacemaking and Liberalization*, (eds.) Gershon Shafir and Yoav Peled, Westview.

Shapira, Anita 1995: "Politics and Collective Memory: The Debate over "the New Historians" in Israel", *History and Memory*, 7, 1.

Shapira, Anita 2000: "Hirbet Hizah. Between Remembrance and Forgetting", *Jewish Social Studies*, 7, 1.

Shavit, Yaacov 1987: *The New Hebrew Nation. A Study in Israeli Heresy and Fantasy*, Frank Cass.

Shenhav Yehouda 2002: "Ethnicity and National Memory: World Organization of Jews from Arab Countries (WOJAC)" *British Journal of Middle Eastern Studies*, 29.

Shimoni, Gideon 1995: *The Zionist Ideology*, Brandeis University Press.

Shlaim, Avi 1988: *Collusion across the Jordan. King Abdullah, the Zionist Movement and the Partition of Palestine*, Oxford University Press.

Shlaim, Avi 1998: *The Politics of Partition. King Abdullah, the Zionist and Palestine 1921-1951*, Oxford University Press.

Shlaim, Avi 2001: *The Iron Wall. Israel and the Arab World*, Penguin.

Silberstein, Laurence J. 1999: *The Post-Zionism Debates. Knowledge and Power in Israeli Culture*, Routledge.

Silberstein, Laurence J. 2000 (ed.): *Mapping Jewish Identities*, New York University Press.

Smith, Anthony D. 1991: *National Identity*, Penguin Books.

Smith, Anthony D. 1998: *Nationalism and Modernism*, Routledge.

Sorkin, David 1987: *The Transformation of German Jewry 1780-1840*, Oxford University Press.

Starr, Deborah A. 2000: "Reterritorializing the Dream: Orly Castel-Bloom's Remapping of Israeli Identity", *Mapping Jewish Identity*, (ed.) Laurence J. Silberstein, University of Minnesota Press.

Steiner, George 1985: "Our Homeland, the Text", *Salmagundi*, 66.

Sternhell, Zeev 1999: *The Founding Myths of Israel. Nationalism, Socialism and the Making of the Jewish State*, Princeton University Press.

Stillman, Norman 1991: *The Jews of Arab Lands in Modern Times*, The Jewish Publication Society.

Taureck, Bernhard 1991: *Lévinas zur Einführung*, Junius Verlag.

Teveth, Shabtai 1989: "Charging Israel with Original Sin", *Commentary Magazine*, 88, 3.

Troen, Ilan and Lucas, Noah 1995 (eds.): *Israel: The First Decade of Independence*, State University of New York Press.

Weitz, Yechiam 1997 (ed.): *From Vision to Revision. A Hundred Years of Historiography of Zionism*, Shazar, (Hebrew).

Whalidi, Khalid 1988: "Plan Dalet Revisited", *Journal of Palestine Studies*, 18, 1.

White, Hayden 1973: *Metahistory. The Historical Imagination in Nineteenth Century Europe*, The Johns Hopkins University Press.

White, Hayden 1978: *Tropics of Discourse. Essays in Cultural Criticism*, The Johns Hopkins University Press.
White, Hayden 1987: *The Content of the Form. Narrative Discourse and Historical Representation*, The Johns Hopkins University Press.
Winther, Judith 2003: "Hebrew", *The Desert Rose and other Short Stories from the Middle East*, (ed.) Claus V. Pedersen, Museum Tusculanum, (Danish)
Wisse, Ruth 2000: *The Modern Jewish Canon. A Journey through Language and Culture*, The Free Press.
Yehoshua, A.B. 1968: *Facing the Forest*, Hakibbutz Hameuhad, (Hebrew).
Yerushalmi, Yosef Hayim 1989: *Zakhor. Jewish History and Jewish Memory*, University of Washington Press.
Young, Robert 1990: *White Mythologies. Writing History and the West*, Routledge.
Zerubavel, Yael 1995: *Recovered Roots. Collective Memory and the Making of Israeli National Tradition*, The University of Chicago Press.
Zertal, Idith 1998: *From Catastrophe to Power: Holocaust Survivors and the Emergence of Israel*, University of California Press.
Zipperstein, Steven J. 1993: *Elusive Prophet. Ahad Ha'am and the Origins of Zionism*, Peter Halban.